From the
CENTER
OF THE RING

From the Center of the Ring

An Inside View of Horse Competitions

Arizona Instructor/Trainer Al Dunning on the classic reining horse, Expensive Hobby.
Courtesy of Al Dunning. Fallaw photo.

BY CHERRY HILL
ILLUSTRATIONS BY N. J. WILEY

 A GARDEN WAY PUBLISHING BOOK

Storey Communications, Inc.
Pownal, VT 05261

Cover design by Nancy Lamb.

Book design and production by Oliver & Lake Design Associates.

Front cover photograph by Scott K. Trees of Mozambique, an imported Hannoverian owned by BARA Farms, Anne Callin up. BARA Farms and Scott K. Trees.

Back cover photo of Joe Glo's Yellow Rose ridden by Craig Johnson. *Horseman* magazine photo by Linda Blake-Caddel.

The name Garden Way Publishing has been licensed to
Storey Communications, Inc. by Garden Way, Inc.

Printed in the United States by W. A. Krueger Company

First Printing, August 1988

Library of Congress Cataloging-in-Publication Data

Hill, Cherry, 1947–
    FROM THE CENTER OF THE RING.
    "A Garden Way Publishing book."
    Includes index.
    1. Horse-shows.   2. Horses—Showing.   I. Title.

SF294.5.H55   1988   636.1'0888   87-72355
ISBN 0-88266-492-1 (hard)
ISBN 0-88266-494-8

DEDICATION

*On the occasion of her special birthday, to
Barby Fairbanks Eide, a Virgo out of a Virgo
by a Virgo, who has added organization,
inspiration, and a new perspective to my work.*

*And to my pal Richard for his sincere interest,
generous talents, and great sense of humor.*

ACKNOWLEDGMENTS:

These individuals and associations provided helpful information in the development of this book: Terry Bath, Dale Forbes Bormann, Sean Brevard, Don Burt, Harold Campton, Richard Klimesh, Dave Moore, Steve Schwartzenberger, Susan Sexton, Phil Teeter, Terry Thompson, and Lowell Boomer, Martha Wooster of the United States Dressage Federation, Bara Farms, the American Horse Shows Association, the American Quarter Horse Association, the National Cutting Horse Association, the National Reining Horse Association, the North American Trail Ride Conference, the American Endurance Ride Conference, the United States Combined Training Association, the United States Pony Clubs, Inc., the American Horse Council, the American Vaulting Association, and the American Association of Equine Practitioners.

Special thanks to the following individuals and organizations for providing photos: Sean Brevard, Debbie Cain, Jackie Dewall, Al Dunning, Richard Klimesh, Marjorie Maagoe, Jennifer Meyer, and the *California Horse Review*, Moondrift Morgan Farm, Iris Mosgrove, Susan Sexton, Carol Story, Terry Thompson, Joyce Perry-Williams, Bara Farms, Linda Blake-Caddel, and *Horseman* magazine, the Appaloosa Horse Club, the United States Combined Training Association, the United States Dressage Federation, the National Cutting Horse Association, the International Arabian Horse Association, the American Paint Horse Association, the American Vaulting Association, the American Saddlebred Horse Association, and *Horses West*.

Illustrations designed by Cherry Hill. Artwork by N.J. Wiley with extra thanks for her painstaking attention to detail.

TABLE OF CONTENTS

*Patrick Pulley on Peek At Me circling the cow in the Junior Stock Horse
Class at the Monterey National Horse Show in California.* Photo by
Jennifer Meyer, publisher of *California Horse Review.*

LIST OF ILLUSTRATIONS

PREFACE

OFTEN at a horse competition, after I hand in my scorecard for tabulation, I have a strong desire to walk over to the exhibitors and talk with them. Because of my years as an instructor, I naturally want to communicate my ideas. And sometimes just a few small tips could make a rider or a horse a blue ribbon winner.

But did you know that at most horse shows judges are not allowed to speak with the contestants? There are good reasons behind the ruling, even though the code of silence can be just as frustrating for the judge as it is for the exhibitor. First, it would be unfair for a judge to give comments to only one exhibitor. Second, there simply isn't time during the tight schedule of a horse show for any-

Author Cherry Hill. Richard Klimesh photo.

thing other than judging. In fact, a judge is often looking at the next class while the awards from the previous class are being announced. One of the main reasons I am writing this book is so that I can finally talk with exhibitors, past and future.

Luckily there are certain types of small shows that are specifically designed to allow the judge to talk with the exhibitors. The 4-H, Pony Club, and schooling shows often require that their judges explain the placings of each class so that the contestants can learn from this show-ring experience.

The title of this book refers both to the judge and to the exhibitor. In large group classes, the judge's vantage point is from inside the ring. In other classes that require individual performance, such as reining, trail, hunter, and dressage, the horse and rider are center stage. My role has been that of a competitor and that of a judge. I hope the blend of these two viewpoints will be helpful whether you are new to showing or already competing.

With this book, I'd also like to help you make some important decisions. If you are just getting started, you must first choose the event best suited to your physique and inclinations and then select an appropriate horse for that type of competition.

You shouldn't make your choice of event out of convenience. Just because your best friend is a barrel racer or because the closest stable specializes in hunters doesn't mean that you automatically need to choose one or the other. Please take the time to read, with an open mind, about all of the events described in this book. You may find a wonderful surprise waiting for you in a style of riding that, until now, you never took the time to explore.

Once you have found the event that really interests and excites you, you must select a horse with the conformation and temperament to participate well in that activity. Attempting to force a horse into a mold for which he is unsuited would be like trying to make you a physicist if you have the talent and desire to be a sculptor. Although it is true that many horses are versatile at lower levels of competition, once you begin showing at the bigger or more specialized shows, you must ride a horse that is well suited mentally and physically for his task. If you choose a horse that is a natural for an event, your riding will be more enjoyable and your horse will be happier.

In this book, you will read about trainers, instructors, veterinarians, and farriers. Seek experienced help, especially if you are a newcomer to the horse world. Employ the services of professionals whenever you can. You should never attempt to shoe your own horse, administer medications, or train your horse without supervision. It is essential that you develop a good working relationship with a veterinarian who is an equine specialist and also with a qualified, certified farrier.

I also recommend that you work closely with an instructor or trainer if you aspire to compete. Even our celebrated U.S. Equestrian Team receives regular instruction and coaching. Until you have nothing more to learn (may that day never come), you will need regular help and instruction.

Fortunately, professional assistance does not necessarily mean big dollars. Organizations such as 4-H and Pony Club are good places to get help if you are under twenty-one. And there are always new professionals entering horse-related occupations who are eager to build up a clientele. If you can find the well-qualified new instructor in the neighborhood, you may get a good deal of personal attention for an affordable price.

Finally, I hope this book will take some of the little terrors out of your first show. After all, everyone has to begin somewhere, and there are many more first-timers out there than you might realize. It is a common feeling to think that everyone is staring at you and can see all of your mistakes, and that everyone else at the horse show knows exactly what to do. This simply isn't true!

To prevent the jitters, keep in mind the reason that you want to compete. I hope that it is to demonstrate your dedication to becoming a good horseman and rider. If you approach a horse show as another opportunity to further your experience, it will help you to realize that show day is not the finale, but just a step along the way.

When you have worked diligently to develop good communication with your horse, and you know your performance reflects that, you have reason to be proud. Sometimes the judge will see that your performance, in comparison to the others in the ring, merits recognition. Other times, your competitors may be better prepared or presented. If you enter a horse competition with the attitude of doing your best and learning how to become better, it will be easier to take both winning and losing in stride.

The very best of luck to you! I'll be looking for your top-notch performance from my vantage point here at the center of the ring.

SECTION ONE
GETTING STARTED

The gray Arabian and his fit and knowledgeable rider have been climbing hills, negotiating rocky trails, fording streams, and working energetically on the straightaways since before dawn. With ninety-nine miles behind them and only one more to go, the team continues to work in harmony, synchronizing their every movement. Even when the finish line comes into sight, they proceed at an efficient pace, one that doesn't tax the horse's heart and lungs beyond their capacity to recover safely. Mom and Dad are cheering as horse and rider complete the ride in tenth place. For these partners, finishing is winning.

The showmanship horse must be attentive yet dependable. Brook Baker with Porvenir Gay Bobby. Courtesy Moondrift Morgan Farm. Rob Hess photo.

CHAPTER ONE

INTRODUCTION

ALTHOUGH FORMAL horse showing originated over two hundred years ago as a means of ranking the merit of breeding programs, showing today is primarily a recreational activity. Because the vast majority of exhibitors are nonprofessionals—young people and amateurs—the role of many professionals has evolved to that of coach. Trainers and instructors use the performance arena as a showcase for the horses and riders they have developed.

Showing provides the opportunity for riders to set specific goals for both their horses and themselves. It encourages a progressive training plan aimed at the particular requirements of a competition. The judge's evaluation is a progress check for the horse and rider: an objective opinion that can help the exhibitor plan future training sessions.

Horse care, training, and riding contribute to the mental and physical development of both the horse and the rider. Working with a horse can develop confidence and improve physical fitness, coordination, balance, strength, and rhythm. Since 95 percent of a horse show exhibitor's time is spent caring for a horse and preparing for the performance, it is essential that the horse owner enjoys more than just the moments in the show ring. It has often been said that success in the horse world consists of 10 percent inspiration and 90 percent perspiration.

Showing also offers the participant the opportunity to meet people of similar interests. The sharing and caring that should be a part of showing often provide lifelong associations and friendships.

Although few riders are fortunate enough to make a career in the show ring, some may find employment in related businesses that require firsthand knowledge of competition-oriented horse activities.

But talking first about showing is putting the cart before the horse. The aspiring showman must strive to become a good horseman first and foremost. This means

not only practicing diligently, but also understanding the behavior and needs of the equine companion and partner. The good horseman is hungry for knowledge about the proper management of his or her mount and accepts the responsibility of its care and keep.

Once you develop confidence and competence as a rider, it is time to consider competition. If you enter a horse show with the idea of doing your very best and learning from the experience, you will emerge a winner even if you do not take home the blue ribbon. If you enter a horse show with the intent of taking home the trophy at any cost, you may be headed for trouble.

Competition can do odd things to people. In order to win, exhibitors can lose sight of good horsemanship and sportsmanship. Horses are sometimes treated inhumanely and fellow exhibitors discourteously. I hope that this won't happen to you. But please be aware that you will likely see many routes to the winner's circle. You'll be better off if you do not try to take any shortcuts.

Competition must be viewed from a healthy perspective. Although our fast-paced society seems to require instant success, there is no place for this kind of thinking in the development of a horse and rider. And besides, your involvement with horses is supposed to be a pleasurable activity.

I have seen adults carry their anxieties from the workplace into the show ring. I have seen children pushed and prodded by parents and trainer at a pace that is not conducive to growth and learning. I have also watched the development of other riders over the years who have taken the time necessary to make really solid horses that have lasted for years. These people have also developed a large family of horse show friends. They know the meaning of the advice, "It's not where you are going that is important but how you get there."

I don't mean to say you shouldn't have lofty aspirations and concrete goals for success. Go for that blue ribbon and the cash prize. But prepare for it properly and you will enjoy horses and horse showing for years to come.

We'd all like to have the perfect horse and the very best of tack to help us exhibit our skills. But that simply is not possible. If you make the most out of the horse and tack you can comfortably afford and gradually work your way up, you will be ready for the horse of your dreams when you have the experience to warrant it. A knowledgeable and trusted professional can help you determine when you are ready to advance.

A prospective showman must dearly love riding. Few accomplished horsemen emerge by simply hopping aboard on show day. Time and hard work are required to show, but the benefits are well worth the effort.

WHERE TO BEGIN

If you are new to the horse show world, but enthusiastic about entering it, do a little investigative research before you make any investments. Visit the well-established riding stables and breeding farms in your community. Get a feel for horses in general and some of the specific activities available for your participation. Read all you can on a variety of horse-related topics. There is a list of recommended books and magazines in the appendix that will help you sift your way through the thousands of horse books and over 250 equine periodicals available today.

Be sure to send for the latest edition of the American Horse Council's *Horse Industry Directory*. (Send $5 to the address listed in the appendix.) The annually updated resource guide includes the names and addresses of breed registries, performance associations, libraries, museums, youth organizations, horse magazines, state horse extension specialists, and much more. The AHC promotes cooperation among all breeds and activities.

Attend one of the horse fairs listed in the appendix. These fairs are not competitions, like state or county fairs, but expositions designed especially for you, the aspiring horseman. Horse fairs are an excellent way to get some free education while being exposed to various breeds, performances, horse products, and services. At some of these fairs there are continuous slide presentations and lectures on topics such as first aid, saddle selection, and shoeing. Other sections of the fair may hold live horse demonstrations.

Breed associations, professional groups, and perform-ance organizations send representatives to these fairs for promotional purposes. Merchants of equine wares distribute literature, free samples, and ordering information for products that range from feed supplements to foaling alarms, automatic waterers to show bridles. In addition, there are usually several vendors offering large selections of horse books.

Perhaps the best way to become acquainted with the elements of a horse show is to attend several different types. Check in a regional all-breed newspaper for the dates of hunter shows as well as recognized cuttings, and for large American Horse Shows Association shows as well as small local shows. Be sure to include several breed shows in your itinerary. An Arabian or Appaloosa show, for example, offers a variety of classes all in one day. Walk around the showgrounds and picture yourself in various situations. Do some preliminary research on the events that particularly fascinate you well before you make the major decision of a horse purchase.

If you are under twenty-one years of age, you can get a great start in horsemanship and showing by joining the U.S. Pony Club, the 4-H Club, and the youth programs of many breed associations.

Pony Clubs are designed to give young people a good foundation in horse care and English riding. Together with other members at your level of experience, you will learn proper management and riding skills. Often you can join without even owning a horse because some clubs have horses that have been donated for member use. The term pony is somewhat misleading as most Pony Club members participate with horses. (Horses under 14.2 hands [58 inches] are generally classified as ponies.)

Because all Pony Club instructors are volunteers, it usually does not cost to be involved in a local club, but it does require the dedication of your time. Members progress through nine levels of proficiency in horse management and riding. The D rating is an introduction. By the time the member has reached the HA level (highest proficiency in horse care) and the A level (highest level of proficiency in riding), he or she is able to teach. The annual report and directory lists all of the clubs and those members qualified at HA and A levels. In addition, it contains a list of pony club publications available for purchase. There are more than 400 clubs in the United States with over 9,000 members.

The 4-H is a national network of local clubs that emphasizes agricultural interests, including horses. Clubs are usually organized by parents. Members must keep project record books on the health care and feeding of their horses as well as their training and show records. The 4-H shows offer showmanship and performance classes in both English and Western styles.

Youth Breed Associations are also designed to promote English and Western show-ring competition. Members earn points in classes at approved shows and can compete in national and world championship shows as well as participate in team tournaments and clinics. Often scholarships are available to members. Examples are the American Saddlebred International Youth Association and the Appaloosa Horse Club Youth Program.

Adults often begin their involvement with horses as amateurs or nonprofessionals in various organizations. For example, the American Horse Shows Association and the American Quarter Horse Association both offer amateur classifications. Definitions vary for amateur status, so it is important to check pertinent rules before entering any shows. Amateur generally refers to someone who does not earn money from horse-related ventures. The National Cutting Horse Association and the National Reining Horse Association operate with a similar non-professional classification.

Be aware that the inexperience of the enthusiastic beginner can be taken advantage of by unscrupulous

Joyce Perry-Williams of Livermore, Colorado in the 1986 Tevis Cup 100 mile endurance ride on Too Tall. Hughes photo courtesy of Vetline of Fort Collins.

parties. There is less risk if you are guided through the horse show mystique with a trusted mentor by your side. Ask your friends for recommendations, or contact your state horse extension specialist for the names of reputable trainers and instructors in your area. Your mentor does not necessarily need to be a full-time equine professional, but should be experienced in the horse business. Choose your advisor carefully and then listen to his or her advice.

HORSE SHOWS INSIDE AND OUT

Because the horse world is full of jargon, I am going to try and help you sort through some of the terminology associated with shows. But it is somewhat of an impossible task. If I define a particular term for you, it may be an accurate definition according to some associations but not others. If you carry my definition into the wrong show ring with you, it may cause you disqualification! Please look at the information in this chapter as an overview, not as rules carved in stone. Each association has its own rules, and it is the exhibitor's responsibility to know them. See the appendix for a list of breed and performance associations, and check the glossary for terms.

A breed is a group of horses with common ancestry and conformational similarities. To become registered with a particular breed, there must be proof that a horse has come from approved breeding stock. If a horse is not eligible for registration, it is considered a grade horse. The vast majority of horses today are registered.

Most riding horses are classified as light horses, that is,

they are not draft horses or ponies. Draft horses are generally thought of as cold-blooded workhorses weighing a ton or more. Some pony and draft crossbreds fit into the light horse classification.

Horses are grouped together by type according to their overall body style and conformation and the tasks for which they are best suited. Several breeds with similar makeup may be of the same type. A particular breed can also contain individuals of different type classifications. Be sure to check Chapter 3, "Selecting a Horse," for more information on breeds and types.

The six types are pleasure, hunter, stock, sport, animated, and race. The first five are commonly seen at horse shows. Pleasure horses have comfortable gaits, are well designed for pleasure riding, and are typified by the smooth-moving individuals in any breed. Hunters are long, low movers suited to cross-country riding and negotiating hunter fences and are typified by the American Thoroughbred. Stock horses are well muscled and agile, suited to working cattle, and are typified by the American Quarter Horse. The sport horse can be one of two types: a large, athletic horse suited for one or all of the disciplines of eventing and typified by the European warm bloods, or a small, lean, tough horse suited for endurance events and typified by the Arabian. The animated horse is one with flashy gaits, often suited only for the show ring and is typified by the American Saddlebred.

In order to exhibit the talents of their horses, people have grouped themselves together into either breed or performance organizations. Groups that are designed to promote the versatility of a particular breed offer a variety of classes (hunter, stock, pleasure, etc.) all under the auspices of one organization and open only to horses of that breed. Breed associations generally make their own show rules. The Palomino Horse Breeders Association as well as most other breed associations are set up this way.

Performance groups are designed to promote a particular activity and are open to horses of all breeds. The National Reining Horse Association and the U.S. Dressage Federation are two such groups. Although the

Junior Pre-Training exhibitor Andrea Walnes on Ebony in the Dressage Phase of a Combined Training Event. Courtesy of The United States Combined Training Association. Carol Jean Sostman photo.

NRHA makes its own rules, the USDF is governed by the American Horse Shows Association.

AHSA acts as the governing body for other associations as well, and subsequently its shows offer a wide variety of both breed and performance classes. In addition, the AHSA acts as the National Equestrian Federation of the United States, which is affiliated with the Federation Equestre Internationale and the U.S. Olympic Committee. Equestrian contests have been a part of Olympic competition since 1912.

To prepare for competitions at the breed or performance association level, novices can take advantage of schooling and open shows. Schooling shows are primarily designed to help exhibitors learn and so are informal. Open show classes are usually "open" to any breed. For example, in an open show hunter class, Arabians, Quarter Horses, and Thoroughbreds may compete alongside each other.

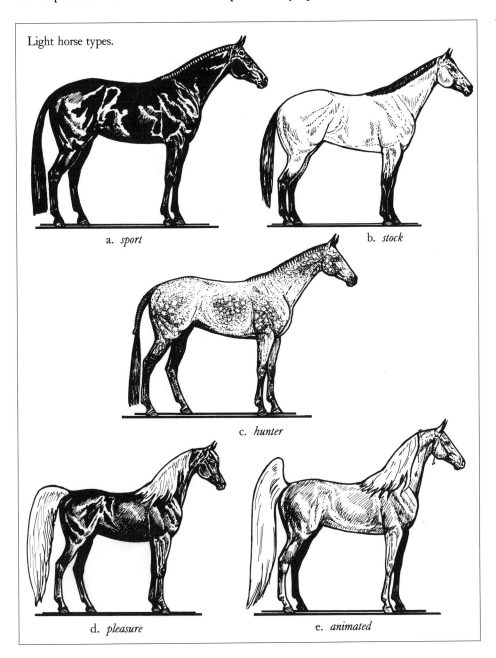

Light horse types.

a. *sport*

b. *stock*

c. *hunter*

d. *pleasure*

e. *animated*

No matter which type of show you enter, there are certain general similarities. The emphasis for judging a class is either on the quality of the horse, its performance, or the quality of the rider's performance.

Conformation, Halter and In-Hand classes all emphasize the quality of the horse. The judge compares the relative worth of the conformation of the horses in the class and ranks them subjectively according to the standard of perfection for the horse's breed.

Classes emphasizing the quality of the horse's performance can be further subdivided into classes that are judged subjectively and those placed by a score. Examples of subjectively judged classes are Western Pleasure, Hunter Under Saddle, and Park Horse. The judge chooses the horse that performs in a manner closest to the ideal for that type of horse. Scored classes, such as Barrel Racing and Jumping, are based on time or faults. There is little subjectivity in such placings.

The rider's performance is evaluated in the three main types of equitation classes: Hunter Equitation, Stock Seat Equitation, and Saddle Seat Equitation. Judges use their knowledge and experience to choose the contestant who exhibits the best overall riding skills while in the ring.

Just what is to be emphasized will be listed in order of importance in the class specifications, located in the appropriate rule book or in the show program. Here is an example of the class specifications for Arabian Park Horses from the AHSA rule book:

"ARABIAN PARK HORSES—OPEN, MAIDEN, LIMIT, STALLIONS, MARES, GELDINGS. To be shown at a walk, trot, and canter. To be judged on brilliant performance, presence, quality, manners, and conformation."

Here you learn what is required: a walk, trot, and canter. You also learn that the judge placings will be primarily based on the horse's brilliance and presence. Quality and manners will also be important. Conformation is the least important of the five criteria in a park horse class. Definitions used in class specifications are included in every rule book.

You may have wondered what all of those additional words meant after the class title. In an effort to separate the park horses into smaller categories, the show will offer separate classes for stallions, mares, and geldings, if there are enough entries. In addition, and only if the number of entries warrants it, a class will be offered for the maiden horse, defined as a horse of either sex that has not yet won a blue ribbon. An open class is one that anyone can enter regardless of the horse's previous winnings. A limit class will specify that a horse may not have won more than a certain number of blue ribbons or cash prizes in previous competitions.

Other classes are defined by the age of the horse or rider. Separate conformation classes are usually offered for each sex in the following categories: weanlings, yearlings, two year olds, three year olds, four year olds, and five year olds and older. A junior horse is one that is four years of age and younger. A senior horse, also referred to as aged, is five years and older. Rider's ages can be divided in many ways (see Chapter 2).

Futurity classes are usually designed for the young horse who has looked promising from birth. Horse owners make installment payments to enter their foals and weanlings in futurity classes in the hopes that their promising youngster will take home big cash winnings. These classes are usually held in the yearling, two-year-old, and three-year-old classifications. Futurities can force horse owners to push their young horses too fast, however, and not allow them to grow up naturally. Some young horses are burned out at a very early age.

Maturities are for aged horses and contribute to the longevity of a horse. Taking care of a horse so that it can continue to win well into its golden years makes a lot of sense.

Most horse activities use some system of further subdividing classes. There are maiden hunter classes for the new hunter and open cutting classes for the horses who have already had big winnings. These subcategories attempt to group horses of equal merit for more equitable competition.

CHAPTER TWO
SELECTING AN EVENT

NOW WE WILL EXPLORE the most popular events in horse competitions today and see what each class entails from the perspective of a judge and a competitor. I will begin with in-hand classes, those in which the horse is led into the ring, rather than being ridden. These classes are judged either on the quality of the horse or the ability of the handler to show the horse.

Riding classes are categorized as either equitation or performance. Equitation classes evaluate the rider's ability. For sake of discussion, I have divided the performance classes into English, Western, and other. Each event has something very different to offer. Once you have familiarized yourself with what each type of competition entails, you will be better equipped to make your first important decision.

SHOWMANSHIP AND HALTER CLASSES
Showmanship Classes

An important skill that every horseman should master is the ability to effectively handle and show a horse in-hand. In showmanship classes, the skill of the handler and the turnout of the horse are being judged rather than the quality of the horse. Turnout is the overall appearance of the horse and includes health, condition, grooming, and the horse's tack. The handler's attire should be neat and clean but not elaborate, and it should not detract from the horse. The horse does not need to be a conformation class winner, although an attractive horse certainly will highlight a good performance.

The object of showmanship is to train the exhibitor for proper halter and conformation class techniques. As an exhibitor, your first goal is to prepare the horse meticulously for the ring. No amount of hair conditioner will improve the appearance of an unhealthy horse. A glossy hair coat begins from the inside with a well-planned

nutritional program, adequate deworming, good management practices, plenty of the right kind of exercise, and a great deal of currying and brushing.

Your horse must be properly trained to perform the various maneuvers required in the class. You must be able to present him to the judge just as instructed. You should not interfere with the judge's view and you should be effective, pleasant, and confident without appearing stiff, false, or aloof. Showmanship exhibitors should perform the required work as precisely as possible with no excess movements or exaggerations. The handler should not invent any unnecessary moves to demonstrate attentiveness. All of this sounds like a tall order, but with practice it comes together relatively quickly.

Judges often evaluate a showmanship exhibitor in four major, equal categories.

1. **Cleanliness**. Is the horse properly clipped for the breed standard? Are there any errant whiskers? Is the bridle path freshly clipped and of the appropriate length? Is the mane shaped, thinned if necessary, and conditioned? Is the tail clean, well-groomed, and natural looking?

2. **Position of the handler**. Was the horseman in a consistent position between the horse's eye and shoulder when the horse was in forward motion? Was the lead shank held at a proper level and used appropriately? Did the horse lug on the chain, or did the handler work the chain excessively? Were the hands carried in a natural and effective way, that is, not way down by the exhibitor's pockets or on top of each other as if carrying a flag? When turning, did the handler move the hand under the horse's head?

In the lineup, could the exhibitor step back away from his or her horse to allow the judge a clear view, or was it necessary to stay close in to the horse in order to maintain control? Did the showman demonstrate an awareness of proper positioning in relation to other horses in the lineup, or was another exhibitor's safety jeopardized by crowding?

Young Halter Showman. Courtesy of The American Paint Horse Association. Catherine Van Der Goes photo.

Did the judge always have an unobstructed view of the horse, and did the exhibitor wait for the judge before moving? Was the showman's response correct when the judge moved from one side to the other when viewing the front of the horse? That is, was the showman aware that his or her movement to the opposite side of the horse should be triggered by the judge crossing the imaginary centerline of the horse?

3. **Performance of the pattern.** Judges are allowed and encouraged to depart from the seemingly standard individual pattern used at many shows: walk out of the lineup, stop, set up, 180-degree turn on the hindquarters, and trot back to the lineup. Keeping the age of the exhibitors in mind, the judge can come up with combinations and variations of showmanship maneuvers that will really separate the contestants.

A unique pattern will immediately show which horse is really well trained and which handler is capable of getting the job done. A challenging pattern is not meant to discourage an exhibitor, but instead to show him or her that competition is tough and in order to win, an exhibitor must be sharp and must practice.

Individual maneuvers are rated in this category, as well as the form throughout the pattern. Was the turn balanced, smooth, and precise? Did the exhibitor aim his or her horse directly at the judge? Was the trotting and/or

walking in a straight line? Was the exhibitor able to bring the horse to a prompt halt, or was the judge forced to move to avoid being run over?

When the exhibitor returned to the lineup, was he or she aware that turning should not take place in the line, but rather in front of or behind it for safety reasons? Did the horse back as a response to movement of the handler rather than to heavy chain pressure? Was the contestant able to set the horse up in an absolute maximum of two to three moves?

Was the pattern correct? Did the exhibitor add or delete maneuvers or perform them in an incorrect order?

4. **Overall impression.** Was the pace appropriate? Did the exhibitor perform in an efficient and effective manner?

Did the exhibitor appear relaxed and poised and in complete control of the horse? Were the handler's mannerisms natural or did they draw attention to the handler and away from the horse? Did the exhibitor overshow in any of the following ways:

• An additional 360-degree turn or other maneuver. Judges often place a large penalty on each extra maneuver.
• Extra steps (often tiny) back and forth as if to keep up exactly with the judge's every breath. A medium penalty.
• Excessive snappiness when moving around the horse, characterized by the military-style "Attention!" stance with a broken forward curve to the back. A medium penalty.
• Hunkering extremely low to the ground when trotting the horse. A minor demerit.
• Looking around or behind as an affectation of attentiveness. A minor demerit.
• Too much eye contact with the judge. A minor demerit.

If showing in a large class, did the exhibitor continually pick at the horse while standing in the lineup, or was the horse allowed to relax, within limits, until the judge was nearby? Was the contestant able to brighten the relaxed horse so when the judge drew near the horse was alert and ready to work?

Was the contestant's clothing appropriate for the age and sex of the exhibitor? Showmanship is not Hollywood and should not be full of tricks or false affectations. Showmanship is the training grounds for tomorrow's halter exhibitors.

Western Showmanship

Each breed and association has its own set of rules for showmanship. The exhibitor's guidelines as outlined by the American Quarter Horse Association are listed on page 12.

You must follow the rules that are specific to the show in which you are exhibiting. The responsibility for knowledge of the rules is entirely yours. It can break a judge's heart to have to disqualify an otherwise lovely performer because of a minor tack infraction. Items to check include, but are not limited to

- Appropriate attire
- Acceptable tack
- Type of hoof dressing or polish allowed
- Shoeing regulations
- Style of mane and tail, length of bridle path, and other customary clipping practices
- Exhibitor's stance in relation to the judge
- Manner in which exhibitor changes direction with the horse
- Type of questions the judge may ask exhibitor as part of the competition

In the stock-type western showmanship class, the exhibitor must move the horse directly toward the judge. The exhibitor is attentive, yet natural. The position in motion is between the head and shoulder. The manner in which the lead shank is carried varies.

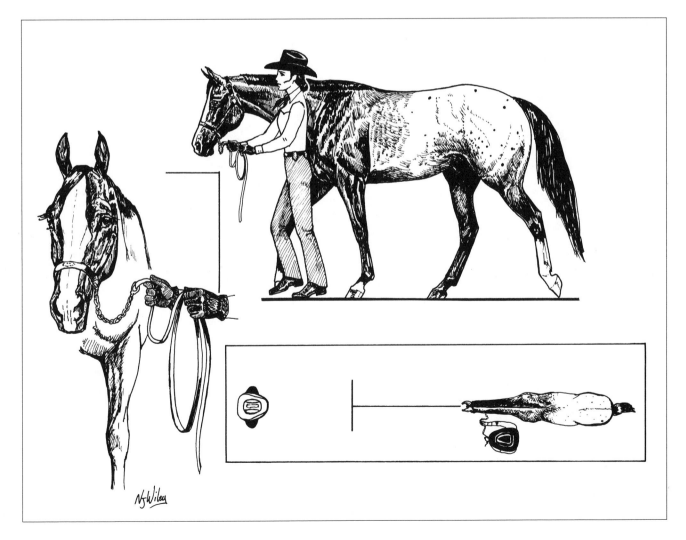

AMERICAN QUARTER HORSE ASSOCIATION
SHOWMANSHIP AT HALTER

APPEARANCE OF HORSE   40 points

A. Condition and thriftiness   (15 points)

B. Grooming   (15 points)

1. Hair coat clean and well brushed.

2. Mane, tail, forelock, and wither tufts free of tangles and clean. It is prohibited to use any ornaments on the aforementioned. Manes, tails, foretops, and wither tufts may be English braided, or manes, foretops, and wither tufts may be Western banded if the exhibitor so desires or the schedule of classes dictates due to time.

3. Hoof trimmed properly. If shod, shoes must fit properly and clinches should be neat.

C. Trimming   (5 points)

1. Manes may be roached but forelock and wither tuft must be left.

2. Inside of ears may be clipped.

3. Long hair on jaw, legs, and pasterns should be clipped.

D. Tack   (5 points)

1. Tack should be neat, clean, and in good repair.

APPEARANCE OF EXHIBITOR   10 Points

A. Clothes and person—neat and clean.

B. Suitable Western clothing.

SHOWING HORSE IN RING   50 Points

A. Leading   (15 Points)

1. Enter the ring leading the animal at an alert walk in a counterclockwise direction unless otherwise directed by the judge. Walk on the animal's left side, holding lead shank in right hand, near halter. The remaining portion of the lead is held neatly and safely in the left hand. A tightly coiled or rolled lead shank will be considered a fault in showmanship. Animal should lead readily at the walk or trot.

2. After the judge has lined up the class in front of the spectators, he will call on each exhibitor to move his horse individually. When moving the horse, be sure that the judge gets a clear, unobstructed view of the horse's action. Allow the horse sufficient lead so that he can move freely and in a straight line. Lead the horse from his left side the required distance, stop and turn to the right around the horse.

3. It is mandatory that the judge post the pattern he will ask for at least one hour prior to the commencing of the class; however, if the judge chooses to bring back exhibitors for consideration of final placing, the finals pattern need not be posted.

B. Posing   (15 Points)

1. When posing the horse, stand toward the front facing the horse, but not directly in front of the horse and always in a position where you can keep your eye on the judge.

2. Pose a Quarter Horse with its feet squarely under it. Do most of the showing with the lead strap. Never kick the horse's leg into position.

3. Do not crowd the exhibitor next to you when in a side-by-side position. Do not crowd exhibitor in front when lined up head to tail.

4. When judge is observing other animals let your horse stand at ease if posed reasonably well.

5. Be natural. Overshowing, undue fussing, and maneuvering are objectionable.

C. Poise, alertness, and merits   (20 Points)

1. Keep alert and be aware of the position of the judge at all times. Don't be distracted by persons or things outside the ring.

2. Show animal at all times, not yourself.

3. Respond quickly to requests from judge and officials.

4. Be courteous and sportsmanlike at all times.

5. Recognize and correct faults of your horse quickly.

6. Keep showing until the entire class has been placed and has been excused from the ring.

In many situations, all of the showmanship exhibitors enter the ring at the same time and walk in a large circle around the judge. Customarily, the judge requests a counterclockwise circle so that the handler's position and attention can be more easily evaluated.

After making one circle around the arena, exhibitors are usually lined up side by side. Then they will probably be asked to perform individual patterns with their horses. Often they may be instructed to come out of the line, trot up to the judge, and set the horse up for a brief inspection.

In all instances, showmanship horses must be well trained to lead at the walk and trot. Depending on the judge's requests, you may need to travel the horse straight to and from the judge or at a distance from the judge to allow a side view of the horse.

In stock-type classes, the horse must trot off willingly and instantly from the lineup and track a straight line directly toward the judge. A common mistake made by the novice exhibitor is making his or her own path a direct line to the judge rather than aiming the horse to the judge. This error puts the horse two or three feet off to the judge's left and requires the judge to take a large step to the side in order to view the horse's travel. Even though the horse's conformation is not actually being evaluated, showmanship classes are designed to prepare the exhibitor to show a horse properly in halter classes.

A prompt halt is required, and the stock horse should stop cooperatively, compactly, and in balance with its feet square. If the horse's feet are out of alignment for its breed type or if it is resting a leg, you should correct its stance within a few seconds so that the judge can begin examining the horse without delay.

During this time specific rules may or may not allow the judge to run a hand along the mane, tail, or hair coat to assess thoroughness of grooming. In some instances, the judge may ask questions of the exhibitor. Questions are usually practical and appropriate for the age of the exhibitor.

When the judge has finished his inspection, you will usually be given a nod. Then you must perform the required turn and travel back to the line. With stock horses, this is performed as a 180-degree turn on the hindquarters. Some showmanship patterns may contain a few steps of backing and a turn on the hindquarters.

In stock-type classes, the turn is always to the right.

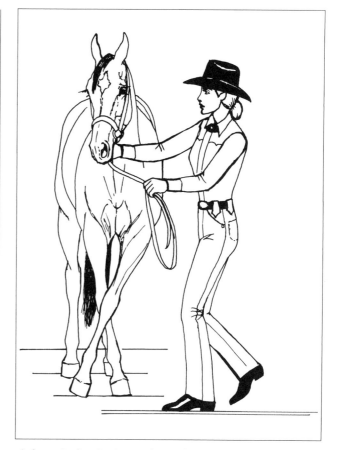

A change in direction in a stock-type showmanship class is accomplished with a turn on the hindquarters.

Stay in position midway between the horse's head and shoulder and exert backward pressure on the noseband of the halter to shift the horse's weight to the hindquarters. The horse should not step backward in this instance; rather it just settles its weight rearward. While maintaining slight backward pressure, move your right hand under the horse's jaw toward the direction of desired movement.

The stock horse ideally settles weight on the right hind foot, which is the pivot in a turn to the right. All other feet walk semicircles around the pivot foot. Some judges will further challenge you and ask for a 360-degree turn to help separate exhibitors in a stiff competition.

Once the horse has been reversed, take one quick glance back toward the judge to be sure the horse is lined up properly, so you can correct your line of travel if necessary.

When the judge has had the opportunity to see all of the competitors individually, he or she may walk through the lineup. Your position in relation to the judge's movement varies depending on the rule book in effect at the show. For safety's sake, some 4-H rules require the handler to remain in one position. In most situations, however, you must have an unobstructed view of the judge at all times and the judge must have a clear view of the horse, yet you should never stand directly in front of the horse. If the judge is standing at the rear quarters of the horse, you must be on the same side of the horse. If the judge is standing at the front quarters of the horse, you should be on the opposite side.

Unnecessary small steps and overshowing detract from the performance. In an attempt to be very crisp and exacting in their moves, young people and amateur exhibitors often become too formal and almost robotlike. Confident moves are efficient and fluid, rather than stiff. It appears as if many exhibitors forget to breathe when they are in front of the judge! Regular breathing will help you relax and make your performance look much more natural. Smiles are a nice addition but must not be forced.

The showmanship horse must be content to stand still for what sometimes seems like an inordinate amount of time. The only way to ensure this capacity is for him to gradually practice standing at home.

English Showmanship

Many of my comments regarding Western Showmanship also apply to Hunt Seat and Saddle Seat Showmanship. Hunt Seat Showmanship contestants usually use hunter- or sport-type horses; Saddle Seat use the animated breeds (Saddlebreds, Arabians, and Morgans).

The attire requirements for the Hunt Seat exhibitor include a hunt cap, boots, coat, and breeches. Hunters are shown in a snaffle bridle, posed with the front legs square and the hind legs slightly separated, with one hind leg perpendicular to the ground. Judges often request a side view of the horse while it is trotting, in order to assess length of stride. The handler may carry a whip.

Saddle Seat attire consists of a solid color suit (coat and jodhpurs in black, blue, grey, green, beige, or brown), derby, and jodhpur boots. Horses are shown in a full bridle (including both a curb and snaffle). The handler guides the horse from the left side by holding the curb reins. The

The English showmanship exhibitor wears attire suitable for either hunt, dressage, or saddle seat and the horse is shown in a bridle rather than a halter. This exhibitor is wearing hunt attire.

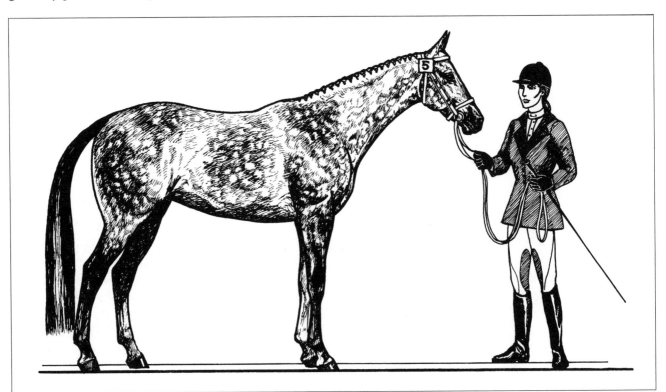

snaffle reins are over the horse's neck, lying on the withers. Horses are shown at a walk and trot, allowing sufficient rein so that the horse can move freely and in a straight line. When the horse is stopped, you should stand in front and face the horse at rein's length. Horses are generally set up with legs somewhat stretched but the judge may ask the exhibitor to bring the horse's legs under the body for inspection.

Conformation Classes

In order to assess the quality of breeding animals, most shows offer conformation classes, in which the horse's overall body structure is evaluated as well as his travel and action at the walk and trot. Horses are exhibited in a halter or bridle by a handler who is on foot.

Before you consider entering your horse in a halter class, be sure the horse is registered and eligible to compete. Then assess the horse's quality with the help of an experienced horseman. Although breed characteristics vary, the overall configuration of a well-made horse is the same no matter what the type.

Judges often view a horse in sections and then put him back together for an overall impression. You can do this with your horse. I suggest that you use one of the two

Peter Mandell with Moondrift Shadow, In-hand. Courtesy of Moondrift Morgan Farm. Rick Osteen photo.

following scoring systems to evaluate your horse. The first method requires that you divide your horse into four functional sections, critique each, and assign each a score of up to 25 points. The four sections are as follows:

1. **Head and neck**. The brain is the master coordinator of the horse's movements, so adequate cranial space is necessary, which is indicated by a good width between the eyes. The head should be clean, not meaty, with well-defined features, a large, warm eye, and adequate nostrils

Susan Lane with Moondrift Carisa, In-hand. Courtesy of Moondrift Morgan Farm. Howard Schatzberg photo.

and windpipe area. The neck functions as a lever to help regulate the horse's balance while moving and should be long and flexible with a slight arching, convex curve to its top line.

2. **Forequarter (shoulder and front legs)**. The front legs support 65 percent of the horse's body weight, so they must be strong and sound. The shoulder should be well muscled without being heavy and coarse. The front legs need to be straight when viewed from the front and rear. Legs when viewed from the side should exhibit a composite of moderate angles, for efficient shock absorption. Exceptionally long, sloping pasterns or short,

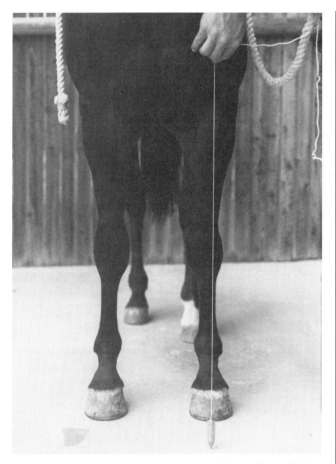

The judge's eye must be trained to assess straightness. Cherry Hill photo.

upright pasterns are to be avoided. Joints should be large enough to allow free movement but devoid of any puffiness. The hoof should be of appropriate size, well shaped, and symmetric.

3. **Middle (barrel).** The midsection houses the vital organs; therefore, the horse must be adequate in the heart girth and have good spring to the ribs when viewed from the front or rear. Spring of rib refers to the curve of the rib; a flat-ribbed horse is not desirable. The back should be well muscled and strong to enable the horse to carry the weight of the rider and saddle. Be wary of the horse with the long back because it is a sign of weakness.

4. **Hindquarter (hip and hind legs).** The hindquarters are the center for power and propulsion. Therefore, muscling must be adequate for the type or breed. Horses may have very flat or very bulging muscles, but the moderate type that tie in low to the hocks are the most versatile. The comments regarding the front legs also apply to the hinds.

Another way to evaluate your horse is outlined below.

When looking at your horse overall, you should check to see that all the parts blend smoothly together and are symmetric. In other words, the halves of his body should be mirror images of each other.

Also the horse must be well balanced. If the forehand is extremely heavy, the horse will tend to pound with his front feet, setting the stage for lameness. When viewing

Quality. Flat bone, well-defined tendons, clean joints, sharply defined features, smooth muscling, overall blending of parts, fine, smooth hair coat. 10 percent

Top line and proportion. The ratio of the top line's components, the curvature of the top line, the strength of loin, the sharpness of withers, the slope to the croup, the length of the underline in relation to the length of back.   10 percent

Angles. The length and slope to the shoulder, croup, hip, stifle, and pasterns.   10 percent

Muscling. Type of muscling, length and position of attachment of muscles, amount of lateral muscling. 10 percent

Head and neck. The size of the head, the face line, the eyes, nostrils, ears, teeth, throatlatch, shape and length of neck, attachment of neck to withers and shoulder.   10 percent

Substance. Weight, height, size of bones, depth of heart girth and flank, spring of rib.   10 percent

Legs and hooves. Straight alignment of bones when viewed from front and rear, large clean joints, high-quality hoof horn, adequate height and width of heel, concave sole, adequate size hoof.   20 percent

Travel and action. Efficient breakover, straight path of foot flight, light, easy landing of hoof, adequate length of stride, desirable flexion of knees, hocks, and fetlocks.   20 percent

the top line, be sure that the withers are at or above the level of the croup. A horse built with withers below the level of the hindquarters is termed downhill and causes the rider to be unbalanced as well as jeopardizing the horse's future soundness.

The balanced horse has equal length of leg and depth of body. Measure your horse from the ground to the underline. This should equal the measurement from the underline to the top of the withers. In a like manner, the leg measurement should also equal the length of your horse's body from the point of the shoulder to the point of buttock.

Avoid a horse whose neck is shorter than its back—it will likely be inflexible. A rule of thumb is that the neck should be greater than or equal to the back and that the rump should be at least two thirds the length of the back. The neck is measured from the poll to the forepart of the withers. The back measurement is taken from the withers to the area above the coupling (the center of the loin) located above the last rib and the front of the pelvis. The rump length is measured from the coupling to the tail head.

Because the legs are the horse's means to perform, they receive a great emphasis in conformation classes. In general, the legs should exhibit clean, flat bone. The term flat bone is a bit misleading. Actually the lower leg bones are round, but they appear to be flat when they have well-defined tendons that stand out cleanly behind them.

Both forelegs and hind legs should appear to bear equal weight. A line dropped from the point of the shoulder or the point of the buttock to the ground should bisect the leg. The toes should point forward and the feet should be

Conformation evaluation begins with a thorough knowledge of the parts of the horse.

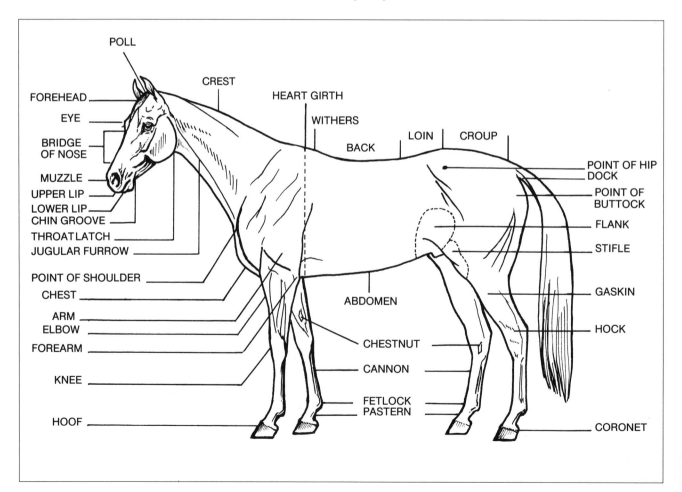

DEFECTS OF THE LEGS AND HOOVES

Splay footed ("toed-out"). When coupled with base narrow it is one of the worst defects. Causes the horse to wing to the inside, increasing the likelihood of hitting the opposite limb. May result in a fracture or recurrent wound.

Calf-kneed ("back at the knee"). Knee is constantly bent backward. Strains the check ligaments and can cause chips in the knee bones.

Buck-kneed ("over at the knee"). Knee is constantly bent forward. May cause less damage to the horse than calf knees. More dangerous for the rider because the horse's knees are always on the verge of buckling forward.

Bench-kneed ("offset cannons") . Cannon does not join the knee at its center. Does not result in a straight column of bones, so medial splints are common and may interfere with proper movement of the knee joint.

Tied-in-knees. Viewed from the side, tendons are pulled in sharply just below the knee inhibiting free movement of the joint.

Cow-hocked. Hocks are closer together than hooves and point toward each other rather than straight ahead. Can result in bone spavin on the inside of the hock.

Sickle-hocked. Also called excess angulation of the hock. Overstresses the ligaments of the hock and often results in curb.

Short, upright pasterns. Increases concussion to the fetlock and pastern joints. Horses tend to form osselets, ringbone, and, depending on the relationship between the pastern and hoof angle, can also develop navicular problems.

Long, sloping pasterns. Results in overstretched tendons causing bowed tendons and damaged sesamoid bones.

Long toe-low heel. Sometimes seen with long, sloping pasterns. May result in bruises to the heel bulbs or damage to the navicular area as the foot strikes the ground.

Flat feet. Hoof is capable of less shock absorption and experiences more sole pressure. Results in sole bruises and abscesses.

Contracted heels. Heels are too narrow and are unable to function during normal hoof expansion. Causes decreased blood supply to the hoof structures resulting in an even more contracted foot.

---

as far apart on the ground as the limbs are at their origin in the chest or hip.

Lameness disqualifies a horse in a conformation class. The majority of lamenesses are found in the front legs, and of those 95 percent are in the knee or below. About three lamenesses will be seen in the front legs for every one lameness found in the hind. You can detect lameness several ways. It is best to conduct the examination at the trot on a hard surface where the feet can be both seen and heard. The unsound foot makes less noise because less weight is put on it.

By viewing a horse from the front and rear, you can watch his head and body for clues that one of his legs does want to bear its share of weight during movement. When a front leg is lame, the horse's head will drop when the sound leg hits the ground. When weight is placed on the unsound foot, the head will rise in an attempt to keep as much weight off the lame leg as possible.

When a hind leg is lame, the head will rise when the sound leg lands. When the unsound leg lands, the horse will pull its head forward and down in an attempt to keep weight off the unsound hind leg. The horse may also "hike" or raise the hip of the unsound leg.

Certain types of conformational defects can predispose a horse to specific lamenesses. Some of the most common defects are listed on page 19.

TERMS ASSOCIATED WITH TRAVEL AND ACTION

Travel. Way of going; the horse's manner of moving. The foot should travel in a straight path.

Action. Style of movement, including the flexion of the knees and hocks.

Gait. Particular footfall pattern such as the walk, trot, or canter.

Pace. Speed at which a horse moves in a particular gait. (A pace is also a specific gait exhibited by Standardbred pacers and some other horses.)

Breakover. Moment between the weight-bearing phase and the movement phase as a hoof hinges forward on the ground. Also refers to the point at which this occurs, ideally the center of the toe.

Length of stride. Distance from the point of breaking over to the point of the next contact of the same hoof with the ground.

Extension. Lengthening of stride in a gait, without increase in tempo; brought about by a driving forward from behind and a reaching in front.

Collection. Shortening of stride in a gait, without decrease in tempo; brought about by a shift of the center of gravity rearward.

Directness. Trueness, the straightness of the line in which the hoof is carried forward.

Rapidity. Promptness, the time consumed in taking a single stride.

Power. Propelling and pulling force.

Height. Degree of elevation of arc of the stride.

Spring. Manner in which the horse's weight is settled upon and released from the supporting structures of the leg.

Regularity. Cadence or rhythmical precision with which each stride is taken in turn.

Balance. Harmonious, precise coordinated form of a horse's movement.

If you think your horse merits being shown in halter, you should present him to the judge with an open mind. If the judge does not place your horse in the ribbons, it may be that you have overlooked a major fault or are simply too fond of your horse to see his flaws.

The judge will inspect the horse for any unsoundness that may disqualify him from placing in the class or that may count strongly against him. A veterinarian can be called in the ring for consultation. Each breed has its own list of unsoundness specifications, which may include but are not limited to the following: totally blind, one nonfunctional eye, parrot mouth, defective hearing, ringbone, sidebone, spavin, thoroughpin, curb, heaves, roaring, bowed tendons, and cryptorchidism (see glossary).

Some judges examine the mouths of all horses for the tooth alignment defect called parrot mouth. This overbite configuration can make it very difficult for the horse to eat properly. The judge will request that you part your horse's lips so that he or she can see the incisors. You'd better be sure that your horse will cooperate for this examination, or it could result in a disqualification.

Another specific examination that may need to be performed occurs in the broodmare class. In order for the judge to assess the suitability of a mare as a breeding animal, he or she will need to view the genitalia under the mare's tail. Often the judge will require the exhibitor to hold the tail to one side for a view. This means that your horse will need to stand still without you being right at her head.

Selecting the best horse involves less guesswork if horses are presented as conditioned athletes, not as fat steers. Fat can hide a multitude of conformation flaws, and is sometimes used to superficially improve a horse's shape. In order for a judge to make an accurate evaluation, the horse should be presented in a fit form.

If a horse is born with less than perfect leg configuration, the time to make adjustments by corrective trimming is usually before six months of age, when the bones are still capable of adaptation. Alterations made after this time may cosmetically improve a horse's appearance but often just shift the stress of imbalance to another part of the horse's body. Altering the hooves or legs of a yearling may get him to stand square enough to win some halter trophies as a youngster, but it will increase his chance for failure as a performance horse. Such unwise practices also contribute to the unsoundness of horses in future generations. The genes for crooked legs are still present in such animals even if the legs have been adjusted to look fine. Such is the story behind a good number of stallions and mares that never were sound enough to have a performance career: They were sent to the breeding shed.

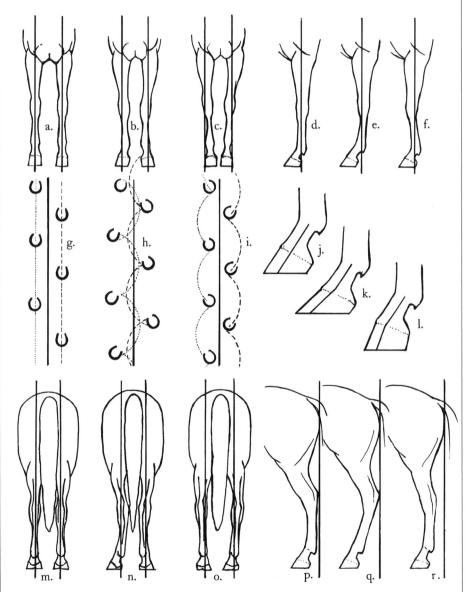

Leg conformation.

a. *correct*

b. *toed-out*

c. *toed-in*

d. *correct*

e. *calf knee*

f. *buck knee*

g. *straight travel*

h. *winging in*

i. *paddling*

j. *normal hoof alignment*

k. *broken back axis*

l. *broken forward axis*

m. *correct*

n. *cow-hocked, toed-out*

o. *bow-legged, toed-in*

p. *correct*

q. *sickle hock*

r. *post-legged*

DEFECTS IN TRAVEL

Paddling. Throwing the feet outward in flight. Often associated with toed-in conformation. Unsightly.

Winging. Throwing the feet inward in flight. Often associated with toed-out conformation. Dangerous because it can result in interfering.

Interfering. Striking a foreleg (hind leg) with the opposite foreleg (hind leg). Associated with toed-out, base narrow conformation. Results in tripping, wounds.

Forging. Hitting the sole or the shoe of the forefoot with the toe of the hind foot on the same side. Associated with sickle-hocked or short-backed/long-legged conformation. Also characteristic of a tired, young, or unconditioned horse or one that has hooves too long in the toe and needs his shoes reset.

Overreaching. Hitting the heel of the forefoot with the hind foot on the same side before the forefoot has left the ground. Also called grabbing. Often results in lost shoes.

Stock Horse Halter Classes

The style of showing various types of horses in conformation classes varies. Most commonly, stock horses are shown to the judge one at a time. Traveling straight toward the judge's line of vision, the horse is walked to the judge, who stands about 40 feet inside the in-gate. The horse may or may not be momentarily set up when arriving at the judge, depending on the judge's instructions. Then the horse and exhibitor trot straight away from the judge, and after about 40 feet drop to a walk and head to the lineup.

Some judges prefer the horses to line up head to tail, and some want to see them side by side. In either instance, you must plan to leave ample space on each side of your horse to prevent accidents and to allow for the judge's examination. When the judge has finished evaluating each horse's travel, he or she will approach the lineup and begin to make a close inspection of conformation and soundness. The stock horse should be standing still and square so the judge can assess the limbs for balance and symmetry.

Hunter On The Line

The conformation hunter is traditionally shown in a hunt snaffle and enters alongside the handler on a loose rein, either at a walk or a trot, depending on the judge's instructions. The horse is trotted past the judge to allow assessment of soundness and length of stride. Then the horse is set up to display the top line to its best advantage. The head and neck are exhibited well in front of the body.

The stock-type halter horse is set up with its feet positioned squarely for the judge's inspection. The exhibitor is holding the shank in a manner common to 4-H shows.

So that all legs are visible from a side view, one front and one hind leg should be offset slightly from the others.

Other Breeds

Morgans, Arabians, and Saddlebreds are exhibited similarly to each other, although there are some important differences, such as whether it is customary to use a show halter or a bridle. Often the judge will evaluate the horses as they circle in a group on the rail to the right and then as they work as individuals. The horse is moved at a walk and a trot directly away from and back to the judge. The way of going and presence are evaluated as well as the ideal standard of perfection of the breed. All horses should exhibit good manners in the ring with no tendency to break gait or resist the handler.

The walk should be rapid, flat footed, four beat, and elastic with an accent of flexion in the pastern. The trot should be animated, elastic, square, and collected. The rear action should be in balance with the front and exhibit no gait impurities. The height of action should not take

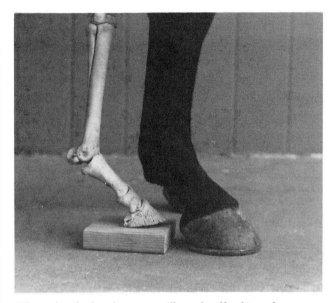

The angles of a horse's pastern will greatly affect his performance. Cherry Hill photo.

precedence over the correct way of going.

Arabians, Morgans, and Saddlebreds are generally required to stand still with all four feet flat on the ground and the front legs perpendicular to the ground. The rear legs may be placed slightly back, rather than in the square

Many judges request a view from the side to evaluate action and/or length of stride, such as with this Arabian exhibitor.

position of the stock horse. The judge may ask the exhibitor to move the hind legs under the horse's body to allow for a normal stance during conformation evaluation. Two handlers are frequently allowed to exhibit a single horse. Both usually carry whips, which are used to encourage the horse to exhibit flashy movement.

EQUITATION CLASSES

Equitation, or horsemanship, is the art of riding, requiring correct overall rider position and proper use of the natural aids: the mind, hands, legs, seat, and upper body. Equitation classes are judged on the performance of the rider, not the horse, although a well-trained horse certainly helps to show a rider's skills.

During equitation classes, errors are bound to occur. A rider's ability is not automatically discounted if the horse makes a mistake. How the rider reacts to the error and corrects the situation is more important. Is the rider aware that the horse has made a mistake? Does the rider allow the horse to continue inaccurately? What is the rider's reaction to the horse's error? Is the rider's response immediate and appropriate? Does the rider not only know how to correct a mistake, but how to prevent it from occurring again? Does the rider retain composure or does the performance begin deteriorating with the first mistake?

The ideal physique of the successful equitation rider is often described as slim, long legged, short waisted, and lithe but strong. The ballerina type does seem to have a natural advantage over the weight lifter in the equitation classes. Anyone can improve his or her equitation, however, in spite of build.

Regardless of height and shape, a rider should never try to force the body into an unnatural position. Each style of riding has its own ideal position. If, in the attempt to attain such posture, and despite lessons and exercises, you find that your ankle or knee turns out more than the ideal, learn to live with it and instead concentrate on the effective use of the aids.

Instructors may differ slightly in the actual names for the natural aids. Some may call the seat the base or the weight, but in essence, the aim is the coordination of the body parts.

The mind is your most important tool. Along with proper training, it allows you to control animals many times your size. Equitation riders need to be simultaneously keen and relaxed. Strong mental preparation and confidence help to make the winning ride.

The upper body assists the rider in maintaining equilibrium during the various direction, gait, and speed changes required. A mere tilt of the head can affect the overall balance of the rider/horse team. Each event requires different uses of the upper body. The center of gravity of the jumper and the reiner goes through radically different changes during a performance and the rider of each must learn the effective upper body position for the particular sport.

The action of the hands on the reins is often overemphasized by the novice but becomes more subtle with experience. Through the bridle, the rider has the power to influence the shape of a movement, the gait, the rhythm of a gait, the rate, the length of stride, and the weight distribution, or to stop forward movement all together. The hands are held according to the head position of the horse and the style of riding. There are many variances among the disciplines, which will be discussed along with each individual event.

The rider's base is comprised of the seat, back, thighs, and overall weight. In general the base transmits signals to the horse's back that help to produce and control impulsion, bending, collection, and extension. The base of the rider should always follow the movement of the horse: If it falls ahead or is left behind, loss of balance and communication result.

The lower legs, acting on the horse's ribs, are the primary motivation for forward movement and engagement of the hindquarters. They are very influential in lateral maneuvers such as the turn on the forehand or side pass because the horse is taught to move away from pressure of the lower leg. In a similar way, the lower leg can also regulate the amount of bend in the horse's body when doing circular work.

The ideal equitation horse is a seasoned horse that is well trained and dependable. It boosts the rider's confidence if the horse's temperament is calm and pleasant. A brilliant but unstable mount is not as good a candidate for an equitation rider as the average performer that is consistent and honest. Although the horse does not need to have spectacular conformation, it should be made well enough to allow it to perform its job well.

Youth equitation classes are usually divided according to the rider's age, depending on the size of the show and the number of exhibitors. Riders under six participate in "Lead-Line" classes. An adult handler accompanies the horse with a lead line while the youngster guides the animal through its paces in the ring. Once the young rider has developed the confidence to ride without assistance, he or she can enter "Walk-Trot" classes that do not require cantering or loping.

The regular youth equitation classes can be divided by age of the rider in several ways, the most popular of which are: twelve and under, thirteen to fifteen, and sixteen to eighteen; or fourteen and under, and fourteen to eighteen.

The hunt seat equitation rider at the sitting phase of the posting trot.

Hunter Seat Equitation

Hunter equitation classes may include group rail work, individual tests "on the flat" (not over fences), and individual tests over jumps. Most breed associations require only group work or group work plus an individual pattern on the flat. However, American Horse Show Association shows offer Hunter Seat Equitation classes that require jumping a course of at least six fences.

Although only the rider is being judged, the horse must be suitable and able to perform the class routine. During group rail work, riders must guide their horses at a walk, trot, and canter both ways of the ring. Extension of gaits may be required of the group as a whole. Riding without stirrups may be requested of the group if the riders are more than fourteen years of age.

Individual patterns are usually selected from a list such

as the following (see the section on Saddle Seat Equitation for a more detailed explanation of the individual tests):

1. Back.
2. Gallop and pull up (stop).
3. Figure eight at the trot, demonstrating change of diagonals.
4. Figure eight at the canter, demonstrating simple change of lead.
5. Ride without stirrups.
6. Dismount and mount.
7. Figure eight at canter, demonstrating flying change of leads.
8. Change of lead down center of arena with simple changes of lead.
9. Serpentine at the trot, showing change of diagonals.
10. Serpentine at the canter, showing simple or flying changes of lead.
11. Half turn (180 degrees) on the forehand or haunches.

In some instances, individual pattern work is timed. If the exhibitor fails to complete the pattern in the allotted

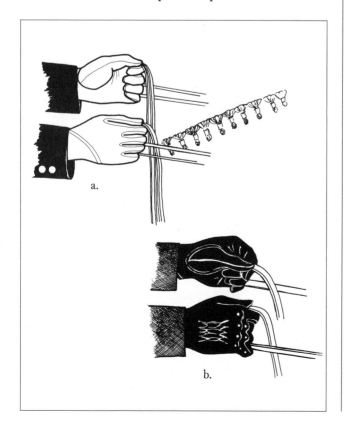

time (e.g., thirty seconds), it is not grounds for disqualification but is judged against the rider. Usually if the rider completes a pattern but it was not exactly what the judge requested, he will not be disqualified but judged accordingly.

In equitation classes requiring course work, there will be at least six fences to jump. Younger riders will not be asked to negotiate fences higher than 3 feet and the older riders not higher than 3 feet, 6 inches. The rider's position and effective use of the aids are evaluated as the horse negotiates the course. The horse's way of moving and style of jumping are not being judged. However, a smoother, more seasoned horse will help the rider with his or her equitation problems.

The judge may jot down general comments regarding a rider's position such as "elbows out," "hands flat," "lost stirrup," "stiff," or "rounds back." The judge may also use a set of symbols to denote the specific elements of the rider's performance (see below).

good fence	rider ducked to one side
rider jumped ahead of horse	rider sitting in the air
	no release
rider left behind the motion of the horse	rider just a passenger
rider looked down at fence	rail knocked down due to rider error
	refusal due to rider error
loose leg	

General Position. Rider should have a workmanlike appearance, with seat and hands light and supple, conveying the impression of complete control.

Mounting and dismounting. To mount, take up reins in the left hand and place it on the withers. Grasp the

---

Two of the various methods of holding the reins, English style:

a. *When using four reins with a double bridle, the rein on the top goes to the curb bit while the rein on the bottom crosses over and on top of the curb rein on its way to the snaffle bit. The hands are held in a near vertical position. Another acceptable variation is with the snaffle rein under the little finger and the curb rein between the ring finger and little finger.*

b. *The snaffle reins are held by hands approximately thirty degrees inside of the vertical.*

stirrup leather with the right hand, insert the left foot in the stirrup, and mount. To dismount, step or slide down. Judge will take the size of the rider into consideration when evaluating mounting and dismounting.

Hands. Hands should be over and in front of the horse's withers, knuckles 30 degrees inside the vertical, hands slightly apart and making a straight line from the horse's mouth to the rider's elbow. Method of holding the reins is optional, and the bight (ends) of the reins may fall on either side; however, all reins must be picked up at the same time.

Basic Position. Eyes should be up, shoulders back, and toes at an angle best suited to your own conformation. Ankles should be flexed in, heels down and your calf in contact with the horse and slightly behind the girth. Stirrup iron should be on the ball of the foot and must not be tied to the girth.

Position in motion. At the walk and slow trot, body should be vertical; posting trot, inclined forward; canter, halfway between the posting trot and the walk; galloping and jumping, same inclination as the posting trot.

Common rider problems include the following:

Rigid hands

Loose rein as with Western horse

Rider loses stirrup(s), then grips with knees

Posting on the wrong diagonal

Exaggerated posting (incline, height, and/or landing)

Broken line at the wrist ("puppy paws")

Hands bobbing

Too much weight in stirrups

Lower legs flap as rider rises to post

Excess curve in lower back

Rider forgets pattern

Western Horsemanship

Western Horsemanship, or Stock Seat Equitation, can be one of the most enjoyable classes for a judge to place and present some of the stiffest competition. In spite of the fact that the rider's ability is being assessed, the young or amateur horsemanship rider should be well mounted. The horse must be cooperative and responsive so it can be guided by imperceptible aids. Although the performance of the horse is not to be considered more important than the method used, it is difficult to win a horsemanship class with an unfinished horse that is young, green, or incompletely trained.

Class routine for group work. Horses enter the ring at a walk or jog trot (as directed), turning to the right and proceeding in a counterclockwise direction (tracking to the left). Class is worked at a four-beat walk, jog trot, and lope both directions of the ring on a reasonably loose rein. Horses should always be on the correct lead. Riders may be asked to extend the horse's normal gaits, reverse away from the rail, back, and ride without stirrups.

In addition, individual work may be required or optional. Examples include but are not necessarily limited to

1. Mount and dismount (except riders twelve years of age and under).

2. Perform figure eights at jog.

3. Perform figure eight at lope demonstrating simple or flying changes of lead.

4. Lope and stop.

5. Execute rollbacks and spins or any other test the judge feels is necessary to evaluate the rider's ability.

Rider's Position. In repose, arms should be in a straight line with the body, with the arm that is holding the reins bent at the elbow. Only one hand is used for reining, and hands should not be changed. Reining hand should be around the reins (one finger between the reins is permissible), above the saddle horn, and as near to it as possible. Position of free hand is optional, but it should be kept away from the horse and equipment and held in a relaxed manner with the body straight at all times. You may hold the romal to keep it from swinging and to adjust the reins, provided it is held at least 16 inches from the reining hand. Bracing against the horn will be penalized. You should sit in the saddle in a balanced, relaxed manner, with a straight back, even shoulders, and arms close to the body. Stirrup should be just short enough to allow your heels to be lower than your toes. Knees should be slightly bent and weight should be directly over the balls of your feet, which turn out slightly. Because the width of the stirrups vary on Western saddles, the judge takes this into consideration when he is assessing whether the rider's weight is on the balls of the feet. Legs must maintain contact to give aids to the horse. The "A-frame" position where the legs are held exaggeratedly away from the horse's sides is ineffective.

Position in motion. You should sit to the jog trot and not post. At the lope, you should be close to the saddle. All movements of the horse should be governed by the use of imperceptible aids. Exaggerated shifting of the rider's weight is not desirable.

Pattern work. Although many exhibitors present a correct picture on the rail during group work, their performance falls apart during the individual pattern. Aside from mistakes that can be directly attributed to a horse's level of training, there are five errors commonly seen in horsemanship classes: going off pattern, executing poor shapes, stiffness in the rider, overcueing, and lack of sufficient control.

Often judges have the choice of either posting a pattern ahead of the class or verbally explaining the pattern to the exhibitors once they have completed their rail work. In either instance, the exhibitor usually has the opportunity to ask the judge beforehand for clarification of any of the pattern's components. Don't be shy about asking questions, especially if you are the first to perform. It is disappointing to a judge too when a rider goes off pattern due to a misunderstanding. Although it is not a disqualification, going off pattern will weigh heavily against you because it demonstrates a lack of experience and unfamiliarity with maneuvers.

Sometimes novice riders will perform off pattern because they forget where they are in the sequence. This disorientation can be avoided by using a combination of the following techniques. If the pattern is posted ahead of time, draw the pattern several times on paper in a rectangle representing the arena. Include any cones or other markers and add the location of the judge, the announcer's stand, or where relatives will be sitting to give you reference points for the actual performance.

If the pattern is verbally explained during the class, you will have to rely on visualization to imprint the pattern in

The Stock Seat Equitation (Horsemanship) rider must ride straight without appearing stiff. This rider is carrying her right arm near the saddle horn in order to maintain shoulder balance.

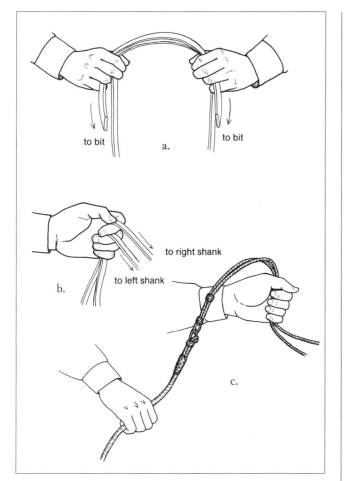

Methods of holding the reins, Western style:

a. *One of the many acceptable two-handed training styles for the western snaffle.*

b. *Split rein.*

c. *Romal.*

Although you should check reference points several times during the running of the pattern, it is poor horsemanship to turn your head every few strides to look at the judge or a marker. That is considered an unnecessary affectation—the good horseman watches where he or she is going.

The size and uniformity of the circles of a figure eight and the junction where they meet can pose problems. Ideally, the two sides of a figure eight should be equal in size and shape. At the center of the figure eight, where the lead changes take place, the horse's body should be straight for one stride before and after the lead change. Because the flying change itself takes up about half a stride, the horse should be straight for a total of two-and-a-half strides at the center of the eight. This requires about 20 feet for a Western horse with an average stride.

Sometimes exhibitors ride the center of the eight in a lazy X configuration. (See illustration on page 30). Typically this results in a less collected change (a front-foot-first or hind-foot-first change rather than a simultaneous change) and destroys the shape of the circles.

Exhibitors often try so intently to assume correct posture that they become stiff, inhibiting fluid communication from the aids to the horse and actually working against an attempt at a correct position. Tension on the stirrup treads or gripping with the knees can lift you right out of the saddle and result in a loose seat. A rigid back doesn't flow with the stride of the horse and communicates tension to the horse. Tight neck and shoulder muscles do not allow the arms to hang relaxed at your side or your upper body to respond to the changes in direction and speed of the horse. An effective rider must be relaxed and follow the movements of the horse. A rigid wrist, caused from trying to hold the hand steady, prevents smooth communication with the horse's mouth via the bridle. Often this creates anxiety in the horse, which will manifest in such things as anticipation of lead changes, nervous tail swishing, avoidance of the action of the bit by "getting behind it," and an overall choppy performance.

The novice horsemanship exhibitor frequently over-cues the horse to ensure that it performs the prescribed maneuvers. Rein cues given outside an imaginary 6-inch square box in the vicinity of the saddle horn will be noticed by the judge, and sweeping cues 12 inches or more to one side or another of the horse's neck will be heavily pen-

your mind. Listen carefully to the judge's instructions, which are usually repeated twice, taking note of where the judge and cones will be located.

Before the run, close your eyes and ride the pattern several times in an imaginary arena to lock the succession of maneuvers in your mind's eye. This should give you a much better chance of knowing what comes next if a performance error causes temporary confusion. Your mind and body will perform much better with a steady supply of oxygen. Several deep abdominal breaths, pushing outward with the diaphragm, may help to calm nerves and prevent memory lapses.

alized. Do not pull the bridle reins in an attempt to back. You should establish contact with the bit instead and back the horse with leg cues. An exaggerated shift of your weight, to initiate a lead change for example, is undesirable because it creates an unbalanced situation for both you and the horse. Although spurs are commonly seen in the show ring, they should be used sparingly. Subtle leg cues are expected for the initiation of lope departs, hindquarter turns or spins, and backing.

Some riders lack sufficient control of their mounts to guide them in individual maneuvers away from the rest of the lineup. This results in a pattern becoming lopsided as the horse performs willingly toward the lineup but

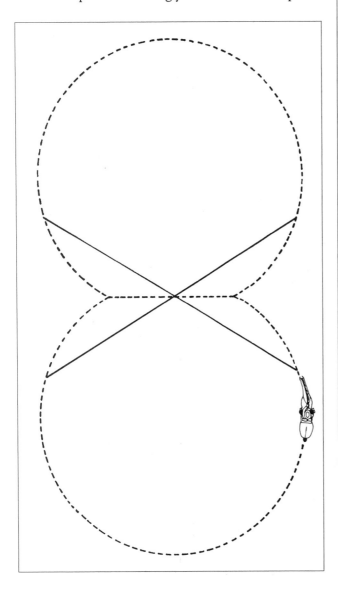

reluctantly away from it. Because the horse is a social animal, he desires companionship with others, especially during times of stress. If the horse is unsure of his rider or the situation, he will want to return to the safety of the rest of the horses in the class. The rider who has developed a confident horse has no problem asking it to work independently.

The Western Horsemanship exhibitor must be relaxed and comfortable when performing precise maneuvers with his mount. The best safeguard against problems in the show arena is to spend plenty of hours riding the horse in a variety of situations.

Saddle Seat Equitation

Exhibitors of American Saddlebred, Arabian, and Morgan horses often show their horses with saddle seat tack and corresponding attire, but many of the comments in the preceding equitation sections are applicable here.

The rail work called for is the same as for Hunter Seat Equitation, but the style is more elevated, animated, and flashy without becoming exaggerated or extreme. The performance should be formal yet light, crisp yet correct, exuberant yet easy. The rider should give the overall impression of competency with style and polish.

The seat of the Saddle Seat Equitation rider should in no way be exaggerated, but it should be thoroughly efficient and comfortable for riding the animated horse at any gait and for any length of time.

In Saddle Seat Equitation classes, riders should convey the impression of effective and easy control and show the judge that he or she has the ability to present a horse. The judge will, in effect, be answering the question, "Which rider would I want to have showing my own horse?"

To show a horse well, the rider should show evidence of ring generalship. Does the rider find good position on the rail? Is the horse being shown to his best advantage? Is the rider in complete control of the situation? A rider who makes full use of the ring yet is courteous to others in the class will make a favorable impression.

Often equitation riders are required to perform a figure eight. Here a western rider approaches the crucial center of the eight. The dotted lines represent the correct shape to the pattern. The solid lines represent an incorrect choice.

Hands. Hands should be held in an easy position, neither perpendicular nor horizontal to the saddle, and should show sympathy with the horse's mouth, adaptability, and control. The height that the hands are held above the horse's withers depends on how and where the horse carries his head. The method of holding the reins is optional, except that both hands must be used and all reins must be picked up at one time.

Basic position. To obtain proper position, place yourself comfortably in the saddle and find your center of gravity by sitting with a slight bend at the knees, without use of irons. While in this position, adjust the stirrup leathers to fit. Irons should be placed under the ball of the foot (not under the toe or with the foot "home"). You should have even pressure on the entire width of the sole of your boot and the center of the iron. Foot position must be natural (neither extremely in nor extremely out).

There should be a straight line from the rider's shoulder through the hip to the heel. The posture should be straight but not rigid. There should be a slight bend at the knee with the grip being in the thigh and knee, never with

the calf. The calf should be in position to give signals, not held out from the horse's barrel in an exaggerated manner. The foot and ankle position should not be distorted.

Position in motion. At the walk, there should be a slight motion in the saddle; at the trot, a slight elevation from the saddle when posting; hips should stay under the body, with neither a mechanical up-and-down motion nor a swinging forward and backward; at the canter you should have a close seat, going with the horse.

Tests from which judges usually choose:

1. **Addressing the reins**. Whip should be held in the left hand as the reins are being threaded with the right hand. Test is usually used for riders under thirteen.

2. **Back for not more than eight steps**. First the horse must be stepped up from his stretch or standing position. Then the required steps backward are taken, the horse is stopped, and then sent forward to retrace the same number of steps. The horse is then stopped and parked. The judge will be looking for the proper adjustment from the rider if the horse attempts to step sideways.

The Saddle Seat Equitation Rider at the trot.

3. **Performance on rail**. Judge may send a rider out to the rail to perform several gaits with precision in a straight line within a limited distance. Change of lead or change of diagonal may be asked here.

4. **Performance around ring**. Rider works on and off the rail, performing such maneuvers as trot, halt, back, canter a circle, trot, and return to the line. A difficult and time consuming test usually reserved for a championship or medal class.

5. **Feet disengaged from stirrups/feet engaged.** (In the lineup only.)

6. **Change of diagonals down center of ring or on the rail**. Horse's body must move forward on a straight line at the trot. The rider, at a point specified by the judge, changes diagonals by sitting or rising for two beats.

7. **Execute serpentine at a trot**. A serpentine is a series of equal-sized left and right half circles off the imaginary centerline of the arena where correct diagonals and changes of diagonals must be shown.

8. **Figure eight at trot, demonstrating changes of diagonal**. Horse begins at the center point of X, proceeds a stride or two straight ahead, bends to the direction of the circle, and completes the first circle. Then he reenters the center line, makes his change at X, and continues as on the first circle, but in the opposite direction. Judge may specify that you start by facing a certain direction or the choice may be left up to you. Judge's instructions may also require you to begin with the left circle first, or the right, or leave the choice up to you. Remember, when circling to the left at the trot, you will be posting on the right diagonal, when moving to the right, you will be posting on the left diagonal.

9. **Serpentines at canter on correct lead, demonstrating simple changes of lead directly on the imaginary center line**.

10. **Figure eight at canter on correct lead, demonstrating simple change of lead.** See comments under figure eight at the trot. For a simple lead change, the horse must be brought to a walk, then restarted on the opposite lead. A full halt change, which is more difficult, would require the rider to bring the horse to a halt before starting on the new lead.

11. **Change leads down center of ring or on the rail, demonstrating simple change of lead**. Changes down the centerline are slightly easier to perform than changes down the rail because the horse tends to associate the rail with a particular lead. When the rail is on the horse's right, habit tells him he should be on the left lead. All leads should be taken with the horse's body parallel to the rail, not angled toward or away from the rail. If a judge requires three lead changes beginning with the left lead, you will have to perform four canter departs to demonstrate the three changes—from left to right, right to left, left to right.

12. **Ride without stirrups, no more than one minute at the trot**. Purpose is to see if the rider is posting correctly from the thigh and knee and assess his or her balance and correctness.

13. **Demonstration ride of approximately one minute on your own mount**. May be used in advanced classes to give the rider and mount the opportunity to show what they can do best. Rider provides a written copy of the demonstration to both the judge and the announcer. The ride is timed. It is better for a rider to do a simple test well than a complicated one poorly.

14. **Exchange horse with another rider**. This is used only to separate the top two riders in a major competition. Riders are usually not asked to perform a test with an unfamiliar horse that they have not already performed with their own horses.

ENGLISH PERFORMANCE CLASSES
English Pleasure

An English pleasure horse is shown either saddle seat or hunt seat at a walk, normal trot, strong trot, and canter, both directions of the ring. The hand gallop may also be required. The judge evaluates the horse on manners, performance, quality, conformation, and presence, in that order. Some breeds specify actual percentages of emphasis for each category. The rider is not being judged, although his or her effectiveness has a great deal to do with the horse's success or failure.

Light contact must be maintained with all reins at all gaits. The horse must perform willingly with ease, cadence, balance, and smoothness. English horses customarily enter the ring at a normal trot, a two-beat gait performed at medium speed with moderate collection. Posting is required. If a strong trot is called, the horse must show an increase in the length of stride, indicating power and the ability to reach. The rate of speed will vary among horses, but the horse should not become quick (short and choppy), strung out, or show exaggerated action in front.

The judge then calls for a walk. It must be a true four-beat gait that is flat footed and exhibits good reach.

The canter must be smooth, unhurried, and with three distinct beats. When viewed from the front or rear, the horse must be traveling straight. The hand gallop is an extension of the canter into a ground-covering stride with the rider maintaining control. All transitions from one gait to another should be smooth and effortless. A pleasure

horse should be agreeable to ride, so cooperation with the rider is paramount. Smoothness of gait and ease of ride are essential.

The Park Horse

Park horses are judged on brilliance of performance, presence, quality, finish, conformation, and manners, in that approximate order of importance. Brilliance is that

Susan Lane on Moondrift Chantilly, English Pleasure. Courtesy of Moondrift Morgan Farm. Howard Schatzberg photo.

sparkling quality of a flashy performer that says, "Look at me—I'm special!" Presence refers to the horse's total aura in the ring. Quality refers to the overall degree of merit of the horse's breeding as reflected by its refinement, cleanness, and correctness. Finish is a combination of tiny details that make a horse's appearance and performance first-rate.

The park horse division is designed as a transition for equitation and pleasure horses that are on their way to the show horse classification. Park horses move with more elevation than pleasure horses and therefore are often not allowed in other performance divisions.

Movement of the park horse should be collected, brisk, and vigorous. Impulsion and power should be evident from the hindquarters, while the front end is light and airy. The shoulder should exhibit free action, with the foreleg able to stretch fully forward with a floating motion. This should be accompanied by hock action that is powerful and well raised.

The Show Horse

Several breeds have show horse divisions that put brilliance of performance at the top of the list. Such animated classes are quite exciting to watch. Because of the common practice of shoeing the animated show horse in an exaggerated fashion, use of this horse is usually limited to the show ring.

Three-gaited and five-gaited American Saddlebred horses have the conformation that lends itself to animation. Some lines of Morgans and Arabians have also been selected for this same type of performance—a straight folding action of the front legs and flexing hocks carried close together, producing a clean, rhythmic action that is brilliant, yet graceful.

The animated horse is being asked to free up his front end by raising his head and neck and drawing it back to lighten the forehand. If a horse has a considerable amount of weight on his forehand, it will be difficult for him to elevate and animate. In addition, a heavy forehand will distort some of the freedom of the leg that is in the air. So, first of all, the animated horse must not have a downhill top line. That would make the horse have to work doubly hard. A relatively level top line is desired.

But what is even more important is the length of the hind leg in relation to the front leg. If an animated horse has extra length to the hind leg, the resulting movement can appear disjointed, as if the two halves of the horse are performing different gaits, or a mixed gait, especially at speed. This type of movement is termed "skatey" or "racky" and is undesirable. If such an imbalanced horse is asked to slow down in an attempt to correct the defect, it will cause the stride behind to become short while the front end has to get very busy to keep up. Remember, the animated horse must perform level, square, and with a unity of movement .

The knee and hock placement is important for the correct folding of the legs. The tibia, the bone which is located between the stifle and hock joints, should be presented in a near horizontal position during the flexion phase of the movement of an animated horse. This is easier to achieve if the tibia is short in relationship to the cannon of the hind leg. Likewise, in the front leg, the relationship of the forearm length to the part below the knee will dictate the knee placement and the ability of the horse to present the forearm in a level position during the movement. Contrary to the selection criteria for most other horses, the animated horse should have relatively long cannon bones.

The overall posture of the animated horse is one that comes back to the rider, or in the vernacular of the Saddlebred trainers, "tips over" or "hinges at the top." One of the key ingredients in getting a horse to assume such a posture is a pliable, long neck that can be raised high and is capable of closing the angle created by the head and neck. This will also be affected by how far the jowl carries into the neck, the thickness of the neck, the cleanness of the throatlatch, and the width of the jowls. In order for the animated horse to close the angle of his head and neck while responding to the bridle, he must have the proper relationship between the top line of the neck and a shorter underline. Horses with top line and underline of nearly equal lengths, such as a hunter or Western horse, tend to carry their head and necks low. But remember, one particular conformational attribute by itself is not going to make a champion. A horse can have a long, well-laid-back shoulder, only to have its effects nullified by a long forearm and short cannon.

The following chart is a description of gaits from the American Saddlebred Horse Association's "Judging Standards for American Saddlebred Horses."

DESCRIPTION OF GAITS CHARACTERISTIC OF ANIMATED HORSES

Adapted from American Saddlebred Horse Association guidelines

Walk. Judging at the walk is based on manners, quality, and natural action; it is not used as a rest period.

Flat Walk. This should be relaxed and elastic, a ground-covering and collected four-beat gait, executed in a brisk manner. It should display the horse's good manners, type of stride, and attitude.

Animated Walk. This can be either a two-beat or a four-beat gait. It is highly collected and animated, at a slow, relaxed speed. It should have snap and easy control and be performed with style and elegance.

Trot. In this natural, two-beat diagonal gait the front foot and opposite hind foot take off from the ground in unison and land simultaneously. A balanced trot should exhibit straight, true shoulder motion of front legs, with flexing hocks carried close together.

Park Trot. In Three-Gaited and Fine Harness classes this gait is executed in a highly collected manner. Speed will be penalized.

Parade Gait. This is a collected trot at a maximum speed of five miles per hour.

Roadster Jog Trot. This gait, again executed in a highly collected manner, should display the purity of motion. Energy should be directed toward animation, not speed.

Gaited Trot. The trot of the five-gaited horse should show speed in form—the maximum rate at which the horse can trot while maintaining proper form, control, and balance.

Extended Trot. This is faster, stronger, and bolder, with a fuller extension of stride to obtain speed.

"Show Your Horse." At this command the driver can show the Fine Harness horse to its best advantage at the trot, but speed will be penalized.

Road Gait. Executed in a highly collected manner, this gait is faster, stronger, and bolder than the Jog Trot with a fuller extension of stride to obtain desired speed.

"Drive On." At this command in Roadster classes, the horse must show speed in form (see *Gaited Trot*, above).

Canter. This three-beat gait, a restrained gallop, is relatively slow and fluid. The second beat is executed by two diagonal legs moving together; the first and third beats are struck by the unpaired hind and front legs. All four feet are off the ground for a brief interval. The canter is executed on the lead that is toward the center of the ring to relieve stress and aid in balance. The lead is determined by which foreleg strikes the final third beat.

Slow Gait. This is a four-beat gait with each foot contacting the ground separately. In the takeoff the lateral front and hind feet start almost together but the hind foot contacts the ground slightly before the forefoot. It is a highly collected gait with most of the propulsion coming from the hindquarters, while the forequarters assist in pulling the final beats. The Slow Gait is *not* a medium rack, but a restrained four-beat gait, executed slowly but with true and distinct precision.

Rack. In this four-beat gait each foot meets the ground at equal, separate intervals. It is smooth and highly animated, performed with great action and speed, in a slightly unrestrained manner. Form should not be sacrificed for speed. It should be performed by the horse in an effortless manner from the Slow Gait, at which point all strides become equally rapid and regular. To be penalized is any tendency to become "trotty," "pacey," or "hitchey gaited" (mixed rhythm).

Hunter Classes

Hunter classes are the show ring approximation of a horse galloping and jumping cross country behind a pack of hounds chasing a fox. A show-ring hunter is shown over natural-style fences: white board fence or gate, natural post and rail, brush, stone wall, chicken coop, aiken, and hedge. Spreads over 4 feet, square oxers, triple bars, hogs backs, or triple combinations are not used in hunter classes.

A good hunter course has a flowing, smooth path with no sharp turns. There must be at least one change of direction requiring a change of lead. One or two easy fences should be located at the beginning of the course, and there should be no frightening or intimidating fences. At least eight separate jumps are required of the horse, with one combination (an in-and-out) toward the middle or end of the round. There should be a different number of strides required in each line of fences but there should be no difficult distance problems on a hunter course.

The hunter must exhibit a steady pace, adequate length of stride, good timing, and a cooperative manner. He must use his body well in a rhythmic, smooth trip around the course and negotiate each fence with style and model form. The hunter's body should make a perfect arc or bascule over the fence as he stretches the neck, rounds the back, contracts the abdominals, folds the knees, and tucks all legs in an organized fashion.

Each judge uses a personal set of symbols to denote a

horse's performance at each fence and between fences (see below).

good fence	jumped with front legs hanging
horse popped fence	hard rap
shortened in front, but jumped OK	quick
dove at the fence	tense
hollowed the back in the air	strong
twisted	overchecking by rider
crash or dangerous	extra stride added
refusal or run out	weaving between fences
knocked rail down	inverted in bridle
jumped flat	no scope
	choppy stride

Besides these specific notations, the judge will also rate the horse's style of moving and jumping ability. The total round is then assigned a numerical score (see below).

0	Not completed or eliminated
40	Two or more major faults
50	One major fault
60–69	Poor performance
70–79	Average performance
80–89	Good performance
90–100	Excellent

Often an assortment of hunter classes is offered. Generally, in order for points earned in flat classes to count toward championships, the horse must be shown over fences later in the show. Be sure to check the rules of the sponsoring organization before entering.

Model hunter. This in-hand (or on-the-line) class is designed for the top-quality animal with elegant grooming and turnout, meticulous shoeing, and ideal conditioning. The class is judged on conformation, way of moving, and soundness.

Hunter Under Saddle. Similar classes may be called Hunt Seat Pleasure and Bridle Path Hack. The Hunter

Arabian Hunter. Courtesy International Arabian Horse Association.

Under Saddle class is often evaluated primarily on quality of movement and conformation and is sometimes thought of as more of a beauty contest than the other two classes. These classes are evaluated primarily on performance, manners, and suitability to ride cross country.

Hunter Hack. Offered in some breed and open shows, this class requires horses to jump two fences that are 2 feet to 2 feet 6 inches. The fences are placed at least 36 feet apart or in increments of 12 feet. After negotiating the two fences, the horse is galloped and pulled up. Horses being considered for an award are then returned to the arena as a group and asked to perform at the walk, trot, and canter in both directions. The judge usually allows a maximum of 30 percent for the flat work when making the final placings.

Junior Hunter. The term junior refers to the rider, not the horse, and usually indicates one who has not yet reached eighteen.

Green Hunter. The term green refers to the horse, not the rider, and indicates the beginning stages of training. Horses in their first year of competition are required to jump 3 feet 6 inches. Horses in their second year of competition are required to jump 3 feet 9 inches.

Regular Open Hunter. Any horse is eligible to

Hunter over fences. Although the turn-out of this horse and rider is very good, the horse has approached the fence off center and at an angle.

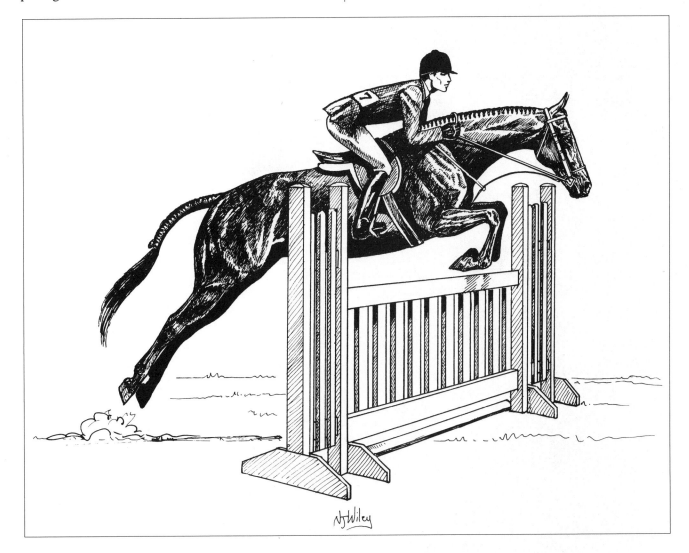

compete in open classes. Open hunters must jump 4 feet.

Handy Hunter. A handy hunter must have prompt response to the rider's aids, as the course is often designed to be tight and challenging (trappy), with at least two changes of direction and at least one combination. Horses may even be required to trot or be led over a fence.

Working Hunter. With less emphasis on conformation, the working hunter is judged on his ability to negotiate a course in a safe and businesslike manner.

Jumper Classes

Jumper classes are judged on the horse's ability to negotiate a course accurately, efficiently, and within the guidelines of the sponsoring organization. Fences for jumpers are more varied, colorful, unusual, higher, and wider than those for hunters, and include spread, plank, stone wall, triple bar, and brush. The course consists of about 50 percent spreads, using striped poles and brightly

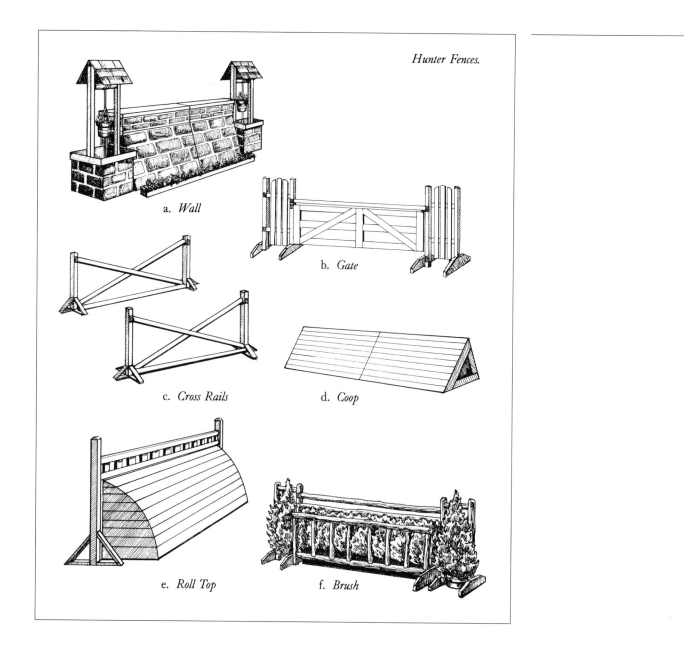

Hunter Fences.

a. *Wall*

b. *Gate*

c. *Cross Rails*

d. *Coop*

e. *Roll Top*

f. *Brush*

painted fences. Fences are usually higher than in hunter classes and square oxers and triple combinations are used. The jumping lines of the course may be tricky, meeting the fences at sharp angles and requiring hard turns.

The rider and horse must be experienced, aggressive, talented, and have heart. The horse's fitness, athletic ability, agility, power, and intelligence are also evaluated in a jumping class.

The scoring of jumpers is largely mechanical, based on faults and sometimes time. Occasionally the judge may have to stop and then restart the time in the event a horse disturbs a fence. The fastest clear round wins. Touches are sometimes figured as a fault, with a greater penalty being awarded for any portion of the horse's body in front of the stifle touching the jump.

Knocking down any portion of a jump constitutes a major fault, usually four penalty points. The first refusal usually produces three faults, the second six faults, and the third is an elimination.

There are a few judgement calls that may be made by the judge, such as noting that the horse lost forward motion, crossed its tracks, or made an illegal circle on the course.

In the event of a tie, there is a jump-off. Jump-offs are held over the original course but may include new obstacles. The sequence of obstacles in a jump-off may be in any order or direction. Obstacles may be raised, lowered, broadened, or narrowed.

The jumper may be any breed, height, or sex but must be a well-trained aggressive athlete capable of pushing on

Appaloosa Jumper ridden by Kathleen Fleagle. Courtesy of The Appaloosa Horse Club. Roberta Wessel photo.

when asked and cooperatively pulling up when required. Because of the difficult course, the horse must be able to lengthen and shorten stride at a moment's notice and make quick turns without losing balance or momentum.

Cash winnings determine a horse's status and eligibility to show in various jumper divisions. Preliminary classes are generally for horses in their first year of jumper classes. Intermediate classes are for horses that have won less than $5,000 since the preliminary division. Any horse is eligible for open competitions, but horses that have won more than $5,000 must compete in open classes. An exception is the amateur-owner class.

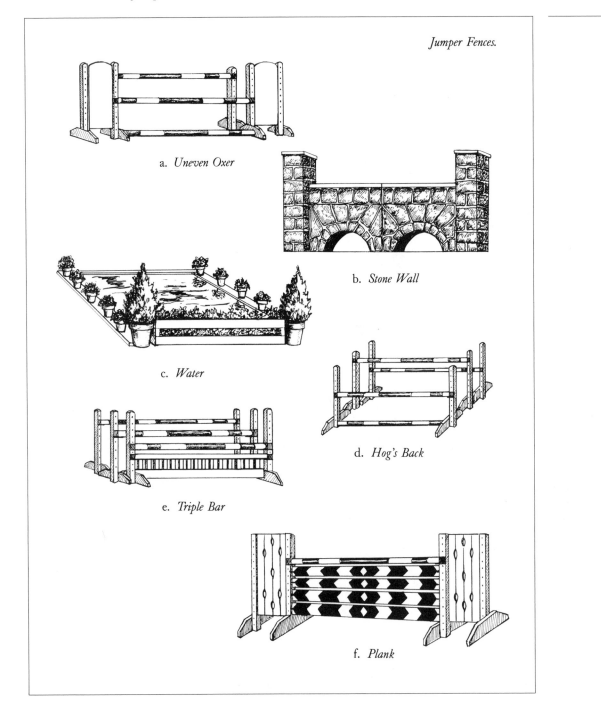

Jumper Fences.

a. *Uneven Oxer*

b. *Stone Wall*

c. *Water*

d. *Hog's Back*

e. *Triple Bar*

f. *Plank*

Dressage

Dressage has enjoyed increased popularity since World War II and a virtual boom in North America since 1970. The white Lipizzan stallions of the Spanish Riding School come to the minds of many people when thinking of dressage. Although the Spanish School represents the classical approach to the discipline, dressage in its contemporary sense is a much more attainable sport.

The term dressage in French means "to train." By systematically guiding a horse through progressive stages, a rider works toward developing a forward free-moving horse that is supple and submissive, calm but keen, and responsive to light contact without resistance or resentment. This elegance and harmony between horse and rider takes years to develop and perfect. Chapter 6, "Training the Horse," is based on classic dressage methods.

Specific goals have been developed for the various levels of the horse's training. The objectives and standards as set forth by the American Horse Shows Association and the International Equestrian Federation are as follows:

Training Level. Introduces the rider and horse to the basic principles of dressage competition. Requires "obedience" to the aids of the rider without fight or evasion when ridden on light contact. Goals are free, rhythmic forward movement with a relaxed and obedient mount stretching into the bit in a calm, receptive manner.

First Level. Verifys the correct foundation for successful training: the horse moves freely forward in a relaxed manner and with rhythm, its spine always parallel to the track of the prescribed movement; he accepts the bit and obeys simple aids of the rider. Also requires that the horse show soft response to the aids, such as softening of the lower jaw, some flexion at the poll, lateral bending, and quiet transitions.

Second Level. Determines the horse has additionally acquired a degree of suppleness, balance, and impulsion. The rider must now add "accuracy" and be able to put the horse to the aids, that is, put the horse on the bit and keep it there without fight or evasion and without shortening the strides. Neck must be relaxed with the nose slightly in front of the vertical.

Third Level (medium difficulty). Determines the acquiring of an increased amount of suppleness, impul-

Dressage—Lower Level.

AHSA DRESSAGE TEST REQUIREMENTS

Training level. Test 1. Working walk, trot, and canter. Halt from walk or trot. Working gaits are regular and unconstrained, energetic but calm, with even and elastic steps. Transitions are gradual: The canter depart is performed from the trot, and transitions into and out of the halt may be made through the walk. Circles at the trot and canter are 20 meters (66 feet).

Test 2. Contains a free walk on a long rein.

Test 3. Requires canter departs at specific letters.

Test 4. Requires a five-second immobility at the halt.

First level. Test 1. Lengthened strides at the trot; 15 meter (49.5 feet) circles at the trot and canter.

Test 2. 10 meter (33 feet) half circle at the trot. Serpentine of three loops at the trot.

Test 3. 10 meter (33 feet) circle at the trot and canter. Leg yield. Lengthen stride in canter. Change of lead through the trot.

Test 4. Leg yield from the track.

Second level. Test 1. Medium walk and trot. Collected trot. Shoulder-in. Rein back three to four steps. Canter depart from the walk.

Test 2. Travers. Medium canter. Collected canter.

Test 3. Collected trot after reinback. Simple change of lead.

Test 4. Rein back four steps. Half turn on haunches. Countercanter.

sion, and balance, so as to be light in hand and without resistance, enabling the rider to collect and extend its gaits. Also requires the attainment of a proper foundation for collection. Horse must show a distinction between paces.

Fourth Level (medium difficulty). Determines the acquiring of a high degree of suppleness, impulsion, balance, and lightness while always remaining reliably on the bit; that the horse's movements are straight, energetic, and cadenced and the transitions precise and smooth. Horses must show complete obedience, relaxation, collection, and

extension and must go fully on the bit without evasion of any kind. He is prepared to proceed to the International Level Tests.

Prix St. Georges (medium difficulty). Shows submission to all the demands of classical equitation and a standard of physical and mental balance and development that enables the horse to carry them out with harmony, lightness, and ease.

Intermediare 1 (relatively advanced standard). Leads horses from the correct execution of the Prix St. Georges to the more demanding exercises of the Intermediare 2.

Intermediare 2 (advanced standard). Eases the path for horses on their way to the Grand Prix and its fundamental "airs and graces" of the Classical High School.

Grand Prix (highest standard). Competition of artistic equitation that brings out the horse's perfect lightness characterized by the total absence of resistance and the complete development of impulsion. Includes all of the school paces and the fundamental airs of the Classical High School but does not include the fantastic paces based on an extreme extension of the forelegs. For this reason, the school leaps, obsolete in a great many countries, do not figure in this test.

The American Horse Shows Association (AHSA) is responsible for designating the contents of the tests through Fourth Level, and the International Equestrian Federation (FEI) governs the tests beyond that. Requirements may change from time to time, so it is important to keep posted on rule changes. To help you get started, the current requirements for training through second level are listed. You can get a complete set of test requirements by joining the AHSA or the USDF.

Training Level tests can be ridden in a small-size dressage arena (20 by 40 meters or 66 by 132 feet). First Level and above are usually performed in a standard-size arena (20 by 60 meters or 66 by 198 feet). The arena is marked by letters that provide exact reference points for the movements in the test.

Horses are trained and shown in snaffle bridles through Third Level. In Fourth Level, either a snaffle or double bridle is allowed.

When training, the rider works on various segments of a particular level rather than practicing a pattern. In competition, however, a pattern must be ridden exactly. In most competitions, the rider has the option of memorizing a particular test or having a "reader" call out the movements from the side line.

Each movement is evaluated by a trained assessor. His or her scores and comments are voiced to a scribe who records the information on a separate score sheet for each exhibitor. Scores can range from 0 to 10 for each component as follows:

10 Excellent

9 Very good

8 Good

7 Fairly good

6 Satisfactory

5 Sufficient

4 Insufficient

3 Fairly bad

2 Bad

1 Very bad

0 Not performed, or fall of horse or rider

In addition to the scores for individual movements, marks are given for overall impression of the gaits, impulsion, and submission of the horse, and the rider's position, seat, and use of aids. The total of points earned is divided by the total possible resulting in a percentage score. Scores of more than 75 to 80 percent are rare.

A dressage horse must be sound and symmetric. He should be able to track straight when moving in a straight line and arc when moving on a curve. He should not have the tendency to develop hollow spots or bulges as a compensation for imbalances. He must have a strong loin, hindquarters, and hock so as to be able to balance the majority of his and the rider's weight rearward. This shift of weight-bearing from the forehand to the hindquarters is progressive as the horse develops through the levels. (See the section on circle of muscles in Chapter 6.)

There are nearly one hundred U.S. Dressage Federation group member organizations around the country. The national organization provides information about local groups and additional information about dressage as well.

Combined Training

Combined training, or three-day eventing, is a comprehensive testing of all-around training and horsemanship. Originally a means for testing military horses, eventing was first included in the Olympics in 1924. In past years, the competition tested dressage on the first day, speed and endurance the second day on the cross-country course, and stadium jumping the third day, thus producing the phrase "three-day event." Today, competitions may span only one or two days and may be called trials, three-phase events, or combined training events.

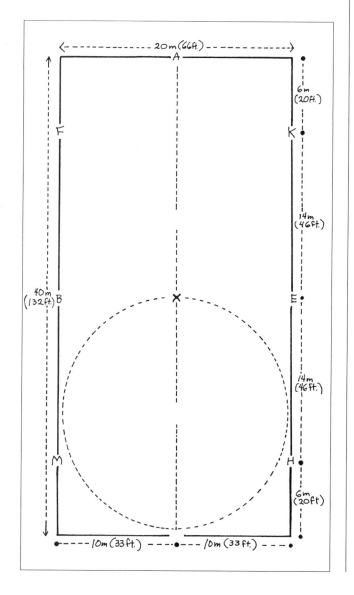

A 20-meter x 40-meter dressage ring with letters.

The governing body for today's horse trials is the U.S. Combined Training Association (USCTA). It was organized to promote American horse competitions in order to develop riders capable of representing the United States in international competitions. Along with the American Horse Shows Association, the USCTA regulates horse trials at all levels for U.S. Equestrian Team hopefuls, as well as for competitors who enjoy the lower levels of the sport.

The dressage phase is ridden as described earlier, but it is scored slightly differently. The score achieved is subtracted from the maximum possible, and the result is the number of penalty points assessed.

The cross-country phase is a test of speed and endurance. It is the ultimate challenge for the horse-and-rider team and requires courage, stamina, and fitness. The total distance may be as great as 12 miles or more. There can be as many as four consecutive sections to the cross-country test: First is an approximately 2-mile route over roads and tracks, covered at a moderate trot; second is a 1- to 2-mile steeplechase, which is to be ridden at 26 miles per hour while negotiating up to twelve jumps; third is a longer roads-and-tracks route followed by a compulsory ten-minute halt for a veterinary examination; fourth is the cross-country course of 3 to 5 miles with up to thirty obstacles. Each of the sections must be completed within a specified time or penalties will be incurred. Falls, refusals, and runouts at obstacles are heavily penalized.

The stadium jumping phase on the third day is designed to prove that on the day after a severe test of endurance, a horse has retained the suppleness, obedience, and energy necessary to continue. Before jumping, the horse must be inspected by the veterinarian. The course consists of brightly painted jumps in an arena. Horses are ranked on time and faults.

The penalty points accumulated from each of the three phases are added together, and the competitor with the least number of faults is pronounced the winner.

The Novice Level (also called Pretraining, Green, or Hopeful) serves as an introduction to the sport. The elementary tests are designed to encourage horses and riders. Competitors can move up through Training, Preliminary, Intermediate, and Advanced levels. With each, the challenge for horse and rider becomes greater: more complex dressage movements, bigger cross-country fences requiring more speed, and higher and wider stadium jumps placed in demanding combinations.

There is no reason why a rider can't compete at the lower levels indefinitely. There is less risk, preparation time, and capital investment necessary. This makes combined training an attainable goal for the average person who has a job and family to fit in alongside horse pursuits.

WESTERN PERFORMANCE CLASSES
Western Pleasure

A pleasure horse should look as though he is enjoyable and comfortable to ride and must be well trained and reliable. He should have naturally smooth gaits and an efficient way of moving. The Western horse should show a good deal of expression as he works and should move naturally, not mechanically. Judges place the easy-riding horse that appears to enjoy his work. Overall, the most thoroughly trained, natural moving horse wins.

With often more than sixty classes to place in eight hours, judges can't spend a great deal of time studying any one class, so often the pleasure horses are worked rather quickly. The routine must satisfy class specifications and provide the judge with adequate opportunity for observation.

As soon as all of the horses have entered the arena and are tracking left at the walk, they are usually jogged, then brought back to the walk before the lope. They are reversed at the walk and often loped and then jogged right into the lineup. Horses are required to back individually and are checked for illegal bits and curb straps. This bare minimum routine fulfills the class requirements. Judges can ask for more transitions and call for certain gaits to be repeated.

Sometimes a judge will save the jog in the second (clockwise) direction as an "ace in the hole" to sort out any problems that have surfaced with the right lead. Often a judge may have selected the top horse(s) from the rail work in the first direction. The horse tentatively in first place after work in the first direction may have, in a particular judge's opinion, a 10-point lead over the other horses in the class because of its quality of movement and good attitude. If that horse bobbles the right lead but then picks up the correct lead on the second try, it may still be in contention for the blue ribbon. The demerits received for errors are weighed against the previous credits earned. If the horse shows a superior trot in the second direction, he may still win the class.

In Amateur and Youth classes, especially, the horse must be shown in a safe and sensible manner. Even though a slack rein is characteristic of the Western style, it does not mean the reins should slap the horse's knees. This jeopardizes safety and usually results in the rider continually lifting up on the rein to check the horse, which detracts from the overall impression that the horse is a pleasure to ride. Although the reins should not be tight, neither should contact with the horse through the bridle be "thrown away."

The gaits are often emphasized more than the transitions in a pleasure class, as it would be virtually impossible for a judge to view every transition for each horse. In a close class, the judge may need to compare the ease with which the horse changes gaits, but, normally, the quality of the three gaits is a much more equitable basis for comparison.

The walk should have four distinct beats, and the horse should appear to be going somewhere. Some exhibitors feel that they must keep their place on the rail and consequently make their horse walk too slow and appear half asleep. Show-ring etiquette requires that riders look out for the other riders. Judges usually do not penalize an exhibitor for passing, if the horse is moving in a manner that is appropriate for his build.

During the jog trot, the horse should travel in a square, cadenced, and collected manner. He should be round over the back with his hind feet well under him and travel with energy, yet be relaxed. It is hard work for a horse to jog slowly with collection, and some of the bigger horses will have to pass the smaller horses on the rail in order to move naturally. At many shows, the judge has the option to ask Western pleasure horses to extend the jog. Horses can be disqualified if no increase is noted by the judge.

Artificial training methods that make a horse afraid to pick his head up or move out are usually easy to spot. The horse's overall attitude is sour, with no expression or interest. His movements are short-strided and mechanical, not smooth. There are a few naturally low-headed pleasure horses, but most horses are not designed to travel with their heads below the level of the withers.

For a horse to be balanced when the leading foreleg hits the ground, especially in the lope, he must be allowed to use his head and neck freely to keep from falling heavily on the forehand. With the neck slightly curved and above the withers, the poll even with the top of the saddle horn or higher, and the head at the vertical or several degrees in front of the vertical, a horse can bring his hind legs underneath his belly. A horse forced to carry his head lower and neck flatter than is natural will travel "strung out" behind, that is, the hind end will trail too far behind the body, rather than be working up underneath it. Moving strung out tends to break up the diagonal pair of legs at the lope, resulting in a four-beat gait. This "trotting behind" at the lope constitutes a major fault for the pleasure horse. In addition, artificially forcing a horse to carry his head low results in the horse being extremely heavy on the forehand.

Young horses entered in futurity classes, especially early in the season, characteristically make more mistakes, and judges are usually more forgiving of these errors resulting from inexperience. Most judges try to help the exhibitors show their young horses to best advantage and prevent them from getting "ring sour." A horse can quickly learn the class routine and will anticipate the rider's cues when it hears the announcer call for a gait change over the loudspeaker. The horse also knows the class is over and it will be able to rest when it is headed into the center of the ring, so it may try to veer there during the class. Horses also will learn where the gate is, and they know that it represents the end of work and perhaps a rest and some feed.

By allotting more time for walking and trotting, judges allow the young horses to become sufficiently warmed up and familiar with the arena. After loping and trotting the futurity horses in the second direction, the judge will often return the horses to a walk and let them go around the arena before coming in to line up. This helps prevent the youngsters from anticipating the end of the class and making a beeline for the center of the ring.

The pleasure horse ideal is constantly changing. Often a judge is presented with a diverse group of training styles and frames (the manner in which the horse carries its body) in the same class. The class may contain "mechanical" or "fixed" horses, horses that are well trained, and also several horses that are just out there for the experience. However, a horse doesn't merit a blue ribbon just because it is nonmechanical. And therein lies the pinch for a judge. Often with no alternative, judges must choose a horse that is far from the ideal but is the most consistent and best-trained horse shown in that class on that particular day.

Determining which horse is truly a pleasure to ride is one of the most subjective and controversial topics in the judging business today. The criteria are usually spelled out clearly in the class specification of each organization.

Trail

A good trail horse is sensible, cooperative, calm, and responsive to his rider's aids. The most placid horse does not necessarily make the best trail horse. A certain intensity and alertness is necessary for the concentration required by the activity.

Training any horse to negotiate obstacles will make him a more useful mount, whether for show-ring competition or pleasure riding. Working on puzzles can help to alleviate boredom for the arena horse and the rider. The Trail Horse Class at horse shows was originally designed to test a horse's reaction to situations he would normally encounter on the ranch or along the trail. Unfortunately, the practi-

Terry Thompson on Plaudits Honey Bun. Harold Campton photo.

cal origins of the class are sometimes forgotten when today's courses are designed. A show committee can dream up a respectable test or a sheer nightmare. Competitors soon learn the suspense involved in waiting for the trail pattern to be posted.

Overall obedience is a necessary foundation before a

A Sample Trail Course:

a. *The horse enters the arena as the rider works the gate.*

b. *The horse jogs to the bridge.*

c. *The horse walks over the bridge.*

d. *The horse walks to the ground rails.*

e. *The horse steps between the rails.*

f. *The horse lopes on the left lead into the circle.*

g. *The rider dismounts, ground ties or hobbles the horse, walks around the outside of the perimeter of the circle, and remounts.*

h. *The horse jogs to the T.*

i. *With head facing the mailbox, the horse sidepasses to the right over the first pole. At the junction of the T, the horse performs a turn on the forehand so that the hind feet pass through the center opening. Then the horse sidepasses the second pole to the right. The horse sidepasses the second pole back to the left. At the junction, the horse performs a turn on the hindquarters so that the front feet pass through the center opening. The horse's hindquarters are now facing the mailbox as it sidepasses the last pole to the left. To face the slicker, the horse performs a 180 degree turn on the hindquarter.*

j. *The horse walks over to the slicker which is hanging from the rail.*

k. *The rider removes the slicker from the rail, puts it on, takes it off, and returns it to the rail.*

l. *The horse jogs to the mailbox.*

m. *The rider takes the mail out of the box, unfolds the newspaper, folds it up, and returns it to the box.*

n. *The horse exits the arena by walking to the out gate.*

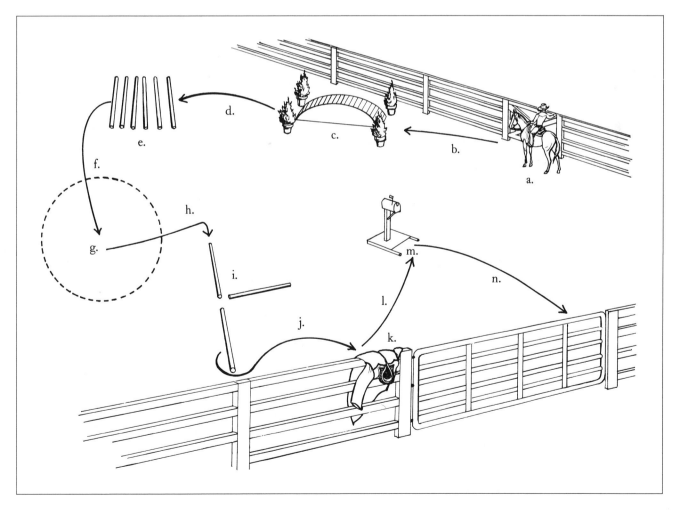

horse is ever introduced to an obstacle. The first essential is respect for the command "whoa." Whether the horseman is mounting, taking the mail from a mailbox, or putting on a slicker, the horse must stand still on a slack rein.

A horse with good basic training will react honestly when he is asked to negotiate a new obstacle. If he refuses to look at the new object, fidgets, or pulls back, he must be taught that when he encounters an obstacle and his trainer pauses that he should inspect it quietly. Not even one step backward or sideways is allowed, and the horse must go forward when the rider decides it is time.

Trail obstacles can be grouped according to the type of challenge they create for the horse. Generally, most will belong in one of the following categories:

• Overriding natural fears
• Resolving optical illusions
• Demonstrating coordination and kinesthetic sense
• Performing intricate maneuvers

Many obstacles combine elements from more than one category.

NATURAL FEARS

• Bridge
• Unusual animals
• Plastic
• Newspaper
• Sack of cans
• Trailer (loading and traveling)
• Motorcycles, unusual vehicles
• Restrain, hobble

Horses are innately wary of unfamiliar sights and sounds and of restraints that inhibit their main means of defense—flight. Hobbling, then, is the supreme sacrifice of mobility and, to allow it, a horse must feel confident with his training and surroundings.

Bridges, horse trailers, ditches, and swampy ground present questionable footing to a horse and spell danger. Be careful not to push a horse to his panic threshold, or you will overload his stress tolerance. Rather than becoming stronger, he will weaken. Use good judgment when asking the horse to do something new.

The trail horse negotiating logs.

MANEUVERS NECESSARY FOR TRAIL

Back. When a horse is backing with energy and alertness, he lifts diagonal pairs of legs and sets them down in unison. The predominant cue for backing is a squeeze with both of the rider's legs, just like the cue for moving forward. The only difference is that the rider precedes the leg cue with a simultaneous shortening of both reins so that the bit makes contact with the horse's mouth and prevents forward motion.

Turn on the forehand. In some situations, such as the gate or the T, the rider wants to move the horse's hindquarters around a stationary forehand. When teaching an inexperienced horse, use a snaffle and two hands (see illustration on page 103). Tip the horse's nose slightly away from the direction in which you want the hindquarters to move. The horse's nose is bent to the right and his hindquarters are moving to the left. The left rein helps to retard forward movement. The rider's right leg is applied at or behind the cinch to move the hindquarters to the left. The horse walks around his right front leg, which remains relatively still. In more advanced training, the horse is taught to perform a turn on the forehand with the head and neck straight or with a slight bend into the direction of movement.

Turn on the hindquarter. Many English and Western maneuvers require the horse to move his forehand around his hindquarters. With a snaffle and two hands, tip the horse's nose into the direction of movement. In the illustration on page 112, the horse's nose is bent to the right and the forehand is moving to the right. The left rein helps to shift the weight rearward and toward the right hind pivot foot. The rider's left leg is applied at or in front of the cinch to move the forehand to the right. The horse walks around his right hind leg, which remains relatively still.

Side pass. Once a horse has mastered the turn on the hindquarter and on the forehand, the side pass comes easily (see illustration on page 50). If side passing to the left, a horse should always cross his right legs over in front of his left legs. The left legs "uncross" by moving behind the right legs. If given the proper cues from a square halt, a horse will first cross the right front over the left front. In the next phase, the left front will "uncross" at about the same time the right hind crosses in front of the left hind. The cycle is completed as the left hind "uncrosses" and the right front begins again by crossing over in front of the left front. Generally, to teach a horse to side pass in a snaffle, the head is tipped slightly away from the direction of movement, that is, to the right if side passing to the left.

Eventually the horse should side pass in either direction with the body straight. When side passing to the left, the rider's right leg is the predominant cue. The temptation is for the rider to lean the weight to the right also, but it is better to keep the weight directly over the center of the horse so he can stay balanced in the maneuver.

OPTICAL ILLUSIONS

- Water
- Plastic
- Mirrors
- Ditches, holes

Because the construction of a horse's eye is not the same as a human's, his view of the world is different than his handler's. Horses use both eyes to see objects directly in front of them but see separate images on each side of their head. At the junction of these two fields of vision, objects appear to jump when they pass from the binocular field (straight ahead) to one of the monocular fields (on the side). When a horse sees something unusual up ahead and approaches alertly with ears and eyes intently examining it, and then shudders or sidesteps just as he passes the object, it may be because the unusual object appeared to move. Experience eventually teaches the horse that certain

objects are not dangerous even if they flicker due to visual distortions. It is a good idea to allow a horse a variety of opportunities to gain this important experience.

Blind spots exist directly below a horse's head and to his rear. In addition, the focusing apparatus of the horse's eye requires him to raise or lower his head to get a sharp image. These two facts explain a horse's sometimes annoying head and body movements when he is reading the environment. Letting an honest horse have a free rein to inspect is only fair.

The structures in the horse's eye that regulate light intake are believed to have slower mechanisms than ours. Horses take a little longer to adapt to the bright sunlight when stepping out of a dark barn or, conversely, need a little longer to adapt to the dark interior of a horse trailer before feeling safe stepping inside it during daylight hours. These adaptation structures are probably also partially to blame for the suspicion a horse displays when he approaches water. The glare is initially blinding.

Coupled with the difficulty in adapting to differing light situations, it also appears that horses lack depth perception. When they are asked to step across a ditch or a sheet of plastic, or, as one show required, aluminum foil, they act unsure of how deep the "hole" is or of whether it even has a bottom.

COORDINATION

- Ground rails
- Jump
- Brush pile
- Rocky slope

Sidepass to the left.

The ability to know where body parts are without actually having to see them is termed the kinesthetic sense. It includes the message relay system from the nerves and muscles to the brain that tells an animal that he is upright and moving forward. Because a horse can rarely see where he is putting his feet, he must trust his last visual image of the terrain he is approaching to dictate how high he must step, how long the steps must be, and whether he needs to alter the speed of his gait to negotiate safely.

Some horses are masters at weaving in and out of log jams or tire piles while others stumble over a single pole lying on the ground. Regardless of innate ability, improvement is possible even for the clumsy horse. Using cavalletti or ground rails set at specific distances will teach the horse to pick up his feet.

Leading or riding a horse over a log or a jump further tests his obedience and coordination. Almost any horse can easily clear a 2-foot jump without prior experience. A 12- to 18-inch log can be negotiated at a walk, but anything much higher will require the additional energy and engagement of the trot. Most horses can trot over an 18-inch jump without banging the rail, but others prefer to hop over and land in lope or canter. Preparing a horse for a jump with a few appropriately spaced cavalletti and/or a ground line at the base of the jump will help the horse visually gauge his task.

MECHANICAL SKILLS

- Gate
- Sidepass
- T
- Square
- Backing through barrels or an L

If the rider has a good sense of geometric shapes and enjoys analyzing specific maneuvers and their components, intricate maneuvers come more easily. The horse must side pass precisely, back with turns, turn on the forehand, and turn on the hindquarter in various sequences and shapes.

Exhibitors are sometimes asked to side pass a single pole, either on the ground or raised by bricks, buckets or bales; to back through a simple alley created by two parallel poles; to back with turns through an L-shaped configuration or barrels set in a triangular configuration; and to perform a 360-degree turn in a 5-foot square.

The Gate. A combination of maneuvers is required to operate the gate. In order to help the rider to open a gate from horseback, the horse must not be afraid of the gate or of what might happen in the event of an error. Some riders use the gate to help teach the horse to side pass by pulling the gate toward the horse as the rider gives cues to side pass. But it is easy to accidentally bump the horse's legs with the gate and frighten him. If you often make an error like this at home, it will show up in a performance, so take your time and be careful. Some horses hurry through the gate pattern without waiting for cues from the rider. This rushed performance is usually characteristic of a frightened horse or one that is bored or nervous and anticipates the pattern. It is nice to see a patient, cooperative horse that is waiting for signals from his rider.

The rider can either approach the gate by riding closely up to it or by stopping parallel to it and then side passing up to it. To begin opening the gate, the rider usually pulls it toward the horse and opens it wide enough to ride through. The horse then is cued for a turn on the forehand. After the turn on the forehand, the horse should be parallel to the gate on the opposite side. The rider then moves the horse forward enough steps so that the horse's hindquarters will clear the gate post. The gate is closed by the horse side passing once again. A few steps back will put the rider in position to latch the gate.

To prevent anticipation, the gate exercise can be varied by pushing the gate away from the horse. Also practice backing through the gate rather than riding through forward. It is a good idea to run through all the possible ways of operating a gate before a show.

The T. The T is one of the most precise obstacles required in the show ring. To negotiate such an obstacle successfully, a horse must be able not only to side pass, and turn on the forehand and hindquarter, but to execute these maneuvers in a very limited space (see illustration on page 47 and instructions for the T).

It is the show committee's responsibility to make sure that all obstacles are safe and fair. However, you must make up your own mind whether or not your horse is capable of performing the course. Not only can an insufficiently prepared horse and rider get hurt, but the horse's confidence can also be permanently damaged if he is frightened by an unnecessary accident.

A flying change from left to right lead taking place correctly between the cones of the Western riding pattern.

Western Riding

An event that combines elements of Western pleasure, reining, and trail, Western riding is sometimes referred to as Western dressage. The pattern requires that the horse negotiate a gate, jog over a pole, and then begin lope work with flying lead changes. The horse must perform with a stride in keeping with his conformation. The class is not based on time, but the pattern should be executed with reasonable speed. Lead changes should be made as near the halfway point between the markers as possible. Eight flying lead changes take place in about two minutes, so to be a good candidate a horse must be very well trained and not anticipate. The pattern ends with the horse stopping and backing in the center of the arena. Rather than the sliding stop and rapid-fire back of the reining horse, the Western riding horse should perform these maneuvers with less exaggeration and more in the manner of a ranch horse.

Reining

Number 16 enters the arena and walks on a slack rein to the far end where the pattern will begin. There is a sense of relaxed concentration in both the horse and the rider as they turn to prepare for the first rundown. Starting from a standstill, the horse lopes with an increasing rate of speed until he is running flat out. With delicate balance, the rider transforms the thundering energy of the run into a rollback. The horse breaks at the loin; his hindquarters melt into the ground. As his hind end locks up, the power of the run sends the horse sliding forward while his front legs initiate the change of direction.

With no hesitation, the reiner keeps the horse's weight settled on the hindquarters and gathers the horse for a 180-degree turn. Jumping out of the rollback with balance, precision, and speed, the horse repeats the sequence at the other end of the arena, performing a rollback in the opposite direction. This time, the horse runs at speed past the center of the arena and performs a sliding stop. He then backs to the center of the arena, where he hesitates before performing spins in both directions.

With the weight borne by the inside hind or pivot foot, the horse's body whirls around so fast that the mane and reins fly out horizontally. Front legs are reaching

and crossing over with precision in the fast but smooth turnarounds.

Next the horse demonstrates his ability to perform perfectly shaped circles. The first circle to the left is small and slow, followed by a larger, faster circle. The horse works on a slack rein, showing no resistance or anticipa-

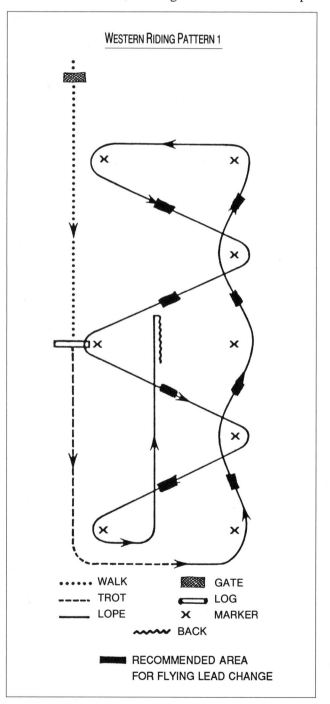

tion. Credit is given for smoothness, finesse, and a good overall attitude. The horse then performs a flying lead change at the center of the arena and does a small, slow circle to the right and then a larger, faster one. Passing through the center the final time, the horse again changes leads and then runs with speed along the wall opposite the judge. A sliding stop leaving tracks of 20 feet or more completes the performance. The horse walks on a slack rein to the judge, where the bridle is dropped for inspection.

This describes one of the nine patterns outlined in The National Reining Horse Association (NRHA) rule book. (See NRHA Pattern 2.) Months of training and conditioning have prepared the horse for this three-minute performance. Large sums are often at stake during a reining. It is not uncommon to see a reining with an entry fee of $750, resulting in an estimated purse of $175,000. The NRHA Futurity, open to horses in the fall of their three-year-old year, has an entry fee of $1,000, payable in ten installments. With an estimated purse of $600,000, the open winner is guaranteed $100,000.

The demands in reining competition are great, and champions combine qualities of strength, agility, and levelheadedness. Successful reining-horse showmen are aware of the potential stresses involved and tailor their programs to produce a healthy athlete.

The horse industry's ideal of the reining horse has changed over the last few years from a deeper-muscled individual to one with longer muscling that ties in low to knees and hocks. Even though the modern reiner is a more fluid mover, the body style still consists of thicker muscles than many other performance horses.

Throughout the training program, there is an emphasis on hindquarter development. Loping in circles not only teaches the horse to carry himself balanced in an arc on the correct lead but also serves to keep the horse legged up for the strains of the more taxing maneuvers. Circle work strengthens the muscles, tendons, and ligaments of the inside hind leg in preparation for pivots, spins, and stops. Loping develops stamina and wind. It is not uncommon for the reiner to be loped thirty minutes each day, interspersed with small work sessions on other maneuvers. Backing develops gaskin muscling, while progressive turn-around lessons improve coordination and hone agility.

Besides a conscientious conditioning program at home,

reining-horse trainers pay special attention to pre-performance warm-up. Maybe thirty minutes before they are to enter the arena, they trot and lope the horse to distribute the blood throughout his muscles. Strategically, they allow a few minutes near the end of the warm-up to ask for a soft stop or a quiet spin and then let the horse catch his breath. If it all works out as planned, the horse is warm but full of wind and has enough energy to deliver a performance with some sting. After his run, the horse is allowed to catch his breath, walked for ten to fifteen minutes, tied until his body heat dissipates, and then is hosed off.

The ideal arena for reining has a clay base with about 4 inches of freshly worked sandy loam. This provides a solid footing with a semislick surface. A lot of reining horses really like to stop, and good footing will make it easier and more enjoyable.

An inspection of the reiner's hind shoes reveals another way to make sliding stops comfortable for the horse. Sliding plates are usually handmade by a farrier from flat stock ¾-inch wide to 1¼-inch wide. The shoes have characteristic extended long heels called trailers, which increase the shoe's surface area and add to the horse's stability and balance. The nailheads are countersunk and filed off flush with the shoe, if necessary, after they are nailed to the horse's hoof. This reduces friction so the horse can glide across his sea of sand. These shoes won't teach a horse how to slide, but they certainly can make it easier. Putting too wide a shoe on a horse too soon in his training may frighten him and may make him reluctant to slide.

Not all Western horses are suited to become reiners. It takes an alert but tractable individual with a willing, go-ahead attitude, a cool, tolerant mind, and a cooperative nature. Couple these qualities with the previous physical requirements and it is no wonder that there are precious few premier reining horses.

Futurities require that the two year olds be started on a regular training schedule. Obedience is the first lesson. A reiner must learn when to run and when not to run. In a way, his mind must be disciplined to be part racehorse and part pleasure horse.

When bringing a three year old along in his training, the rider increases pressure consistently to build up the horse's ability to cope with it. He uses more leg and asks

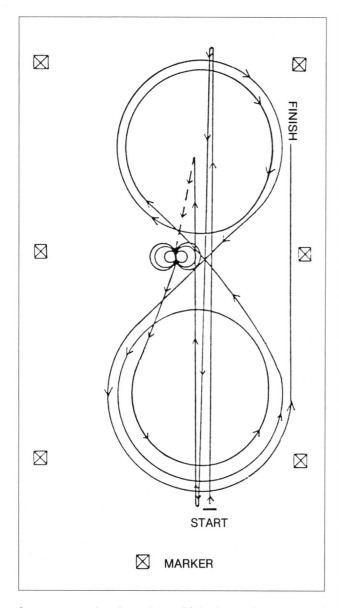

FINISH

START

☒ MARKER

NRHA PATTERN 2

1. Run at speed to the far end of the arena past end marker and do a left rollback—no hesitation.

2. Run to opposite end of the arena past end marker and do a right rollback—no hesitation.

3. Run past center of the arena, do a sliding stop, back straight to the center of the arena. Hesitate.

4. In the center of the arena complete three spins to the right.

5. Complete three and a quarter spins to the left, so that the horse is facing left wall or fence. Hesitate.

6. Begin on left lead and complete two circles to the left. The first circle small and slow—the second circle large and fast.

7. Change leads at the center of the arena.

8. Complete two circles to the right. The first circle small and slow—the second circle large and fast.

9. Change leads at the center of the arena, and begin a large fast circle to the left. Do not close this circle. Run straight down the side of the arena past center marker and do a sliding stop approximately twenty feet from wall or fence.

10. Rider must drop bridle to the judge.

---

performance arena.

Reining patterns have been likened to dressage tests with speed. With balance and fluidity of motion, the reining horse is willingly guided through a specific set of maneuvers with finesse and complete control. Freestyle, a recent addition to reining competitions, is somewhat like a dressage musical kur. The horse and rider design their performance to music with innovative costumes and choreography.

Amateur reiners have such varied backgrounds and abilities that about the only thing they have in common is their desire to ride a finely tuned horse. Although amateur status indicates that the exhibitor has not been paid, it does not necessarily imply that an amateur is an inexperienced horseman. To successfully guide a reining horse with subtlety through a precise and demanding pattern at speed, an exhibitor can hardly be a beginner.

As a pleasure-horse rider, you may have developed good techniques for keeping a horse steady on the rail, but the first time you sit on a reining horse, you will discover a whole new meaning for the words speed and balance!

for more speed and precision. If the horse shows signs of overload, the trainer can back off. Trail riding or pasture work at the walk or long trot will provide exercise and will allow the reiner to also just be a horse. Usually a horse shows great improvement after an intense training session and a "day off."

To keep a good reining horse fresh, knowledgeable trainers practice few actual reining patterns at home. Instead, the mature horse is kept "legged up" (fit) with pasture and hill riding, loping circles, and participation in other events. A season of ranch work can do wonders and make a good reiner even more keen when he returns to the

A tolerant horse with a cool mind may lack the sizzle a professional wants for performance, but he may be the best type for the amateur to learn on. Later, when a rider's talent warrants it, the trainer can help in the selection of a horse with the potential to go out and win at a tougher level of competition.

In the interest of sparing a well-trained horse the miscues and imbalance of a novice amateur, some professionals will allow the amateur to climb on only at competitions. This may work if the amateur is a top hand and has a practice horse to help him keep his timing and feel. More often than not, this isn't the case. Most trainers insist that their riders spend a lot of time riding their horses out of the show ring.

The cutting horse moves as a mirror image of the cow he is controlling.

Cutting

The show-ring performance event of cutting originated on large Western cattle ranches. Horses with cow sense made a cowboy's work much easier, so breeding programs were developed to preserve the family lines with this savvy. Because there are few opportunities today to really use a good cutting horse on the ranch, cutters have evolved into show-pen exhibitors. Entry fees and cattle charges make cutting one of the most expensive Western sports in which to compete—and one with the richest winnings.

Although local cuttings may charge as little as $25 or $50 entry per class, plus a $10 cattle charge, exhibitors entering the National Cutting Horse Association (NCHA) Futurity pay a $2,000 entry fee plus a $100 cattle charge. However, $200,000 is added to the exhibi-

tors' fees to make for a very attractive total purse. The NCHA World Championship Futurity is the richest indoor equine event in the world. The 1987 Futurity had seven hundred entries and a purse of $1,600,000.

The performance of an exhibition cutting horse is governed by NCHA rules. Each contestant is allowed two and a half minutes to show his horse's ability. With the rider's guidance, the horse must enter a herd of from twenty to forty cows and show that he can work quietly without disturbing the cattle. The rider indicates to the horse which cow he would like to cut out of the herd, and together they drive the animal a sufficient distance out in front of the herd so that working the cow will not disturb the others. Once the cow is isolated near the center of the arena, the rider loosens the rein and allows the horse to show his inherent cow sense and physical ability. The cutting horse reacts with a mirrorlike instinct to the cow's every move.

It is the horse's responsibility to prove that he can keep the animal from returning to the herd. Usually the cutter works two to three cows in the two and a half minutes allowed. Although fresh cattle are preferred for cutting competitions, sometimes a particular cow may not offer the challenge necessary for the horse to show his abilities to the best advantage. It is in the exhibitor's best interest to quit a sour or lazy cow and choose another from the herd. When scoring, judges consider the degree of difficulty required to prevent a particular cow from returning to the herd.

The performance is also rated on eye appeal and the amount of courage shown by the work. The NCHA has specific rules and penalties for the various errors committed by the rider or the horse that are deducted from the overall score. Scores range from 60 to 80, with 70 denoting an average performance. Large competitions are evaluated by a panel of five judges. After each performance the judges turn in their final numerical scores for the rider. The highest and lowest scores are discarded, and the remaining three are averaged. Small competitions often require only a single judge.

Reined Cow Horse

The working cow horse, or reined cow horse, is often thought of as part reiner and part cutter. During a class, each contestant must perform a "dry" reining pattern as well as cow work. The dry work is a somewhat abbreviated

The working cow horse must show that he can hold the cow at the end of the arena. Billy Martin on Nevada Commander winning the Open Stock Horse Class at the prestigious Salinas Rodeo. Photo by Jennifer Meyer publisher of California Horse Review.

reining pattern but with most of the same components. The specific cow work, however, is very different from cutting, although it requires related talents and abilities from the horse.

A single cow is let into the arena with the contestant. The exhibitor must show that the horse is watching and can control the animal at one end of the arena. Then the cow is allowed to run down the side of the arena, and the contestant must turn the cow at least twice each way along the fence. Once this has been completed, the contestant takes the cow to the center of the arena and circles it once each way.

Scoring for the dry work and the cow work are from 60 to 80 points each, with a total possible score of 160.

OTHER COMPETITIONS
Competitive Trail Riding

A horse of any breed, type, or conformation can participate in competitive trail riding. Animals must be sound and possess the stamina for trail work. A competitive trail ride is not a race. The horse is judged on performance, fitness, and manners, not speed. Horses are evaluated by at least two judges: one veterinarian and one horseman. In addition to the horse being rated, the rider is scored on horsemanship skills and horse care. Separate awards are usually available for both riders and horses.

Divisions are set up according to the age and experience of the horse. The open division is further divided by the weight of the rider and tack. The distance covered daily is between 25 and 40 miles depending on the division and the terrain. Each horse begins the ride with a perfect score of 100 percent based on 40 percent for soundness, 40 percent for condition, 15 percent for manners, and 5 percent for way of going.

Typically, competitors arrive at a campsite designated as "Ride Headquarters" on a Friday afternoon. After getting settled in for the weekend, the horses are presented to the official for a thorough physical examination. In the evening, a riders' briefing is held. Maps are distributed and important details regarding the trail are outlined.

On Saturday morning, each horse-and-rider team leaves the starting line separately at intervals of about thirty seconds. Riders negotiate the course at their own pace, following lime marks on the ground or colored

Cee Wolf on one of her competitive mules. Cherry Hill photo.

ribbons that have been tied to trees. During the ride, horses are observed and pulse and respiration are recorded in order to evaluate their condition. There is a mandatory lunch break, and then the ride continues. Horses must maintain forward motion for the final two miles to ensure that all horses reach the finish line at a similar state of physical exertion for the vet check.

On Sunday morning, riders again present their horses to the officials so that any adverse effects of the previous day's work can be noted. Then the teams set out on a shorter course covering different trails. Again they are evaluated upon return. After the officials have compiled the information from all three days, winners are chosen, and an awards ceremony takes place on Sunday evening.

Competitive trail riding does not require an expensive horse or expensive tack. All that is necessary is a fit horse and a rider who enjoys trail riding and would like to emphasize his or her good horsemanship and horse care. For more information, contact the North American Trail Ride Conference listed in the appendix.

Endurance Riding

Another sort of trail competition is endurance riding, which is a race. Horse and rider must cover a specifically measured course within a prescribed amount of time and the fastest entry that also conforms to the ride's soundness guidelines wins. Rides must be at least 50 miles per day, with a maximum distance of 150 miles in three days. Endurance riding is open to all breeds of horses and mules. Many competitions include a Novice ride consisting of 25 or 30 miles, intended as a training ride for new riders and young or inexperienced horses, although it is open to everyone.

A typical 50-mile ride might have a preride check, a vet check at 10 to 15 miles, a thirty- or sixty-minute stop (with vet check) at 25 miles, a vet check at 35 to 45 miles, and a postride vet check one hour after finishing. The winner of the ride is the first horse-and-rider team that completes the rider "successfully," meaning that the horse must meet all the criteria of the ride veterinarians.

The preride check is designed to identify horses that are not fit or sound enough to compete. The vet checks along the course are for monitoring the horse's condition, providing mandatory rest stops, and noting any unsoundnesses that have developed with exertion. The postride check includes the following: a pulse recovery to a specified rate, a respiration recovery appropriate to the environmental temperature and humidity, and soundness at the walk. In addition, a horse should not have required medical treatment of any kind prior to the final examination.

An additional award will usually be available for the horse that completes the course in the prescribed time and is judged to be in the best condition.

Speed Events

Barrel racing, pole bending, and the keyhole race are three of the most popular timed events, also collectively know as gymkhana. Competitions are usually run against the clock, but in Appaloosa Horse Club shows, winners are often determined by racing horse against horse.

For barrel racing, three steel barrels are set in a triangle. Distances between barrels vary according to the association sponsoring the event. The contestant starts and finishes at a designated line. Most rules allow the rider to run to either the right or the left barrel first. Then, running in a cloverleaf pattern, the rider makes a tight

Leslie Pederson performing a "Kur" (Freestyle). Courtesy of Timberline Vaulters.

turn at high speed around each barrel before turning for the sprint to the finish line. Touching or knocking down a barrel carries different penalties with various associations. Usually the penalty is either a disqualification or five seconds added to the contestant's time.

Vaulting

Vaulting is gymnastics performed on the back of a horse that is circling at a trot or canter on the end of a 25- to 30-foot longe line. The American Vaulting Association (AVA) has fifty recognized teams in the United States. Often members get started in vaulting through 4-H or Pony Club. There are individual and team competitions at the local level all the way up to the International World Championship contest (first held in 1986) and vaulting is recognized by the International Equestrian Federation. See the appendix for the address of the AVA.

The Nez Perce costume is judged on authenticity.

Costume Classes

The Arabian Costume Class is designed to display a well-mannered horse and rider in colorful desert regalia, including such adornments as fringe, tassels, flowing capes or coats, pantaloons, headdresses, scarfs, and sashes. Gaits called for are the walk, canter, and hand gallop. Reckless speed is penalized, and the horse must stand quietly and back readily. Judging is 75 percent on performance and 25 percent on appointments.

The Appaloosa Costume Class covers quite a broad range of historical characters: Spanish conquistadors, fur trappers, buffalo hunters, missionaries, and Indians. However, it is the history and dress of the Nez Perce Indian that suits the Appaloosa horse especially well. The authenticity of trappings and equipment, attire of the rider, and markings and colorful qualities of the horse are all considered. Horses must walk and trot under control and stand quietly so that the judge can evaluate the authenticity of the costume. The careful selection of appropriate materials and artifacts and the painstaking work involved in making a Nez Perce costume is evident in the accompanying illustration.

Driving

Ponies and horses of all breeds can be exhibited in driving classes. Vehicles include single passenger two-wheeled carts, buggies, and coaches. Harnesses can range from a delicate fine harness to the heavy, elaborate trappings of the draft breeds.

Classes will specify how many horses are to be in the hitch. Single is as it says. Pairs are exhibited side by side unless it is stipulated to be a tandem pair, which is one horse in front of the other. A pair led by a single is termed a unicorn. Four horses are called a four-in-hand.

The American Driving Society (ADS) regulates driving competitions in conjunction with AHSA and also promotes the sport of driving for pleasure. Breed associations also offer various types of driving classes.

Pleasure driving. The pleasure driving horse must show that it is cooperative and suitable to provide a pleasant drive. Horses are required to perform a walk, slow trot, working trot, and strong trot both ways of the ring. Change of direction is performed on the diagonal of the arena at the walk or the normal trot. After the rail work, horses are lined up side by side in the center of the ring. An assistant, called a header, is sometimes allowed to enter the ring at this time to stand at the horse's head for safety. Horses are required to stand quietly and back readily. The class is judged on manners, quality, and performance.

In a Turnout Class, the fit and appropriateness of the harness and the driver's attire, as well as the overall impression of the horse and vehicle, are emphasized more than in a regular Pleasure Driving Class.

In a Reinmanship Class, the ability and skill of the driver is assessed. Using the same routine that is called for in a normal pleasure class, the judge evaluates the rider's control and posture, and his or her handling of the reins and whip. The condition of the harness and vehicle and neatness of the driver's attire are also judged.

The Concours d'Élégance class awards the exhibitor whose overall impression shows careful maintenance and thoughtful restoration. The elegance of the vehicle and appointments, as well as the appearance of the driver, passengers, and grooms are assessed.

Pleasure Combination Classes require a horse to be driven as well as ridden. There are several variations, some requiring work on the flat and others work over fences.

Pleasure driving horses may also enter a trail class of sorts called the Obstacle Class. Using traffic cones, show management sets up a course consisting of the following: U-turn, L, T, backup, figure eight, and twist. In addition horses may have to negotiate a bridge and pass animals in a pen. There is a different time allowance for four-in-hands than there is for singles and pairs.

Combined driving. If you thought pleasure driving sounded like a great sport, and you have a little bit of the dressage, event, or endurance rider in you, you may want to check out Combined Driving. Here the real talents and skills of the driver and horses come out as they are tested in three very different phases of competition.

On the first day, the entry is presented and must be at the peak of perfection regarding grooming and cleanliness of harness and attire. Then the contestant performs a dressage test at a level appropriate to the competition and in an arena appropriate for the size of the team and vehicle.

The second day is the marathon, a test of fitness and stamina. The course requires that several miles be negotiated in a specific time limit. Along the way are gates, sharp turns, water obstacles, and steep hills.

The obstacle test is the third phase designed to test fitness, obedience, suppleness, and condition of the horses after their exertion of the previous day. Using some of the same obstacles described in pleasure driving, the contestants must finish the test within a specific time limit without touching any of the cones. See the appendix for the address of the ADS.

CHAPTER THREE
SELECTING A HORSE

LEASING

LEASING HAS ITS advantages. It allows the newcomer to try out the experience of showing a horse without the investment of purchase price. In addition, it can protect the newcomer in the event the horse becomes unusable for use during the term of the contract.

For an agreed-upon monthly or annual fee, you (the lessee) can arrange for exclusive use of an animal. For an additional fee, the horse's owner (the lessor) may provide care and keep, or may require you to make other satisfactory arrangements for the horse's board. As long as you fulfill the obligations of the lease agreement (paying fees and providing proper care), you are not usually held liable for lameness or illness.

The problem with leasing is that you may develop a good relationship with a horse but then be unable to renew the contract. Ultimately, the owner makes the decisions about the horse's future. The bottom line is that the horse is not yours. In addition, many leases contain clauses that restrict use of the horse in certain areas and for certain types of activities. And because the cost of the horse's upkeep is your responsibility, it may seem that a lot of money is going down the feed tubes for a horse that is not your own.

INSURANCE

Lease agreements sometimes require that the horse be insured during the term of the lease. (Insurance may also be required in horse-buying situations that involve deferred payments.) Mortality insurance pays the value of the horse if the horse dies or if the insurance company agrees that the horse should be put down (humanely destroyed). Limited or restricted policies cover specific situations only, such as death by fire or lightning. Full mortality insurance covers all causes of death, including illness and injury. A thorough physical examination is required before the full mortality policy is issued and, even if the horse passes the examination, the insurance company may have standard exclusions for certain causes of death, such as colic.

A permanent loss of use rider can be added to a policy. At the time of issuance, the intended use of the horse is stated on the policy in specific terms. If the horse is injured and can no longer be used as intended (for jumping or breeding, for example) the owner of the horse can collect about 50 percent of the value of the horse, but the insurance company may have the option to take the horse.

The value of the horse is almost always based on the purchase price, but it can be increased by listing performance records. Insurance rates are based on the value of the horse and vary according to the breed, age, and use of the animal. In general, rates range from 1 percent to 6 percent of the policy value of the animal.

Due to recent horse insurance frauds and unscrupulous activities regarding horse deaths, insurance companies find it a great risk to insure horses. Some companies no longer offer mortality insurance, and others have been forced to increase rates to protect themselves.

HORSEKEEPING

Before you actually obtain a horse, you need to decide whether the horse will be boarded out or kept at home. Keeping a horse at home on a small acreage or farm has great appeal and allows you to be involved in every detail of the horse's care and keep.

Because the maintenance costs for a $500 horse and a $5,000 horse are virtually equal, it pays in the long run to invest in the best-quality horse you can afford. By the end of the second or third year, you may have spent almost $5,000 for horse expenses. The conscientious, innovative person, however, can find many ways to cut these costs without compromising quality of care.

Your county agent can supply you with pamphlets that describe desirable horse facilities: blueprints of sample horse barns, necessary space requirements and suggestions for sheds, fence recommendations, barn and stable equipment, ventilation, sanitation, and more.

BOARDING

Boarding your horse with your trainer or at a commercial stable can simplify your responsibilities, but it will increase monthly costs. Boarding arrangements can be made with various levels of care. From most expensive to least expensive they are complete care, full board, limited board, stall rent, and pasture rent.

Complete care caters to the horse's every need and the owner's too. All that is required of the owner is to pay the bills and ride when the mood strikes. Full board is similar, except that the owner must groom and tack the horse before riding. Limited board requires the horse owner to perform some specified horse care and stall cleaning tasks. Stall rent merely allows the use of the stall space. Pasture rent is a low maintenance option where a group of horses live together in a herd.

Before deciding on a particular establishment or plan, make several visits to prospective stables at different times of the day and notice details. Are the horses fed on a regular schedule? What is the condition of the horses? Is there adequate space for turnout? Do you notice any unusual horse behaviors or attitudes such as weaving, cribbing, or pacing? How are the fences constructed? Are they well maintained? Is there evidence of wood chewing? What are the riding facilities like? Are they indoor or outdoor? What is the size of the arena? How is the footing? What equipment is available? What is the riding schedule? What are the hours? What is the attitude of the other boarders? Be sure to talk to several. Probably most important of all: Is the manager of the facility conscientious and concerned about proper horse care? Is he or she competent and knowledgeable? If you have trouble answering any of these questions, ask your mentor for his or her advice.

No matter what arrangement you decide upon, a formal contract is the best assurance of a good relationship for all parties. Some of the items that should be discussed and listed in the agreement are

Hay. Type, quality, amount, and frequency of feedings.

Grain. Type, amount, and frequency of feedings.

Supplements. Who pays and who feeds.

Water. Availability and quality.

Veterinary. Which veterinarian is used? How are farm call charges divided? Who is billed? How are payments made?

Farrier. Which farrier is used? How are appointments made? How are billing and payments handled?

Stall. Size, construction, stable mates (and their habits).

Bedding. Type, frequency of addition.

Stall cleaning. Who is responsible and how often is it done?

Turnout. Frequency, facilities, companions.

Additional exercise provided. Longeing, riding, etc., by qualified employee.

Grooming and stable care. Mane, tail, blankets, bandages.

Pasture. Condition, number of pasture mates.

Tack storage. Accessibility, security, insurance.

Riding facilities and privileges. Indoor or outdoor arena, size, footing, equipment available, schedule, and hours.

Insurance. Amount and type of coverage.

Lessons. Availability, cost, instructor's specialty and qualifications.

Health program. Incoming requirements and herd health program.

Amenities. Lounge, rest room, first aid kit, wash rack.

SELECTING A HORSE

Once tentative decisions are made for the care and keep of your horse, it is time to start shopping. Of course, it may take quite some time for you to find just the right horse. As a matter of fact, being in a hurry is one of the most common pitfalls of horse buying. Another is the faulty thinking that a green horse and a green rider can learn together. Nothing could be further from the truth.

A novice needs a well-seasoned, dependable mount. Often a beautiful, spirited, but untrained horse will catch the novice's fancy, and it may be difficult to look at other, less flashy prospects with objectivity. It is best, however, to follow your head rather than your romantic heart when choosing your first horse. Although you may end up with an older, plainer, but wiser horse than you originally dreamed of, the resulting pleasant and safe riding experiences will be the basis for a deep affection. Later, when you are more experienced, you may be ready to progress to the untrained spirited beauty.

When buying, it is wise to ask for and pay for professional advice—and then listen to it! When your instructor or veterinarian cautions you about a horse, it is for a reason. Conversely, if you are given the "go-ahead" to buy and then you get cold feet, you may not find as good a horse again. When procuring advice, it is best to use the view of an objective professional rather than the enthusiastic recommendation of an equally inexperienced friend. Stay focused. Keep in mind that you are selecting a horse for a particular performance event. There are many decisions and compromises ahead, so it helps if you set your priorities clearly at the outset.

If the overall purpose of the horse is to teach you how to ride, rather than how to win, the selection process will emphasize different traits. If the horse is intended to be a long-term project rather than a stepping-stone, you will have to invest more time, effort, and money in your purchase.

Once you have determined the largest sum you can spend for the horse, begin narrowing the field by considering what determines a horse's price. Rearrange this list to suit your specific situation.

Temperament. The single most important requirement for a novice's horse is a willing and cooperative temperament. The horse should be calm and sensible yet keen. He should be alert and ready to work but under control at all times.

Soundness. For a performance prospect, soundness is essential. Be sure to consider the fact that some conditions might render a horse unsound for one use but not for another.

Conformation. The overall structure of the horse must be suitable for its particular event. However, many fine performance horses do not have the potential to be competitive in halter classes, and many halter horses have no athletic ability. Review the comments regarding conformation in Chapter 2 and consider them again when you read the comments on type.

Breed or type. A weekend trail horse will not command as great a price as a high-level dressage horse. An imported registered horse will likely cost many times more than the farm-raised grade horse. If you do not need a registered horse for your performance event, you may do well to check grades or some of the breeds that are currently less in vogue. What is most important is to select the type of horse that is best suited for your proposed event (see chart on pages 64 and 65).

Manners. Note the horse's behavior in the privacy of his stall and as he is handled from the ground. Bad habits may lower his price but provide you with more exasperation and aggravation than the discount is worth. Horses that are hard to bathe or are slightly grouchy to cinch but perform beautifully under saddle may be an acceptable bargain. Remember, however, that the horse's habit may be at its lowest intensity because of a professional's guidance and may worsen with handling by a novice. Stall vices or bad habits can be dangerous for the novice and should be carefully considered before purchase. Vices include but are not limited to cribbing, wood chewing, stall kicking, weaving, pacing, pawing, rearing, and tail rubbing. Bad habits include balking, nibbling, biting, striking, kicking, bolting, halter pulling, rearing, and shying.

Sex. Geldings usually make the most suitable horse for a novice because castrated males are reputably more steady in their daily moods. Stallions should not be considered for a first horse unless they are purchased with the intention of castrating them and then sending them to a professional for thorough training. Mares often make brilliant performers but are usually more expensive because of their breeding potential. With a mare, there also can be a period of silliness, irritation, or fussing each month as she experiences hormonal changes due to the estrous cycle.

Health. Many health problems are temporary, and sick horses can sometimes be purchased at a discount. The buyer who plans to nurse a horse back to health must realize, however, that what is saved in purchase price may be expended in time, labor, and supplies. There is also a chance that veterinary bills will be high, as well as a further risk of complications or the development of a chronic condition. Some health problems are permanent and may require a lifetime of care.

Age. Horses in the prime range of five to eight years old usually command the highest prices. They have matured enough mentally and physically to be useful, have hopefully already been trained properly, and have many years of service left. Younger horses cost less because of their lack of training and experience and because of the risk of unsoundness. A horse that has made it past five years old and is still sound will likely remain sound. The assurance is not so great with a two year old. An older horse may have only a few performance years left but may

SELECTING A HORSE FOR AN EVENT
Types and performance events this type is suited for.

Type of horse	Temperament and other Characteristics	Conformation
Pleasure (Western Pleasure, Hunt Seat Pleasure, Trail)	Calm, dependable.	Well-balanced, smooth, attractive, prominent withers so saddle stays put, good angles and tendons for gait elasticity.
Hunter (Hunter Under Saddle, Working Hunter, Hunter Hack)	Coordinated, cooperative.	Neck must be long and supple and tie relatively high at withers and chest to assure greatest length of stride, no exaggerated knee and hock action, knees must be correct, not set back or over, not tied-in.
Stock (Reining, Cutting, Working Cow Horse, Gymkhana)	Energetic but levelheaded, cow sense.	Well-muscled hindquarters, good lateral muscling overall, inverted V at chest, equal gaskin muscling inside and out, strong hocks and back with rounded croup. No massive shoulders or chest, no sickle hocks, no small hooves.
Sport (Dressage, Stadium Jumping, Eventing, Combined Driving, Endurance)	Keen to aggressive, competitive but tractable.	Long, well-set neck with clean throatlatch for flexion, elevated forehand, strong hind legs, good substance of bone throughout. Short back and long underline for increased stride from behind, no long backs or weak stifles. Tough hooves with concave soles, no long, weak pasterns. For jumping, steep croup; for endurance, level croup.
Animated (Park Horse, Three Gaited and Five Gaited)	Flashy, charismatic.	High-set stylish neck, long well-laid-back shoulder, clean, free-moving joints. Straight legs with long cannons (crooked legs will result in injury at speed). Tennessee Walkers can have shorter, steeper croup and more set to the hock; Saddlebreds, Arabs, and Morgans should have level croup.

be the perfect choice for a novice. Many fifteen-year-old horses still have a substantial number of active years ahead.

Level of performance training and accomplishments. Here is where the price tag can shoot skyward in a hurry. A horse capable of performing consistently at the amateur level, and especially one who has a record to prove it, commands high prices. Although awards and points earned in competitions do not tell the whole story, they do separate the horses who are said to have potential from the ones who already have a proven record.

Performance requirements	Examples of breeds that excel in this category
Efficient, comfortable mover at all three gaits.	Certain individuals in all breeds.
Ability to negotiate obstacles 4 feet high with balance and efficiency.	Thoroughbred, Connemara.
Explosive bursts, lateral maneuverability, and in some cases, cow sense.	Quarter Horse, Appaloosa, Paint.
Ability to shift weight rearward. High levels of stamina.	Thoroughbred, Warm blood, Arabian.
Exaggerated flexion of joints with precision and speed.	American Saddlebred, Morgan, Arabian.

Size. Big horses generally cost more because they can accommodate a wider variety of rider sizes. When considering a small horse, be sure to note whether your legs can be positioned properly for effective use of the aids. Refer to the equitation illustrations for the suitability of size between a horse and rider.

Quality. Refinement, class, and presence all increase the price. Finely chiseled features, smooth hair coat, clean bone, and charisma all contribute to the horse saying, "Look at me!" and because many people do, the price goes up! Because pride of ownership is a large part of the reason behind buying a horse in the first place, it's nice to own an attractive one.

Blemishes. Scars and irregularities that do not affect the serviceability of an animal are called blemishes. Although they are not considered unsoundnesses, they lower the price of a horse. Old wire cuts, small muscle atrophies, and white spots from old injuries may detract from the horse's appearance and save the buyer money.

Pedigree. For the most part, the bloodlines of a horse's ancestors dictate his quality and suitability for a particular event. Using the family name as the sole selection criterion is a poor system, but using it along with other observations can be helpful. Certain family lines become fashionable from time to time and command higher prices. Examples of family lines are Secretariat in the Thoroughbred breed, Bask in the Arabian breed, and Poco Bueno in the Quarter Horse breed. Although all of these stallions sired many performance champions, they sired some poor horses too. Be sure you have a good horse in front of you first and then look at the papers.

Color and Markings. Although often the first thing one notices about a horse is his body color and points, it is really the least important criterion for selection unless you are considering the horse for use in halter classes in one of the color breeds.

BUYING THROUGH A PROFESSIONAL

When a buyer uses a professional to help in the selection and purchase of a horse, an unwritten code of ethics is in operation. Understanding the basis of buying and selling etiquette can allow both sides to emerge as winners from the transaction.

An instructor or trainer assisting a client in purchasing a horse has a more long-term incentive than immediate sale profit in mind. Choosing a mount that will work successfully with the student is far more important than a one-time commission. The professional should not be expected to perform his valuable services, however, without appropriate compensation. Looking at horses, testing them, and eventually buying one is time consuming and requires many miles. The professional's reputation is put on the line every time he or she helps to choose a horse.

If you get a professional trainer or instructor involved in the buying process, you will have to pay for this person's experience and expertise. The fee may also cover the cost of having the professional be your official representative and negotiate the business transaction for you. Some instructors add a flat commission of 10 percent to the price of a horse that they have found for a student. This works fairly well for horses in the price range of $3,000 to $15,000, but it may be inappropriate for horses on either side of that range. A flat fee of $300 could be charged for horses under $3,000 and a negotiable percentage may be used for horses above $15,000.

If you are interested in cutting, choose a horse that shows natural talent like Montana Suzanna the 1986 AQHA World Champion Senior Cutting Horse. Midge photo.

A finder's fee, on the other hand, is a seller's way of saying thank you to another professional who has referred a customer to him or her. For instance, you may contact Trainer A for a particular type of horse, and he or she may send you to Trainer B from whom you end up buying a horse. It is in Trainer B's best interest to send Trainer A a check for about 1 to 5 percent of the resulting sale price.

If you only want to employ a professional's assistance for specific portions of your search, you should expect to pay customary expenses including mileage, meals, and lodging and a looker's fee of perhaps $25 to $50 per horse evaluated. If, after six horses, at $25 per look plus expenses, the instructor finds you a $6,000 horse, he or she may subtract the $150 perviously paid from the $600 finder's commission.

If you are a prospective buyer and a regular client of a particular instructor, here are some guidelines for dealing with a seller. (In some cases, your instructor may be the seller.)

Before you narrow the field, you need to make an accurate statement of your goals and financial capabilities. This provides the professional with essential information and helps to assure a successful purchase and an efficient transaction. Listen to an instructor's advice. A certain horse may have great visual appeal but may not be a practical mount. The instructor should be objective enough to see such distinctions. But if the instructor and the seller are the same person, do not count on his objectivity. Employ another professional for an opinion.

You must be realistic about price. If you want a top-class show horse but have a small budget, you must be willing to compromise, usually from both ends. Many instructors report that a very time-consuming aspect of horse buying is learning what a buyer really likes. A solution may be for you to do the initial looking. You can narrow the choices down to what you can afford and would be proud to own. This substantially minimizes the instructor's time involvement. If you use this approach, however, you run the risk of missing a prospect that a more experienced eye might have recognized. Like other professional services, you get what you pay for.

STEPS IN BUYING A HORSE

Start by phoning ahead to schedule an appointment.

Most competent sellers will then have the requested horses clean and clipped. It is discourteous to arrive unannounced and ask to see everything in the barn. Some sellers will allow you to assist in the grooming and saddling of the horses to aid you in temperament evaluation.

Before you take the first trial ride on a horse, the seller may ask you to sign a release or disclaimer of liability in case of accident. Although such a waiver may not hold up in court as a legal document, it does outline your risk in specific terms and proves that said risk was pointed out to you by the seller. The seller is usually equipped to provide you with the appropriate tack to test ride the horse, but often you can use your own saddle if you have one. I recommend that you wear a protective hard hat during a test ride.

A horse will usually be either longed or ridden for you, so you can see the horse's movement. The trainer can best exhibit a horse's talents and level of training.

If the horse seems to be a possible candidate, however, you and/or your instructor should try him out.

In one way or another a seller gives valuable information about each horse in his barn. If you observe carefully and listen attentively, you can gather interesting facts and draw important conclusions about the manners and personality of the horse you are considering.

The relationship between buyer and seller should be courteous, positive, and businesslike.

Even if you wish to try the horse out more extensively, few sellers will allow you to take a horse home on trial.

The seller would prefer you indicate your serious intent by signing a prepurchase agreement, which will also clarify items in writing that you have discussed.

Sometimes a deposit is required in addition to the contract. A deposit is designed to reduce risks for both parties. The deposit will compensate the seller if he loses a sale to another customer because the horse was off the market. It will also provide a guarantee to the buyer that the horse will not be sold to anyone else while the contingencies are being met and will fix the price at the one originally quoted. A well-designed contract with a deposit is really a protection for both the buyer and seller.

THE VETERINARY EXAMINATION

A prepurchase veterinary examination is most often

scheduled and paid for by the buyer. Ahead of time, the seller may point out a condition of the horse that causes it to fail the vet exam but allows it to still be suitable for the buyer's purpose. If you and the seller have discussed such a condition, like cribbing, and list it on the prepurchase agreement, then you have accepted the horse as a cribber if everything else checks out all right. So, even if your veterinarian suggest that you do not buy the horse because it is a cribber, you have already acknowledged and accepted the condition. Be sure that you fully understand any habit or condition before agreeing to accept it.

The prepurchase exam should be performed by an equine specialist and may include the opinion and services of an American Farrier's Association certified farrier as well. Understandably, the greatest emphasis in the examination of a riding horse is centered around the legs and hooves. In examining the hooves, the veterinarian may request that the shoes be removed, so it may be necessary to schedule a farrier to be present to pull the shoes and reshoe the horse.

There is no standard prepurchase exam. The veterinarian should be informed of the proposed use for the horse,

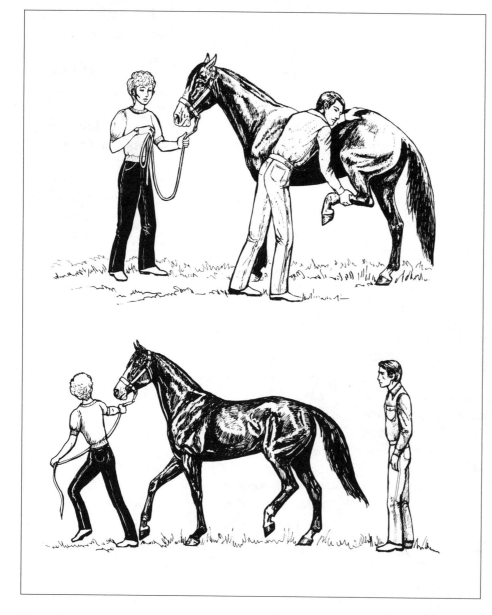

The flexion test. The veterinarian holds the hock in a flexed position for two minutes. The horse is then immediately jogged away and checked for soundness.

PREPURCHASE AGREEMENT AND SALES CONTRACT

This agreement is made between _____ ,
hereinafter referred to as BUYER and _____ ,
hereinafter referred to as SELLER.

This agreement is entered into between BUYER and SELLER for purchase and sale of the horse described below on the following terms and conditions of sale:

DESCRIPTION OF HORSE. Registered name _____
Registration number and association _____
_____

Tattoo, brand, or other identification (state which) _____
_____

Date of birth _____ Sex _____
Color and markings _____

PRICE. For the total sum of $ _____ , SELLER agrees to sell BUYER the horse described here, and BUYER agrees to buy said horse on the terms set forth here.

PAYMENT TERMS. A deposit of $ _____ (10 percent of purchase price) is to be paid at time of offer. This deposit will hold the horse for the BUYER for _____ days or until the results of a veterinary prepurchase exam are available, whichever is sooner. This deposit is not refundable if the horse is described as sound for BUYER'S purpose and BUYER does not complete the purchase. This deposit is refundable if the veterinarian fails to pass the animal for BUYER'S intended use. BUYER'S intended use is _____ .

The balance of the purchase price $ _____ shall be paid by the BUYER at the time of possession, no later than _____ days from the date of veterinary results. Daily board from the time of offer to the time of possession at the rate of $ _____ per day is also due at time of possession.

CONTINGENCIES. This contract is contingent on the described horse passing a veterinary prepurchase and soundness examination at the BUYER'S cost with the intended use for the horse being stated as _____ . BUYER understands that the offer is based on the fact that BUYER has knowledge that the horse has the following blemishes, unsoundnesses, conformation defects, vices, or unusual behaviors _____
_____
_____
_____

BUYER states that he knows what the above conditions represent and although discussion of them with a veterinarian is encouraged, since the conditions have been previously noted and accepted by the BUYER, the conditions stated above can not be basis for veterinary exam failure for the purpose of this contract.

WARRANTIES. SELLER warrants that he has clear title to the horse and will provide a bill of sale, appropriate registration transfer papers, and necessary health and transport papers at time of possession.

Signed this _____ day of _____ , 19 _____

_____   _____
              (Seller)   (Buyer)

IMPORTANT NOTE: Every state has its own laws regarding the necessary content of contracts. The sample contract in this chapter is designed to give general guidelines. Check with your attorney or modify a standard lease contract purchased from a business supply or stationery store to fit your specific needs.

and then you and the veterinarian should confer about what tests will be required to make such a determination. Costs for the exam can run from $30 to well over $300, depending on the number of radiographs required, what lab tests are ordered, how many miles the veterinarian must travel, and how much time is involved in the exam.

A general overall health check is the minimum that should be performed. After palpation and observation, the veterinarian will provide either a written or oral report.

The temperature, pulse, and respiration are taken before and after moderate exercise. The veterinarian listens to the heart, lungs, and intestines to note any irregularities. The teeth are checked for bite alignment, the presence of wolf teeth, and any sharp edges on the molars that may need to be floated. While examining the mouth, the veterinarian often presses a finger onto the gum and then notes the number of seconds required for blood to return to the spot. This general circulatory indicator is called the capillary refill time. The eyes are checked for inflammation and scars, and the pupillary light reflex is noted. The skin is examined for fungus, any blemishes are noted, and the limbs and back are palpated for soreness and/or swelling.

Before more specific limb exams, the veterinarian usually watches the horse move in-hand, on the longe line, and under saddle. Gait defects show up more markedly in the circle required by longeing and under a rider's weight.

In addition, flexion tests are performed most commonly to the knees, pasterns and fetlocks, and hock-stifle-hip. The veterinarian or assistant holds the joint in a flexed position for one or two minutes and then asks the handler to trot the horse off immediately. Irregularities in rhythm or stride are noted and may indicate the need for further evaluation.

If any of the flexion tests raise suspicion, the veterinarian may suggest X rays. Because the cost for each area ranges from $30 to $50, X rays are limited to joints that indicate degenerative bone problems or arthritis. Not every unsoundness shows up on an X ray and not every abnormal mark on an X ray indicates an unsoundness. Previous X rays of the same area may help to spot a progressive problem. The radiographs of many horses over the age of twelve show some signs of arthritis even though the horse may be perfectly usable.

Laboratory tests can be quite sophisticated and expensive. One of the most common blood tests is the Coggins test, which checks for the presence of Equine Infectious Anemia (EIA) antibodies. A positive test indicates that the horse has been exposed to EIA in the past and is a potential risk. This test costs about $20, and the results take about three days.

Veterinarians usually do not give a hard and fast pass or fail; rather he or she will give you a report in light of your intended use for the animal.

When a horse has cleared the vet check, you will have a certain number of days to complete payment and pick up the horse. During this time it is the seller's responsibility to have the horse cleared by a brand inspector in states where it is required. The seller must also have the necessary transfer papers available so that at the time of sale the registration papers can be signed over to the new owner.

If the horse passes the vet exam and the buyer does not follow through with the purchase, the deposit is normally forfeited to the seller for his inconvenience and the horse's time off the market. If the horse does not pass the vet check the deposit is refunded, or the horse's price can be negotiated in light of the veterinarian's findings.

CHAPTER FOUR

SELECTING TACK AND ATTIRE

WESTERN SADDLES

THERE ARE MANY features to consider when selecting a Western saddle. The tree is the framework or skeleton on which the saddle is built, and its features, overall style, and construction should be chosen specifically for its intended use. Tradition calls for a hardwood frame covered with rawhide. This is the best bet, as the tree should have give to it. Lightweight synthetic frames are also available but they are usually inflexible. The shape of the tree greatly influences the final exterior features of the saddle.

The slope of the seat is a result of the "ground work" that is added over the tree. Saddle makers add plates of rawhide or metal and layers of leather to achieve the desired seat style: very flat or cupped deeply or high rise to the front.

Some so-called equitation saddles have an extremely built-up front to the seat that supposedly locks the rider in the proper position. What such a saddle actually does, however, is provide a false sense of security rather than develop a foundation for good horsemanship. These saddles do not allow the rider to shift the weight forward and backward as is needed in various maneuvers called for in horsemanship patterns. The best bet is to choose a saddle with a balanced, versatile seat.

Swells can range from slick to full: the former are popular with ropers, the latter with cutters, and moderate swells are common on most general purpose saddles. Horns come in various heights and widths, and with assorted types of caps. A cantle can be low (roping), moderate (pleasure) or high (comfort cantle for trail riding). Stirrups can be ordered in assorted weights, shapes, and tread widths. The underside of the saddle is usually either genuine sheepskin or the less desirable acrylic fleece.

Rigging is traditionally double, that is, Western saddles use both a front and rear cinch. The position of the front cinch varies from full to center-fire position (see illustration on page 72). Full double-rigged saddles fit heavily built horses and are often required to stabilize the saddle for roping. Seven-eighths rigging is the most commonly used today and fits most horses with a moderate shoulder and a longer, more prominent wither.

There are two popular ways of attaching the rigging to the saddle. Ring rigging consists of cinch rings suspended from leather straps that are firmly attached directly to the tree. The latigo (cinch strap) is fastened to the cinch ring. Although ring rigging makes a very strong saddle, because the ring and latigo are located right under the rider's leg, the bulk can interfere with subtle communication between the rider's leg and the horse's side. To counter this, skirt rigging has become popular. It consists of a metal plate or reinforced leather slot located at the bottom of the saddle skirt (See illustration on page 72). Bulk is reduced but so is the potential strength of the rigging.

Cinches are often provided with Western saddles. The front cinch is made of from thirteen to twenty-seven strands of mohair, cotton, or synthetic. The cinches range in length from 22 to 36 inches; average is approximately 30 to 32 inches. Hardware on the cinches should be solid stainless steel or brass. Forged metals are much stronger than cast ones. Brass-plated and chrome-plated hardware is also seen but is less desirable. Two small D rings are sewn at the middle of a Western cinch. One is for the attachment of the rear cinch connecting strap, and the other provides a point of connection for a breast collar or martingale.

Western Saddle Types

There are five main types of Western saddles, ranging in weight from 20 to 45 pounds.

Roping and all-around ranch saddle. Saddle of

heaviest construction. Often made with a laminated oak tree covered with two layers of bull hide. Stiff fenders with stirrup leathers lock into position and add to the rider's stability when standing to throw a loop. Low cantle allows the rider to get off quickly and easily, and smooth swells prevent the rope from getting hung up. Ropers use tall, stout rawhide-covered or rubber-wrapped horns and heavy stirrups.

Competition cutting saddle. High swells and cantle and a low flat seat. Locks the rider in position for the sharp, fast turns characteristic of a cutting horse's performance. Seat size usually 1 to 2 inches longer than other Western saddles. Narrow oxbow stirrups securely anchor the rider's foot.

Pleasure and equitation saddle. Between a roping saddle and a cutting saddle in style and construction. Equitation stirrups are set farther back than reining or cutting stirrups, allowing the equitation rider to attain a more balanced position.

Barrel-racing saddle. One of the lightest of Western saddles. Made with a lightweight tree and minimal leather. Sports a short seat and has narrow stirrups similar to those on a cutting saddle.

Competition trail saddle. Riders are concerned

A Western Ranch Saddle.

a. *Parts of the Tree*
b. *Rigging Positions*
c. *Parts of the Saddle*

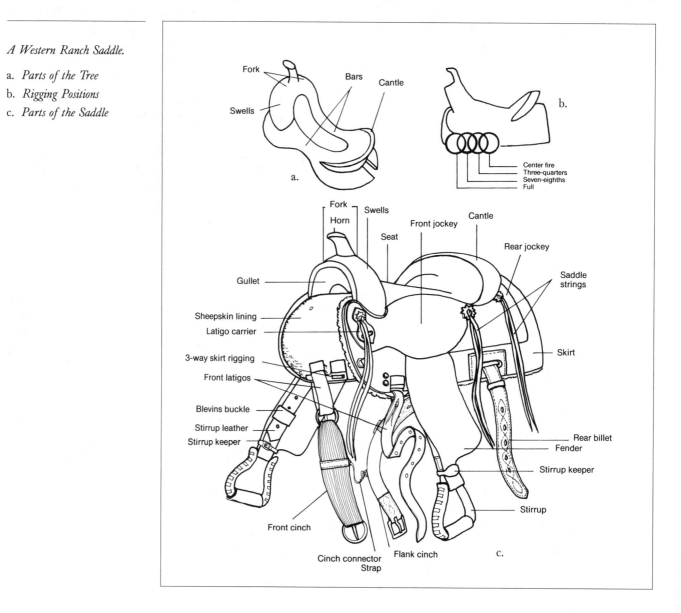

72

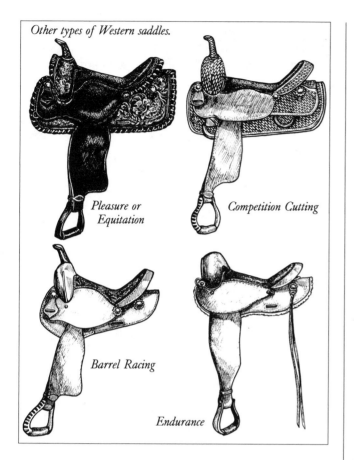

Other types of Western saddles.

Pleasure or Equitation

Competition Cutting

Barrel Racing

Endurance

with minimal weight, so saddles are lightweight yet durable. Often have no horn and have thin stirrup straps instead of fenders.

ENGLISH SADDLES

English saddles are built on either rigid or spring trees. The rigid wooden tree has very little give and results in a stiff, flat seat. The spring tree, most popular today, has two spring steel plates running the length of the wooden bars (see illustration on page 74). These plates yield to pressures of movement, and so result in some shock absorbency and greater comfort for the rider and the horse. Spring trees characteristically have deeper seats than rigid trees do.

The head of the English saddle is the portion of the pommel above the withers of the horse. The head may be vertical, sloped back, or cutback to accommodate various types of withers. A vertical head might fit an Arabian with low withers but may bruise a Thoroughbred with promi-

nent withers. The Thoroughbred may require a saddle that has the ceiling of the head cut out, allowing the withers to protrude. This cutback head is a good investment for the person who owns horses with varying types of withers.

Stirrup bars are metal brackets that attach the stirrup leathers to the saddle. Most have a safety latch allowing the stirrup leather to slip away from the saddle in the case of an accident. Forged steel stirrup bars are preferable to cast metal because of superior strength. The position of the stirrup bars dictates the position of the stirrup leathers and consequently the rider's leg, so check to be sure that the position will be appropriate for the style of riding you are pursuing.

The panels, the stuffing on the underside of the saddle, are referred to as the bearing surface, which distributes the rider's weight over the horse's back. Panels come in various shapes covering differing amounts of surface area and should be examined for evenness and symmetry.

Some dressage saddles have knee rolls or thigh rolls to stabilize the rider's leg. Saddles for hunters and jumpers almost always have a knee roll to keep the rider from moving forward off the saddle while negotiating a jump. Close contact saddles, which are primarily used for eventing, have no rolls.

English saddles are usually made from premium cowhide and some have a pigskin seat. Traditionally saddle leather is a tough, durable oak-tanned leather. However, some dressage saddles are being made today with butter-soft bag leather, so the saddle fits like a glove from the first day.

Girths, stirrup leathers, and stirrup irons are purchased separately. Girths may be string, web, or leather. String and web girths are less expensive and can be easily washed, but are not as durable as leather. A contoured leather girth with elastic buckle straps is a good investment. Stirrup leathers are relatively standard in width, with some variation available in length. There is a great difference in quality, so choose a smooth, close grained, and durable leather that is not too thick and avoid those made of stretchy leather.

There are some stirrup irons on the market that promise to fix problem leg positions. It is best to use a standard stainless steel iron and learn how to ride properly. Choose one with ample room for your boot. Tread widths are available in the 4½- to 5-inch range. Rubber stirrup pads are an option that increase grip and stirrup security.

English Saddle Types

There are four types of English saddles.

Dressage saddle. Designed for flat work (not jumping) and allows the rider to assume a vertical position with a rather straight thigh and a deep seat. Has a deeper dip to the seat and requires a slightly shorter seat to accommodate

the rider. Vertical flaps are long to correspond to the long, straight dressage leg position.

Jumping saddle. Has short forward flaps, often with suede-covered knee rolls or "pockets" to help stabilize the rider's leg while going over a jump. Seat is not as deep as on a dressage saddle because the rider must "get out" of the seat when negotiating a jump.

All-purpose saddle. Combines the qualities of the dressage and jumping saddles. Allows a rider to do reasonably well in several disciplines with one saddle. Close

An English Jumping Saddle.

a. *Parts of the Tree*
b. *Parts Under the Flap*
c. *Parts of the Saddle*

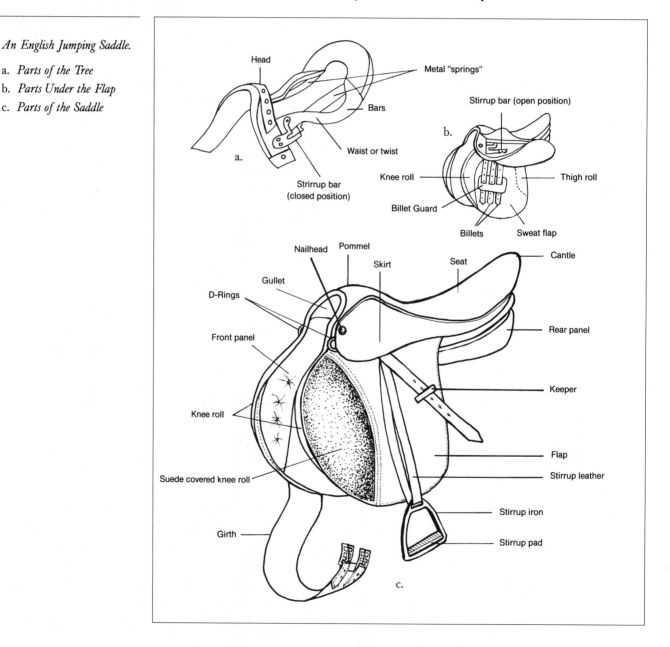

contact all-purpose saddles made of minimal material are popular with experienced riders because they provide maximum communication with the horse. Because the saddle does not have thigh or knee rolls, the novice may feel less secure when using one over jumps.

Saddle seat or Fox Lane show saddle. Used on three-gaited and five-gaited horses and other animated pleasure horses. Positions the rider the farthest back of any saddle in order to maximize freedom of movement of the forehand. Exhibitor rides with a more horizontal thigh than do other English riders, yet uses a very long stirrup leather, thus requiring a long seat.

FITTING THE SADDLE TO THE HORSE

The tree determines how well the saddle fits the horse. Most saddles, both English and Western, come in the same general tree types. The wide tree (called full Quarter Horse in Western saddles) is designed for a horse with heavy, low withers and a well-muscled back. The medium tree (semi Quarter Horse) fits a horse with moderately high and narrow withers and medium muscling of the back. The Arabian tree has flat short bars to fit the wide, short back of the Arabian. English saddles are also available in very narrow trees to accommodate the horse with very thin, tall withers and a razor back.

The gullet must be tall enough to allow the mounted rider to put three fingers between the saddle and the horse's withers. "Cutback" English saddles have a portion of the pommel removed to accommodate horses with higher withers.

The width of the gullet must allow a saddle to ride balanced from front to rear without pinching the withers and with no weight actually being borne by the backbone or the withers.

The rider's weight is transferred to the horse via the bearing surface of the saddle. There must be adequate room between the bars to fit the width of the horse's back. A saddle with bars too close together for a particular horse will perch on top of the horse's back rather than nestling down on it. The set (also called the twist) or angle of the bars should also allow the saddle to lie uniformly on the horse's back with an even distribution of weight. If a flat-backed horse is forced to wear an A-frame-shaped saddle, only the edge of the tree will contact a small portion

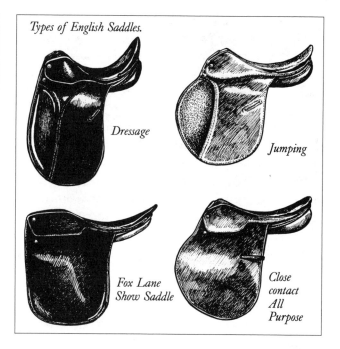

Types of English Saddles.

Dressage

Jumping

Fox Lane Show Saddle

Close contact All Purpose

of the horse's. When the maximum surface area of the bars bears the rider's weight, it is more comfortable for the horse.

On Western saddles the bearing surface is the sheepskin covered bars; on English saddles it is the panels. A Western saddle has a larger bearing surface than an English saddle and may be more appropriate for training unbalanced riders, young horses, or horses with sensitive backs.

The sweat marks of a properly fitted saddle are symmetric and the hair is slick. If used for a workout, the ill-fitting saddle will leave dry spots or ruffled hair on the horse's back. Weight concentrated on a particular spot (or spots) in the area of the withers or back may cause pain, swelling, and possibly open sores. This may later be evident as spots of white hair.

The length of the bars must correspond to the length of the horse's back. Short-backed, close-coupled horses, such as Arabians, require saddles with shorter bars and perhaps rounded skirts instead of long square skirts. Forcing a short-backed horse to wear a long saddle can damage his kidney/loin area or imbalance the saddle forward and cause all of the rider's weight to be borne at the withers. Using a short saddle on a long-backed horse, on the other hand, simply does not conform to the maximum-bearing surface rule.

The best way to see if a saddle will fit a horse is to set the saddle without any pads on the horse's back and observe from the front and the rear, checking for wither and backbone clearance. Then place the saddle on the horse's back again with a blanket, cinch it up, mount, and see if it passes the three-finger test.

If you cannot bring the saddle to the horse or vice versa, you can make approximations of the horse's back and take it to the saddle for comparison. Using an 18-inch piece of stiff but malleable wire, make an A-shaped mold of the horse's withers. Form the wire around the withers and then affix a crosspiece to help the mold hold its shape in transit.

Or you can trace the wire form onto a piece of cardboard and cut it out. Make a second mold about 9 inches back of the withers. Trace and cut out. Make the third and final wire form and cardboard template to correspond to the place where the back of the saddle will rest, just in front of the loin. Measure how far the first template is from the

third; this will be the approximate length of bars. Take the templates and measurements to the saddle shop and see what type of saddle will work best.

If you are considering a specific saddle, you may want to make some other measurements to see if the saddle will fit your horse. A Western saddle should be measured in several places. In the gullet, measure between the spots that are directly under the two front saddle strings, and record that figure. If there are no saddle strings, measure between two spots located 1 inch above the lower edge of the bars directly below the saddle horn. This will give you the same figure, the approximate width of the gullet. Most horses will do fine with a 6-inch to 7-inch wide gullet.

With the aforementioned line as an imaginary horizontal axis, measure the distance up to the bottom of the gullet. This vertical line is the height of the gullet. The average horse needs about a 2½-inch high gullet. Thoroughbred-type withers may require up to 5 or 6 inches for clearance.

English saddles can be measured in a similar fashion using the point of the bars as the comparable "saddle string" spots and continuing as outlined for Western saddles.

Choosing a saddle that is too wide or too low in the gullet with the intention of adding extra blankets to rectify the situation is not wise. Adding more padding just puts the rider farther away from the horse and makes more bulk between the rider's aids and the horse. It also makes the saddle unstable and can cause the rider to ride off balance. Besides, the saddle still fits improperly; the pressure has just been transferred and possibly intensified by the addition of the thick layers.

FITTING THE SADDLE TO THE RIDER

Lengths of saddle seats range from 12 to 21 inches in half-inch increments. However, a 15-inch Western saddle is not the equivalent of a 15-inch Lane Fox show saddle! The seat length of Western saddles are generally measured

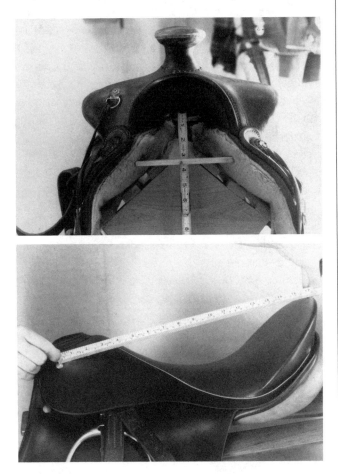

Above: *The height of the gullet provides room for the horse's withers and is the distance between the top of the gullet and the gullet-width line.* Cherry Hill photo.

Below: *The seat size of an English saddle is determined by measuring from the nailhead to the cantle.* Cherry Hill photo.

from the swells to the cantle. English saddle seat measurements are taken from the nailhead to the cantle. Following is a list of approximate seat sizes for a rider in the following range: 5 feet 4 inches to 5 feet 8 inches and 110 to 155 pounds.

Type of Saddle	Measurement for Average Rider	Where to take Measurement
Western ranch	15 inches	Midpoint of bottom of swells to top of cantle.
Cutting	16 inches	"
Barrel racing	14 inches	"
Jumping	17 inches	Front nailhead to top of cantle.
Dressage	17 inches	"
All-purpose	17 inches	"
Saddle seat	20 inches	"

Saddles come with varying widths to the seat, depending on how the ground seat layers have been added underneath. A wide seat is fatiguing to the hips and thighs but may be necessary for riding a wide horse. An extremely narrow seat can make the rider feel as if he or she is riding a rail.

When ordering a saddle, the rider should include the following personal information: height, weight, inseam, and possibly a sitting measurement. Sitting far back in a straight chair, measure from the back of the chair to the tip of the knee. This thigh-length dimension is often helpful to the saddle maker for determining seat size and stirrup length.

CHOOSING A SADDLE BLANKET

The material for a saddle blanket should breathe and be absorbent, washable, and able to conform to the horse's back. Wool is often preferred for its cushion and superior wicking ability, although it requires some extra care during washing.

Cotton, quilted or in thick sheets, satisfies most criteria but is not very resilient or fluffy. Synthetic fleece is soft and thick but is notoriously slippery. Felt is self-conforming

The double twisted wire snaffle (top) is much more severe than the thick mouth O-ring snaffle with bit guards (bottom). Cherry Hill photo.

but compressess quickly with sweat, and its washability is questionable. Closed-cell rubber provides good grip and shock absorption but is not absorbent. Wool or wool blends are the favorites for Western; wool felt and the synthetics are popular with English riders.

BITS, BRIDLES, AND OTHER TACK

The list of necessary tack items seems endless when you are first accumulating horse equipment. It is imperative, therefore, that you be absolutely sure of what you need. Not all snaffle bridles are created equal! Look through several tack catalogues and become familiar with the photos and descriptions. There are usually choices to be made regarding size, leather finish, color, and embellishments. Your trainer or instructor may allow you to try various pieces of his or her tack in order to determine what type and size will work best for your horse.

With your instructor's advice, buy the very best quality tack that you can afford and take good care of it. You will probably find that it is most expedient and economical in the long run to have a complete set of everyday schooling tack and some separate pieces especially for show.

Be sure to check with the rule books of your specific association for lists of prohibited and legal equipment. For example, although the use of a mechanical hackamore is legal for competitive and endurance trail riding and most

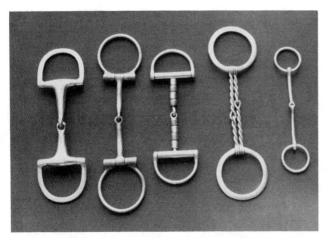

Snaffle bits from the left: Hollow mouth eggbutt dressage snaffle, Don Dodge, copper and stainless roller D-ring, double twisted wire, and Bradoon. Cherry Hill photo.

gymkhanas, it is prohibited in many other competitions. As another example, most show associations have a rule book that specifies the minimum width of curb straps and the minimum diameter of the mouthpiece of a snaffle.

A thorough knowledge of bridles and their mechanical actions will help you to make wiser choices when tack shopping and add to your overall horsemanship. For sake of discussion, I'll divide bridles into three categories: the snaffle, the curb, and the bitless bridle. All three types are seen in English and Western classes.

A snaffle bit is one with a solid or jointed mouthpiece and works with principles of direct pressure only: The reins make a direct line from the mouthpiece to the rider's hands. A snaffle does not have shanks.

There are nine factors that affect the action of a snaffle bit: the rider's hands, thickness of the mouthpiece, weight of the bit, texture of the mouthpiece, bit's design, type of metal of the mouthpiece, width of bit, type of sidepieces, and adjustment of the bridle.

The rider's hands have the capacity to turn the mildest bit into an instrument of abuse or the most severe bit into a delicate tool of communication. Above all, good horsemanship is the key to your horse's acceptance of the bridle.

When choosing a snaffle, thicker mouthpieces are generally selected for young or very sensitive horses. The thinner the mouthpiece, the smaller the surface area that receives pressure from your rein aid (the same intensity of

pressure is concentrated over a smaller area and the sensation is more intense). Measurement is officially taken 1 inch inward from the rings and is often required to be ⅜ inch or thicker. I caution you, however, from thinking that if thick is mild, then thicker is milder. There is a point where a bit can be excessively fat. Some thick bits marketed for young horses simply contain too much metal to fit comfortably in a horse's mouth. Avoid such extremes.

Often thick mouthpiece snaffles weigh more because of the additional metal involved in making them. Although weight stabilizes the bit in a horse's mouth, extreme weight can tire the horse and contribute to heaviness on the forehand. Some large mouthpiece bits are made hollow to provide mild action without excessive weight or top line.

The texture of the bit's surface affects its severity as it comes in contact with the bars, tongue, and lips. A smooth-mouthed bit makes even contact with the skin surfaces and underlying nerves. In contrast, a twisted wire bit's surfaces make rough, rubbing contact that may get a horse's attention but can also jangle its nerves and produce raw tissues if used indiscriminately. Smooth mouth bits are recommended.

Because the mouthpiece of a bit rests mainly on the tongue, it must be designed to keep the horse's tongue comfortable and responsive. Due to the variation in mouth structure, some horses need more space for their tongues and require a roomier design. Others with a shallow palate may need a solid bit that will not peak in the mouth. A nervous horse may perform better with the pacifying effect of "tongue toys." Others may need a bit that helps to moisturize the mouth.

Nerve impulses, which are tiny electrical transmissions are most efficient when sent through moist tissues. A moist mouth is potentially a more responsive mouth. Metals vary in their chemical and physical properties and their subsequent effect on salivary glands.

Copper traditionally leads the list of saliva producers. The nickel alloy Never-Rust, a yellowish soft metal, is popular in hunter bits and enhances salivation. Stainless steel and cold rolled steel also encourage moist mouths. Aluminum and chrome-plated bits are undesirable as they tend to produce a dry mouth.

The width of the horse's mouth at the corners of the lips determines the width of the bit to be used. Five inches is average. Fine-muzzled or young horses require narrower bits; warm bloods and draft crossbreds need wider ones.

The width of the bit can affect comfort and, inadvertently, severity. A bit that is too wide for a horse may hang low and bang the canines or incisors, or may peak and scrape the roof of the mouth. Bit guards can be added

to the sides of a bit that is too wide to make it usable, but it's best to select a bit that fits your horse perfectly. A bit that is too narrow can pinch the corners of the horse's mouth and put constant pressure on the bars and tongue.

Other bridle adjustments can also affect severity. Buckling the headstall too short and creating too many wrinkles in the corners of the horse's mouth can cause the

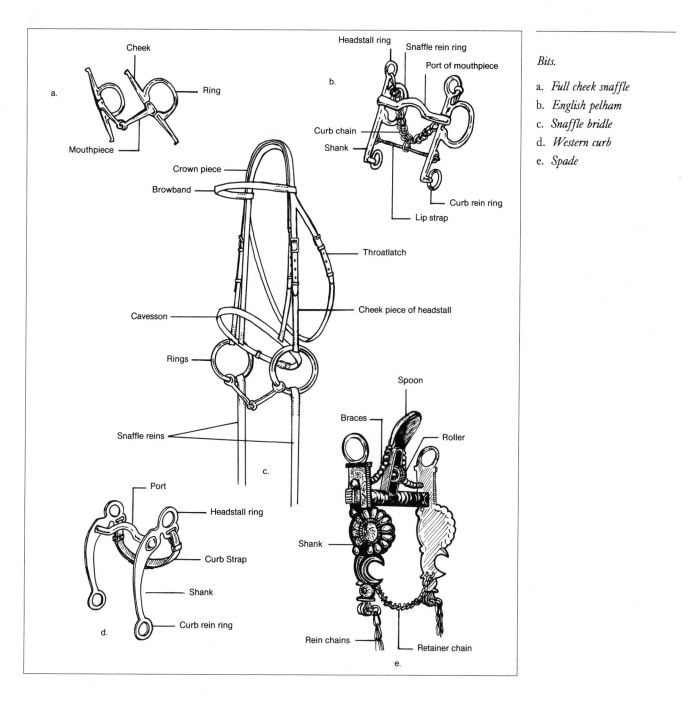

Bits.

a. *Full cheek snaffle*

b. *English pelham*

c. *Snaffle bridle*

d. *Western curb*

e. *Spade*

A ring snaffle with flash noseband.

snaffle to ride against the premolars or desensitize the skin at the corners of the mouth. Letting the bit sit too low in the horse's mouth can cause the bit to hit the canines or incisors.

A noseband used in conjunction with a snaffle increases control and communication by exerting pressure on the nassal bone and chin grove when the horse attempts to open its mouth. This prevents the horse from avoiding the action of the bit and also retains mouth moisture. The cavesson noseband is popular for hunt classes (see illustration on page 79); the figure eight for eventing (see illustration right); and the flash for dressage (see illustration above). A noseband should never be used with a curb bit.

Sometimes a horse will put its tongue over the bit because of inexperience, discomfort, or to avoid the pressure of the bit. Buckling the headstall a little shorter than normal or using a noseband with the snaffle usually stabilizes the bit and prevents the horse from developing this bad habit.

The sidepieces of your snaffle may be rings of various sizes and shapes, or prongs called spoons or cheeks. A full-cheek snaffle comes with a prong (spoon) both above and below the mouthpiece of the bit. Half-cheek snaffles are also available, with a prong either above or below the bit. These prongs should not be confused with shanks. The reins do not attach to the prongs. When a rider pulls

a left rein, the right prong presses into the right side of the horse's face further persuading it to turn left.

In a similar way, D-ring snaffles exert a sideways pressure on a horse's mouth. Eggbutts have less of that effect, and O-ring snaffles exert very little sideways pressure on a horse's mouth. Eggbutt and D-ring snaffles are constructed to avoid skin pinching. The swivel mechanism is located in a place on the ring that does not contact lip skin. Loose ring snaffles or bradoons have the potential to pinch the corners of the lips. However, if they are fitted properly, they are one of the most versatile bits.

The gag snaffle is set up differently than a regular snaffle. The reins and headstall of the gag are virtually one continuous piece. When the rider pulls the reins, the headstall shortens and exerts pressure on the poll and corners of the lips. This is an arrangement that allows a rider to control a headstrong horse.

A typical snaffle might be described as follows: a stainless steel 5-inch wide, ⅜-inch thick jointed mouthpiece with 2½-inch rings.

Any bit with shanks is classified as a curb: a type of leverage bit with a solid or jointed mouthpiece, solid or loose cheeks, and shanks. The severity of the curb bit is affected by the factors listed above for the snaffle, in addition to others specific to the curb.

As the reins of the curb bit are pulled back, three things

A full cheek snaffle and figure eight noseband.

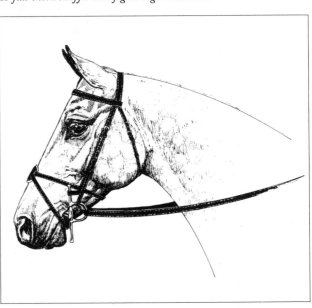

happen: 1. Pressure is exerted on the tongue and perhaps the bars of the horse's mouth; 2. The action of the shanks moving backward shortens the headstall and exerts pressure on the horse's poll; and 3. The curb strap or chain tightens across the chin groove.

As the length of the shanks increases, so does the leverage factor, which multiplies the pull of a rider into a much greater force. Shanks are measured from the center of the mouthpiece at the corner to the center of the rein loop. Five to 5½ inches is average.

The shank ratio will also affect the curb's action. Shank ratio is the relationship between the two following measurements: 1. The length of the shank from the mouthpiece of the rein ring; and 2. The length from the mouthpiece to the attachment of the curb strap or chain. The normal ratio is 3:1. The larger the ratio, the more severe the leverage action.

The shape of the shank also determines the severity of the curb bit. Straight shanks can exert stronger forces than a shank that is curved backward, such as the Western grazing bit. A bit with swept-back shanks rotates very little in a horse's mouth.

The mouthpiece of a straight bar bit has the potential of being harsh because of its constant compressive action on the tongue with no space for relief. The mullen mouth curb has a mildly curving mouthpiece that conforms more to the horse's tongue, so it is not as severe as a straight bar bit. A Western sweet water bit's shape applies little or no tongue pressure and has an extremely low and wide port, so is very mild.

The port is the protrusion in the middle of the mouthpiece of a curb bit. When the reins are tightened, the port will rotate forward toward the roof of the horse's palate and, in some cases, can also compress the tongue. Ports 2 inches or higher generally contact the palate. A rule of thumb: the higher the port, the more severe the action of the bit on the palate; the narrower the opening at the base of the port, the less tongue relief is possible, so the more severe the bit. Extremely high ports will contact the roof of the mouth; extremely narrow spaces at the base of the port leave no room for the tongue.

Spade bits have a hooded port or a spoon from 1 to 3½ inches in height (see illustration on page 79). The spoon is designed to rest against the palate and create suction that helps a horse keep the bit properly positioned in

A jaquima: Bosal with browband headstall, fiador and horse hair mecate.

his mouth. Such a bit must be handled with experience and delicacy.

English curb bridles are ridden with two hands. Western curb and spade bridles are ridden with one hand using either the split rein or romal method (see illustration on page 29).

Just as there are tongue toys on snaffles, so there are on curbs. Copper rollers mounted in the center of the port are popular in Arabian and half-breed bits to encourage the horse to mouth the bit and salivate.

A double bridle consists of two headstalls, two sets of reins, and two separate bits: a thin snaffle called a bradoon and a curb. Such a bridle is used on advanced horses in the dressage and saddle seat classes.

A pelham is a curb bit with extra rein attachments at the junction of the mouthpiece and the shanks (see illustration on page 79). A pelham attempts to combine the action of the curb and the snaffle in one bit. The rider uses two sets of reins: the curb reins to affect vertical maneuvers and the snaffle reins to affect lateral movements.

A bitless bridle, such as a hackamore or a bosal, controls the horse by exerting pressure on the nose and the underside of the jaw. The authentic Spanish bitless bridle seen in the show ring today is an Americanization of "la jaquima," but it is commonly referred to by the name of one of its components, the bosal.

The jaquima actually consists of a bosal, a browband headstall, a mecate, and possibly a fiador (see illustration page 81). The bosal is a ⅜- to ¾-inch rawhide noseband, suspended on the horse's nose by a browband headstall, with the leather throatlatch often removed. The mecate, 22-foot rope made from horsehair, is wrapped around the base of the bosal to form reins and an 8- to 10-foot lead line. Mecates are commonly available in ⅜- to ¾-inch

rope. Mane hair is preferred over tail hair as it is softer and more flexible.

A knotted rope throatlatch, the fiador, is part of the jaquima outfit but is often omitted in the show ring in order to present cleaner lines to the horse's head. If used, the ¼-inch fiador rope is tied into a hackamore knot that slips over the heel button of the bosal. Then a fiador knot is tied 6 inches above the hackamore knot. The rope throatlatch is secured on the horse's head with a sheet bend.

Martingales:

a. *English Running martingale with hunting breast plate*

a¹. *Keeper which prevents running martingale rings from getting hung up on rein buckles.*

b. *Standing martingale*

c. *Western running martingale*

c¹. *Keeper (see a¹)*

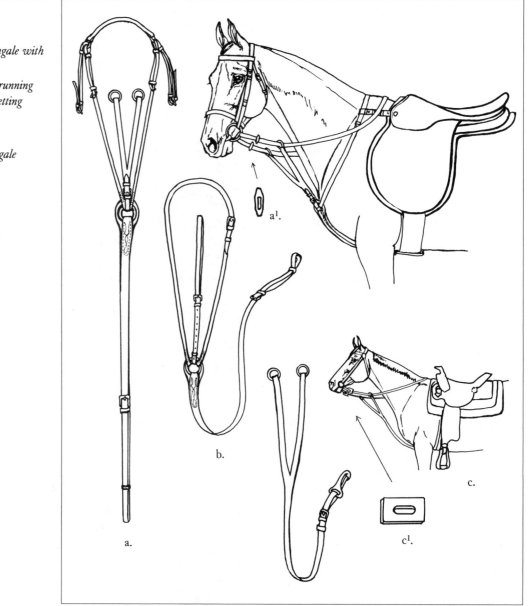

A mechanical hackamore is a modernization of the jaquima. It consists of a headstall and a noseband with long metal shanks and a curb chain. Mechanical hackamores are often used in speed events such as barrels and poles and for competitive and endurance trail riding.

Martingales are frequently used in conjunction with snaffle bridles, but rarely with curbs (see illustration on page 82). The standing martingale is a strap connecting the noseband of the bridle to the girth, and prevents a horse from raising its head past the point of adjustment. Standing martingales are often used with jumpers. Rodeo horses are frequently ridden with a type of standing martingale called a tie-down in combination with a curb bridle.

A running martingale has two leather straps with rings on the ends, one strap running to each bridle rein. The reins passing through the martingale rings. The running martingale is inactive until the horse raises its head, and then the downward pull created on the bit discourages upward movement of the horse's head. It is important to use leather or rubber keepers on the reins. Keepers prevent the martingale rings from becoming hooked on the rein buckles, which could cause the horse to panic. Running martingales are used primarily for training and are prohibited in many classes.

TACK CARE
About Leather

Leather is the preferred material for boots, gloves, and tack. It is comfortable because it breathes, allowing evaporation and ventilation; is self-conforming to the rider and horse; and is durable if it receives proper care.

Good leather has substance to it. The weight of the leather in relation to its thickness indicates a high fat content. Fat is the life blood of leather. A gray tinge over the leather indicates a desirable grease content. Quality leather is pliable and flexible and will not crease or crack when bent. It has high tensile strength and is firm, not soft or pappy. When it is bent, it does not bubble and it returns to its original shape.

Quality leather has a fine-grained, smooth flesh side with open pores but not loose or rough fibers. The pores of the grain side should have become sealed during processing, which makes the surface nearly waterproof.

Caring for Leather

Leather's greatest enemies are water, heat, sunlight, dirt, and the salt from sweat. Fine leather articles should be stored at room temperature out of direct light. The humidity should be moderate, and the room should be well ventilated and as dirt free as possible. Leather that is kept dry, clean, and supple is more comfortable for horse and rider, lasts longer, is safer during stress, and has a first-rate appearance.

Leather should be wiped after each use, thoroughly cleaned weekly, and appropriately greased or oiled about once or twice a month, depending on the climate. Leather loses some of its fat every day from water, heat, and air and needs to be fed. However, overfeeding leather can create a limp, flabby, greasy article with deteriorated threads and weakened fibers. Routine light feedings are far superior to a one-time saturation.

Exactly which leather dressing to use for a particular article varies. Few brand-name products are made from one pure oil; rather, they are blends of several oils and other ingredients. Beware of compounds that contain petroleum-based products, as they can emulsify the fats in the leather and cause them to evaporate, which dries the leather, weakens the fibers, and can rot stitching. It makes sense to condition an animal's hide only with animal fats. The traditional favorite, pure neatsfoot oil made from boiling the feet and bones of cattle, is good, but if used indiscriminately can soften leather too much and can deteriorate linen stitching and leave tack feeling oily. It is beneficial for restoring an old saddle or for breaking in a new one. Lanolin is a superior conditioner but in its pure form is sticky and difficult to apply, so it is best used in a compound. Mink oil is useful for areas that require waterproofing.

Steps in Cleaning

The first step in a thorough cleansing is to open the pores of leather and remove the sweat, dirt, and previous application of saddle soap and oil. A Turkish towel, warm water, and a neutral pH soap do the best job. Ivory soap, Castile soap, or Murphy's Oil Soap work well for the initial cleansing. Detergents contain harsh synthetics that actually dry out the leather.

"Jockeys" or dark spots of dirt that can appear under stirrup leathers and other places may need to be gently rubbed with a wooden match or a dull knife to loosen them, before cleaning with soap and water.

Once the leather is thoroughly cleaned and rinsed of soap residue, it should be allowed to partially dry. While it is still damp, the flesh side of the leather should be nourished with oil or grease. Damp leather absorbs oil more readily by drawing it into the pores as the water evaporates.

When the oil has had time to dry, it must be sealed into the leather. Using glycerine saddle soap and a slightly damp sponge, create a stiff, thick paste. Spread it all over the grain side of the article. Let it dry and then buff and polish the piece with a chamois. (A chamois is a soft under split of a sheepskin without wool that has been oil-tanned and suede-finished.) This final wax coat not only locks in

the oil that was added to the tack, but it also makes daily removal of sweat and mud much easier.

Cover leather articles with fabric rather than plastic when not in use. Fabric provides protection from accumulation of dust and dirt as well as allowing adequate ventilation.

ATTIRE

Fortunes can be spent on a rider's wardrobe but with a little forethought, you can keep expenses to a minimum. First of all, be absolutely sure that you are buying what you need. If you invest adequate time in careful shopping, you

Eventing tack and attire. Junior Novice Event rider Stephanie Cooper on Holley-4-Barrels. Courtesy of The United States Combined Training Association. Kathi Lamm photo.

GENERAL ATTIRE GUIDELINES

Hunter

Coat: Dark gray, blue, brown, or pinstripe; tailored; of wool melton (closely woven wool) or polyester.

Pants: Beige, light gray, canary, or rust breeches; children—jodhpurs with brown leather garter straps.

Shirt: Long or short sleeve; white, pastels or pinstripe; with choker or white stock tie.

Hat: Black velvet or velveteen-covered hunt cap with safety harness.

Boots: Tall black hunt boots; children—jodhpur boots.

Accessories: Gold stock pin; no jewelry; hair nets; dark gloves; spurs without rowels are optional; stick is optional.

Hunter on the Line Same as Hunter except:

General: Men may wear business suits and women sportswear such as skirt and blouse.

Accessories: No spurs or stick.

Jumper Same as Hunter except:

Coat: Black; in FEI classes, scarlet.

Pants: Often white breeches.

Hats: Protective headgear.

Dressage

Coat: Lower levels (AHSA), hunt coat usually black. FEI levels formal shadbelly coat with tails.

continued

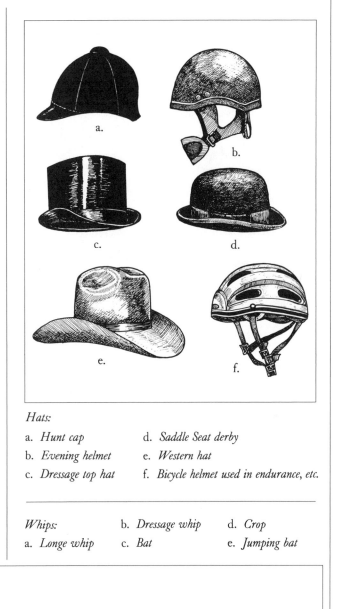

Hats:

a. *Hunt cap*
b. *Evening helmet*
c. *Dressage top hat*
d. *Saddle Seat derby*
e. *Western hat*
f. *Bicycle helmet used in endurance, etc.*

Whips:
a. *Longe whip*
b. *Dressage whip*
c. *Bat*
d. *Crop*
e. *Jumping bat*

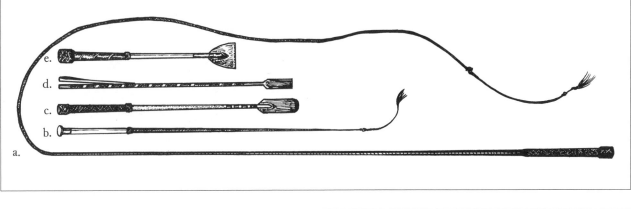

Pants: White breeches, often full leather seat.

Shirt: White with white stock tie, although choker OK too.

Hat: Lower levels (AHSA), hunt cap, bowler, or derby. FEI levels—top hat.

Boots: Black hunt boots with longer dressage top.

Accessories: Gold stock pin; black gloves lower levels and white gloves, upper levels; spurs optional at lower levels, mandatory at upper levels; 4-foot maximum length whip optional through fourth level.

Saddle Seat Check for variations between breeds such as Arabian, Morgan, American Saddlebred, and Tennessee Walking Horses.

Coat: Three-piece suit with vest. Dark solid colors or herringbone or pinstripe, wool preferred. Equitation dress more conservative than other classes. Formal classes after 6 P.M. are more conservative than informal classes. In other than equitation classes, women may wear dress coats of contrasting color.

Pants: Kentucky jodhpurs

Shirt: White dress shirt with visible collar and cuffs.

Hat: Derby, homburg, snap brim. Top hat for formal classes.

Boots: Elastic-sided black leather jodhpur boots.

Accessories: Man's tie, not clip on; gloves optional; whip optional; unrowelled spurs in equitation, rowelled in other classes; boutonniere optional.

Saddleseat Showmanship Same as Saddleseat except:

Coat: Often removed to reveal well-fitted vest.

Accessories: No spurs

Western

Coat: Tailored vest or short jacket optional.

Pants: Plain (not designer) jeans or Western-style pants. Chaps optional in some classes. Chaps should be custom fit, shotgun style.

Shirt: Well fitted, Western style, long sleeve.

Hat: Western, felt or straw, felt preferred.

Boots: Western boots

The topnotch Western equitation rider, Tiffany Baker. Courtesy Moondrift Morgan Farm. Rick Osteen photo.

Accessories: Necktie, kerchief, bolo, or ribbon. Thin scarf tied in square knot preferred. Belt optional. Gloves optional. Spurs optional.

Western Showmanship Same as Western except:

Pants: No chaps

Coat: Coat or vest is almost always used here for dressier look.

Accessories: No spurs.

Cutting Same as Western except:

Pants: Batwing chaps

Gymkhana Same as Western except:

Coat: Coat or vest rarely worn

Pants: Chaps rarely worn

Hat: Western hat must only be on head when entering ring. Safety helmet recommended under hat.

can end up with a classic outfit that is capable of a wide variety of appearances with only minor accessory changes.

The key words in attire are neat, clean, and classic. Conservative, well-tailored clothes suited to a horseman are what attract the judge's eye, not bright colors or current fashion trends. Although white gloves are acceptable for upper level dressage, be wary of wearing them for other classes unless you want to call attention to your hands. Flouncing scarfs, feather hatbands, and Day-Glo colors may make an impression on a judge in a large class, but it may not be a favorable one. You should design a tasteful outfit that accents your strong points and deemphasizes your weak points.

Hair nets are a real help for any exhibitor with long hair. Bouncing hair, no matter how healthy and shiny, detracts from the impression that a particular horse is a smooth mover. Loose, flyaway hair can also interfere with the rider's vision, creating a safety hazard. Be sure your hair never covers up your number. It may make it impossible for the judge to record the score of your performance. Showing a horse is creating a pleasing picture for the judge. It doesn't make sense to work diligently on a horse's training and your equitation to then undermine the performance with billowing scarfs, loose hair, or clanking jewelry.

Choose clothes that will withstand the abuse that only a day at the showgrounds can give. Be wary of dry-clean-only items creeping into your wardrobe. Most clothing should be made from washable material. Synthetic suede

Turn-Out: Proper grooming, tack, and attire add to this horse's performance.

chaps are washable and less expensive than leather, though less durable.

Buy or make clothes with larger than normal hems and seams, especially for children and for individuals with a varying waistline. This way an outfit can last several seasons. Be sure to try on your coats and chaps early in the spring. It is just amazing how the closet environment can shrink these items over the winter!

Select colors that will flatter both horse and rider. In Western classes, for example, most blues and greens look very nice with a palomino; black and an accent color such as red or white with a bay; beige or pastels with a black or dark brown horse. If you ride in English classes, where color choices are more conservative and traditional, stick with the dark coat and light breeches or dark saddle suits. They will always be in style and will save you money in the long run as they stand the test of time.

Mary Alice Malone of Iron Spring Farm on Roemer. Susan Sexton photo.

SECTION TWO
PREPARATION FOR SHOWING

A DANGEROUS GAME

*O*ne day, my farrier invited me to accompany him on an interesting case, and
as I watched him repair a severely cracked hoof I also noted the coming and
going of the boarders at the stable. When we first arrived, a young woman of
about twenty tacked up her horse, managed to get mounted, and rode off. Less than
fifteen minutes later, she returned, untacked her horse, and began grooming him.
She was working in a set of cross ties about twenty feet down the alleyway from
where we were. Because I heard a good deal of movement of the horse's shoes on
the cement floor, I glanced up to see what was going on. The girl had a carrot in
her mouth and was presenting her face to her horse to get a kiss. He was stretching
forward in the crossties to reach the carrot. I instinctively called out to her to stop
the foolish behavior, but my voice was covered by the horror that followed. The
horse, in an effort to get the carrot, and not being able to actually see what he was
doing or to differentiate well with his teeth, had grabbed a part of the girl's face
along with the carrot. When the girl shrieked, instead of letting go, the horse
clamped his teeth in alarm and threw his head up as he pulled back.
The loss of an upper lip and a permanently disfigured nose was a high price
to pay for a "kiss" from a horse.

*To retain your farrier's services be sure your horse behaves
during trimming and shoeing. Richard Klimesh, farrier, shoes
yearling Isaac. Cherry Hill photo.*

CHAPTER FIVE
SAFETY

THE TEN MOST COMMON causes of horse-related accidents are

• Lack of understanding in reading horse body language; lack of experience handling horses; lack of ability or not having a "way with horses."
• Carelessness and overconfidence.
• Working in unsafe facilities.
• Inadequate or improper training of the horse.
• Unsuitable horse.
• Equipment failure.
• Poor equipment fit.
• Lack of skilled assistance.
• Horse spooks, slips, or falls.
• Handler hasn't planned for emergencies.

Most accidents contain common elements. Short-cutting proper safety practices is probably the number one cause of equine-related accidents. A cardinal rule of horsemanship is "Don't overmount," either by riding a horse beyond your capabilities or attempting a maneuver that is too difficult for a particular horse. Riding at your level of competence on a conditioned mount using well-maintained equipment in safe facilities substantially diminishes the chance of accidents.

When a horse is faced with a lesson that he is unable to accept, he usually reacts with an undesirable avoidance behavior. Rushed training can cause explosive reactions such as bucking, rearing, or running away.

Because of their size, strength, and quick reflexes, all horses are potentially dangerous. A horse's power and unpredictability are often underestimated and can surface unexpectedly, especially in an unfamiliar environment with a lot of commotion. Safe habits should be established at shows, as well as at home.

All equipment should be strong, well constructed, and inspected periodically for wear. Stout gear is added insurance that a horse will not develop a bad habit. If a horse learns that he can break a piece of weak equipment and free himself, he may attain a dangerous lifelong habit of attempting to escape.

Therefore, tack should be well stitched and constructed from durable materials that are not fatigued from sweat, weather, or dirt. Hardware should be of the highest quality affordable. Some tack is colorful or attractive, but may not be reliable under severe stress. Make dependability your number one priority.

At almost every horse show, one or two horses are found running loose on the grounds. Invariably, at least one such occurrence is due to a horse wearing a show halter that was tied to a trailer. It does not take much of a tug for a horse to bend the soft silver buckle of the Western show halter or snap the leather of an English show halter. The result is freedom and chaos.

Care should be exerted when passing other horses on the showgrounds or in the ring. A swift kick between two horses is all too common and can prove disastrous to a horse's or a rider's show career. Be aware that there are stallions as well as mares and geldings on the grounds. Do not allow your horse to approach and sniff a strange horse. Often this is the prelude to squealing and more aggressive communication. Stay out of striking and kicking distance of both the front and hind legs of your horse and other horses when you move through the showgrounds.

When riding with other horses, such as in a group lesson or a warm-up arena, take care not to crowd others. When passing a horse that is traveling in the same direction, move off the rail several horse lengths behind the horse and then move well to its near side to pass. Do not return to the rail until you are several horse lengths in front of the horse. When passing a horse that is traveling in the opposite direction, pass right side to right side, with plenty of clearance.

Review the following safety rule list and follow it at home and away.

Safety Rules

APPROACHING A HORSE

- Always speak to a horse as you are approaching it.
- Approach a horse at an angle, never directly from the front or rear.
- Touch a horse by first placing a hand on its shoulder or neck.
- Don't pet the end of a horse's nose; it often encourages the horse to nibble.
- Either walk around a horse well out of kicking range or move around the horse staying very close. Never walk under or step over the tie rope.

HANDLING A HORSE

- Know your horse.
- Let the horse know you are firm but will treat him fairly.
- Control your temper.
- Don't surprise a horse. Let him know what you intend to do by talking to him and touching him.
- Learn simple means of restraint from a knowledgeable horseman and use them to control your horse when he becomes frightened or unruly.
- Stand near the shoulder rather than in front of the horse when clipping and braiding.
- Stand next to the hindquarters rather than directly behind a horse when working on the tail whenever possible.
- Be calm and keep your balance.
- Do not drop tools or tack underfoot.
- Punish only at the instant of disobedience and do so without anger.
- Do not leave a halter on a loose horse as he may hook it on a post or tree when rubbing or on his own hind shoe when scratching his head with his hoof.
- Wear protective footgear and gloves.
- When working in an enclosed space, always take the time to plan an escape route in the event of an emergency.

LEADING A HORSE

- Make the horse walk beside you, not pulling ahead or lagging behind. Somewhere between the horse's head and shoulder is usually the safest position for you to be when standing or walking.
- Turn the horse to the right (away from you) and walk around him rather than having him walk around you.
- Use an 8- to 10-foot lead rope. With your right hand, hold the lead 3 to 4 inches from the snap that attaches to the halter. With your left hand, hold the balance of the lead in a safe configuration such as a figure eight. Although holding the lead in a coil with the left hand is

often seen in the show ring, if a horse suddenly pulls, your left hand may become trapped in the tightened coil. Use your right elbow in the horse's neck to keep the horse straight and to prevent him from crowding.
• Work the horse from both the right and left side so that he develops suppleness and obedience each way and does not become one-sided.
• If a horse resists, do not get in front and try to pull. Instead, stay in the proper position at the shoulder and urge the horse forward with the use of a long whip held in your left hand.
• Never wrap a rope or strap around your hand, arm, or other part of your body. If a horse spooks suddenly and bolts, you may be unable to free yourself and could be badly hurt.
• Teach your horse patience when turning him loose. Do not let him bolt away. If he forms this bad habit, he may pull away before you have the halter fully removed and you and he could become entangled.

BRIDLING A HORSE

• Wear protective headgear when handling the horse's head and ears until the horse is accustomed to the handling.
• Estimate the bridle's adjustment and allow for a little extra room to ensure easy bridling.
• In order to keep control of the horse while bridling, untie the lead rope, remove the halter from the horse's head, refasten it around the horse's neck, drape the lead rope over the horse's neck, and then proceed to bridle.
• With your right hand holding the crown piece of the bridle between the horse's ears, the reins over your left arm, and the bit held in the left hand, present the bridle to the horse. Move the bit into position between the upper and lower incisors, then ask the horse to open its mouth by placing your left thumb in the space between the incisors and molars. Once the bit is in the mouth, put the right ear in the browband and then the left. Fasten the throatlatch and noseband. See the chapter on tack for more information on bridle fit.

TYING A HORSE

• Know how to tie the quick-release manger knot without hesitation.
• Keep your fingers out of loops when tying knots.

Teach your horse to put his head down on command. Richard Klimesh photo.

• Be sure a horse is well accustomed to being tied by other methods before attempting to tie him in a cross tie.
• Tie horses a safe distance from each other.
• Untie a horse and hold him temporarily with the lead before removing the halter. This will help prevent him from developing the bad habit of pulling away.
• Never tie a horse with bridle reins. It would be far too easy for the reins to snap, which could cause damage to the horse's mouth and form a potentially bad habit.
• Always tie at the level of the withers or higher and to a strong post or tie ring, not to a rail that may be pulled loose.

SADDLING A HORSE

• Check the horse and the saddle for foreign objects.

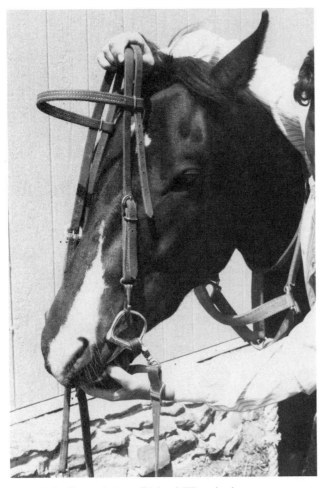

Use safe bridling techniques. Richard Klimesh photo.

• Place the saddle and blanket forward of the withers and slide them back into position. Never slide it forward once it is on the horse because it will ruffle the hair and be uncomfortable for him.

• With a Western saddle, fasten the front cinch first, then the back cinch, then the breast collar and accessories. Reverse the order when unsaddling. If a horse were to spook with just a rear cinch fastened, the saddle could slip under his belly, causing him to buck and resulting in a possible injury to himself and damage to the saddle.

• Buckle the rear cinch so that it is snug but not tight.

• With an English saddle, attach the breast collar and accessories to the girth, then buckle the girth. Reverse the order when unsaddling.

• Tighten cinches and girths gradually. Check them several times before mounting and after riding a short while.

RIDING A HORSE

• Wear a protective helmet with full harness whenever possible. Protective headgear is a must when riding a young or new horse or when riding any horse over jumps.

• Never mount where there is low overhead clearance or projections.

• When mounting, maintain control of the horse through light contact with the reins.

• Confine your riding to an enclosed area until you know your horse.

• Remain calm if your horse is frightened. Give it time to overcome its fear.

• Never fool around when handling horses.

• Don't rush past riders moving at slower gaits.

• Don't crowd other horses.

• Keep all equipment in good repair. Your safety depends on it.

• Stay away from horses when your judgement and reflexes are affected by alcohol, other drugs, fatigue, or illness.

FIRST AID

The type of first aid that should be administered at the scene of an equestrian accident depends on the availability of professional help, the seriousness of the injury, and the supplies on hand. Many of the principles that follow are also appropriate for horse first aid.

Injuries commonly associated with equestrian activities include but are not limited to concussion, sprained or broken wrist or ankle, bruised or broken knee, torn ligaments or tendons, scrapes, scratches, and wounded egos.

Everyone involved with horses should have a good knowledge of first aid practices. Courses certified by the American Red Cross are offered through hospitals, community colleges, and adult education classes.

One of the cardinal rules at the site of an accident is to remain calm. Another is to not move the victim and to control the victim's struggling if necessary.

Whether the rider just slipped out of the saddle during a lesson or suffered a bad fall at the fence, calm the victim and convince him or her to lie quietly and breathe regularly. Meanwhile, make an assessment of the situation and gather your wits and courage.

Do not rely on the injured's opinion of the seriousness of his or her own accident. More often than not, injured riders will say they are OK, when in fact they have broken a bone, wrenched ligaments severely, or suffered contusions that may swell like balloons in a matter of minutes without care. In contrast, some victims panic over minor injuries. It is best to err on the cautious side, however, and treat the person as if seriously injured.

The first part of the action plan is to dispatch someone immediately to secure professional help if warranted. While waiting for help, and depending on the environment and the injuries, it may make the victim more comfortable to be covered by a blanket or cooled by some water on one of the various pulse points. Carefully propping up a bruised, but not broken, limb to reduce swelling or slightly elevating the head if it is bleeding may make the patient more comfortable and reduce complications later. But know what you are doing. Small gestures such as holding a hat over a victim's eyes to block the direct rays of the sun can make a great difference in the patient's outlook.

An attendant to an injured person should be on the lookout for signs of traumatic shock. Shock is common in instances of concussion, great loss of blood, or lack of oxygen. The victim may suddenly turn unusually pale and have moist, clammy skin or he or she may flush and begin to sweat. Breathing may become shallow and quick. The pulse will become rapid. The victim may turn weak and faint. Pain, rough handling, and delay in treatment increase the effects of shock.

Often mild concussions accompany other injuries in rider accidents and provide indisputable justification for the use of hard hats for beginners and all riders participating in jumping activities. Even though a concussion may not actually cause loss of consciousness, it may make the patient behave oddly. He or she may have a hard time remembering what just happened or what you just talked about and may ask the same question over and over again. Be patient and explain what happened as if it were the first time asked. Do not act alarmed at the unusual behavior.

Instead, reassure the victim that everything will be fine and remind him or her to relax and breathe regularly.

It seems like common sense to never say things like, "Your face is covered with blood!" or "I'll bet that really hurts!" or "Oh my God, I don't know what to do!" or "Gross!". However, these are actual exclamations recorded at the scene of various riding accidents. The injured needs to be told that he or she is not stupid, a bother, or a klutz. One of the most powerful tools you have at the scene of an accident is the confidence and reassurance you display.

Bone and joint injuries tend to swell rapidly, so alteration or removal of the victim's clothing in the area of injury may be necessary. Cutting pant leg or sleeve or removing boots will allow the injured area to swell, which is nature's attempt at immobilization. Assist nature's protective process with whatever appropriate materials you have on hand. A heavy saddle blanket may be useful in padding an ankle injury. Aluminum sweat scrapers make good splints for arm and leg injuries.

After application of necessary dressing and some padding, the splint can be attached with tape or tied in place with gauze. Using a sling for a damaged limb will support and stabilize it and allow the victim to rest the muscles surrounding the injury. In an emergency, a long-sleeved shirt works well as a sling. The arms of the shirt are tied at the back of the victim's neck. Adding a safety pin at the victim's elbow will further secure the arm.

As you wait for help, pay attention to the victim's vital signs such as breathing, heart rate, and changes in the eyes and skin. But most important of all, don't put off enrolling in a comprehensive first aid course. If you wait, it could be too late.

ACCIDENTS DO HAPPEN

Today we ask our horses to jump higher, run faster, and execute precise maneuvers at lightning speed. The physical demand on the show horse coupled with the intensity of competition causes an occasional mishap.

After an accident, the first step on the way to recovery is to determine what caused the accident. Was it a hot temper? A horse that was spoiled or too strong for the rider? Lack of experience using a particular training device? Physical failure of an overworked, exhausted animal?

Discussing an accident with several unbiased professionals can reveal valuable insights and help to formulate future tactics. Mental replay and description of the accident can be painful and frightening but is a necessary part of working through trauma.

Preventative measures may include a review of the basics for the horse and/or additional lessons for you. Reestablish manners and obedience during ground work. This can provide the foundation for a better relationship between you and your horse. Grooming and in-hand work can keep communication open until it is time to return to mounted work. If your time out of the saddle is to be brief, perhaps a competent friend can keep the horse exercised. If the lay-up will be extended, however, it would be best to either send the horse to a trainer or give the horse the time off by turning him out to pasture.

Some riders are timid after an accident and some are dangerously bold. Frequently a bold rider begins physical activity before an injury has sufficiently healed. It may be wise to divert energy to other horse-related activities for a while. Customize or remodel an article of tack. Read a book that has been waiting on the shelf. Watch videotapes of trainers and instructors, and (if you are fortunate) critique some tapes of your own riding. Attend clinics and seminars. Go to a horse show with the explicit goal of analyzing every detail. Compare conformation, turnout, and, most important, quality of performance for each rider and horse. Ringside studies are useful when you later are preparing for a show. The pictures you take away in your mind of the top performers can help you visualize your way to a better performance.

A patient must generate the initiative for his or her own healing even if under a doctor's care. Practices followed at home often determine how fast and thoroughly an injury heals. As physical rehabilitation begins, evaluate your past performance as reflected in the following eight areas. If deficiences exist, it is time to plan for positive changes. By the way, the same evaluation can be used for the rehabilitation of your horse.

1. **Suppleness**. Can you bend your body without hurting? If not, begin stretching exercises at least three times per week. Flexibility provides major protection during a fall. The supple body has "give." On impact, well-conditioned tissues yield with temporary lengthening rather than tearing or breaking. Stretching exercises should be done slowly, with proper breathing and no bouncing.

2. **Durability of joints**. Do your knees, ankles, hips, or shoulders ache after riding? Do you normally suffer from arthritis, tendonitis, or weak ligaments? Walking briskly on increasingly deeper, harder, or more irregular surfaces will condition the support structures of your joints. Regular swimming is a good way to exercise joints without the stress of concussion.

3. **Coordination**. Can you orchestrate right leg pressure along with weight in your left seat bone, a right indirect rein aid, and a left direct rein? In any sport, the harmonious functioning of the brain, reflexes, and body parts in complex movements takes time to develop. Riding is the best way to become a more coordinated rider. However, if you are recuperating, swimming, biking, and following directions in an exercise class are good alternatives.

4. **Strength**. Can you move your horse forward, turn him and cue for a canter by using muscle contractions and not spurs? Inner thigh, calf, and lower back and abdomen muscles are areas most riders need to strengthen. With or without weights, repetitions of exercises specific to an area are the best way to increase strength.

5. **Balance**. If your horse abruptly changes direction, do you have the equilibrium necessary to counteract your own weight changes and stay on board? Serious balance problems require a doctor's care, but you can assess and improve your equilibrium with such activities as dancing, bicycling, skiing, and specific balance exercises.

6. **Ability to relax**. When you want your horse to travel with a supple loin, can you communicate that with a relaxed lower back? Riders are required to hold a contraction in the shoulders and hips for long periods of time. Efficient movement is dependent on relaxation. It is counterproductive for the active muscle groups of a particular movement to have to combat tension in antagonist muscle groups. Teaching your body how to relax can be achieved by sitting quietly and concentrating on your breathing. Yoga exercises can help release tension in specific muscle groups. Sufficient rest is essential.

7. **Condition**. Are you muscle bound, overweight, or scrawny? The amount and kinds of tissue in the thighs, seat, abdomen, and chest can make a difference in the effectiveness and comfort of your riding. Although body

type is relatively fixed, condition can be improved, which in turn increases flexibility and strength. Diet and type of exercise have the most influence on condition.

8. **Cardiorespiratory fitness**. Are you out of breath after several minutes of posting? Can you get off and lead your horse on cross-country terrain? Heart and lung efficiency is particularly important in high-energy performances such as dressage, eventing, endurance, and polo. Brisk walking, jogging, and cross-country skiing are good ways to improve fitness.

Look at causes of an accident and make plans to pre-

vent a recurrence. A mishap can be viewed as an opportunity for increased awareness rather than as a setback.

Although safety recommendations can make working with horses sound frightening, having a healthy respect for the large animals you will be dealing with is necessary. It is very easy to become personally attached to a horse and think of him in human terms: "Oh, he is so sweet, he would never hurt me." The fact is, in very few instances do horses actually intend to hurt their handlers. Accidents happen because the handler has not learned horse body language.

Hunter classes require particular attention to safety. Instructor, Sean Brevard, demonstrates good safety practices in this winning round on Time Bandit, First Year Green Hunter. Louise Serpa photo.

Jan Ebeling in a prize-winning performance on Funny Boy, Grand Prix freestyle winner at the Concours de Dressage d'Amite (CDA) *Dressage Show, Scottsdale, Arizona, in April, 1988. Mr. Ebeling is Resident Trainer, Capricorn Breeding Farm, Golden, Colorado. Photo courtesy of Howard Schatzberg, Scottsdale, AZ.*

CHAPTER SIX
TRAINING THE HORSE

WORKING WITH YOUR TRAINER

THERE IS AN IMPORTANT distinction between a trainer and a riding instructor. A trainer teaches an untrained horse what it needs to know by riding it for you. A riding instructor teaches you how to ride a trained horse that belongs to either you or the the instructor. The riding instructor's role will be discussed more thoroughly in the next chapter. Some professionals are both trainers and instructors.

A novice should not attempt to train his or her horse without supervision. Help can be in the form of a Pony Club or 4-H leader, an experienced friend, or a trainer. The person who is in charge of the horse's education, whether a volunteer or a paid professional, is the trainer. It is less confusing for both you or your horse if you choose one trainer and follow his or her advice. Once you choose a trainer, you become, in essence, the trainer's apprentice.

The relationship of owner/horse/trainer makes an interesting triangle. Horse trainers come in all shapes, sizes, moods, types, and specialties. A horse owner should exercise care in selecting one.

The single most important factor to consider in matching yourself with a trainer is the trainer's philosophy of horse use. Are his or her goals compatible with yours? Do they involve improving your equitation, your horse's performance, or both? Does the trainer specialize in futurities (reining, racing, cutting, halter) or maturities (jumping, dressage, etc.)? Is the emphasis on show-ring wins or enjoyment and enrichment? Silver or skills? Is the prospective trainer male or female? Does it matter to you? Would you feel comfortable working with someone ten years younger or twenty years older than you? Someone boisterous or quiet? Can the person you are considering train people as well as horses? Does the trainer continue to take lessons also? This is the sign of a true professional. The best way to find out the answers to these questions is to observe the trainer at work and to talk with his or her customers.

How far away does the trainer live, and how often do you anticipate working together? Some successful relationships bridge continents, but more commonly a trainer should live close enough to the owner for regular sessions.

Set your goals with the help of your trainer. There are a lot of differences in the methods used to develop a child's horse and an open-competition jumper. Don't overwhelm your trainer by expecting your horse to excel at everything. To begin with, what is the main reason you are having the horse trained? Is it to allow you to compete in large shows? To create a family horse that anybody can ride? To make a good cow horse for competition or the ranch? A good trainer will tell you if your horse is suitable for the activity you have in mind.

Now you must make a clear agreement regarding monthly fees. If the trainer is to have complete responsibility for the care and riding of the horse, it will cost more than if you provide the care for your horse and only bring the horse in for occasional lessons. But most trainers will not agree to the latter.

Many trainers will not accept a horse in training for less than ninety days. "Thirty-day wonders" do the owner no long-lasting good and are bad advertising for the trainer. An absolute minimum of three months is required for the basic training of a young horse. Specialization and finishing take many more months. Often horses remain "in training" for their entire performance careers.

Generally, the flat fee for full care and training per month covers board, bedding, feed, and training. Farrier's and veterinarian's bills are handled separately and are the owner's responsibility. Extra feed supplements are an additional charge to the owner. Blankets, leg wraps, and specialized tack are usually provided or paid for by the owner. The cold facts point to a large dollar investment for a horse's basic training. That's why it is to your advantage to buy an already trained horse, and that is why such a horse will cost you more.

An interesting exercise is to start with the trainer's base monthly fee and then subtract the cost of hay, grain, bedding, barn lime, etc. From what remains, subtract labor costs for daily stall cleaning and other barn chores. Divide the resulting figure by twenty or twenty-five, the average number of rides a horse receives in a month of training.

You'll probably come up with a figure somewhere around $10 per session. This is supposed to compensate a trainer for risk and hard work as well as allowing for depreciation on tack, equipment, and facilities. A good trainer certainly earns his or her fee.

Most trainers use a contract to make agreements and arrangements clear to all parties. A training and boarding contract usually contains important itemized information, a statement of requirements for the horse and owner to fulfill before arrival, a discussion of expenses, and disclaimers and protections for both the owner and the trainer.

To begin with, it is essential that the trainer have the owner's telephone numbers and work schedule so that in the event of an emergency, immediate communication and decision making can be accomplished.

Identification information on the horse should be detailed and official, with a copy of the horse's registration papers, identification card, and/or brand clearance attached to the training contract.

Insurance information should list company names and type of policy: mortality, limited mortality, loss of use, etc. Any special terms or limitations should be indicated as well as the value of the policy or policies.

Most contracts state the various conditions that must be met before the horse will be accepted into training. A mortality insurance policy may be specified. Health requirements include but are not limited to a current health certificate (dated within thirty days); a recent negative Coggins test (taken within six months); an acceptable deworming history (listing dates and products used); official records of recent vaccinations for influenza, rhinopneumonitis, and strangles; and proof of yearly boosters for Western and Eastern encephalomyelitis and tetanus.

The contract may require a minimum length of stay for the horse, such as ninety days or a year, depending on the horse's age and the performance program that is planned.

All horses must go through a phase of ground training. Major Lindgren courtesy USDF. Tory Sawyer photo.

Owners should include a provision allowing them to remove the horse from training with just cause and reasonable notice. If your situation changes due to unforeseeable circumstances or if the horse is being ignored, mistreated, or trained incompetently, you must have the right to remove him from the facility, providing that adequate notice is given and bills are paid.

It is unrealistic, however, to expect guaranteed results because each horse and set of circumstances are different. Often such a disclaimer is stated in the contract. The horse may be unsuitable, untrainable, or unworthy and may need to be sent home or to a different program. The trainer needs to reserve the right to terminate the contract.

Trainers also need to be protected in the event of catastrophe or foul play. Usually the contract states that the owner does not hold the training farm liable for any damage to the horse, property, or other persons unless such damage is caused by willful negligence on the part of the trainer.

Once the contract has been signed by all parties, the

trainer accepts all responsibility for the full care and handling of the horse. There is basis for misinterpretation here from the horse owner's point of view. Often owners would like to visit and groom their horses frequently. In order to preserve continuity in the horse's handling and to prevent chaos in stable management, it is best if you check with your trainer's policy. Some feel that it is best if the horse is dealt with consistently and under the auspices of the trainer, assistant trainer, or professional groom.

This is not to say the horse owner will not participate in the horse's training program. Many farms have provisions in the contract stating the availability of lessons. In fact, some trainers require that the owners take lessons before the horse goes home. Owner sessions may range from unlimited riding lessons to observations only. Observation of training sessions may be unrestricted or appointments may be necessary to gain access to the barn. It is best to check farm policy and abide by it. It is more polite to schedule your visits than to arrive unannounced, especially if you require a great deal of the trainer's time. Although talking at length with your trainer about your

horse's progress may seem essential to you, it may not be the best use of your trainer's time.

When your trainer is working a horse, whether it is yours or another customer's, the concentration is intense, and important energy is focused on the successful communication between rider and horse. Distractions can cause the horse's attention to wander. Once you begin lessons, you will appreciate having the trainer's full attention, without interruptions from phone calls or visitors.

The best way for you to get your money's worth from your trainer is to follow his or her advice and instruction during the actual lesson and to ask questions later. Beware of spending too much time on theory when you should be riding. You will have fewer questions on the theory and methods if you take the opportunity to observe the horse's training whenever possible. A dedicated horseman is rarely bored standing at ringside while the trainer works. There is always a detail to be learned.

The cutting horse must have cow sense. Delta Flyer, 1986 NCHA Super Stakes Champion. Courtesy of the American Paint Horse Association. Pat Hall photo.

THE HORSE'S LESSONS

Although there is much variation in the methods and progression of a horse's lessons, most good horse trainers have the same goals. The horse must be obedient to the aids, supple and relaxed, straight in his travel, and balanced in his movements. These classic guidelines for the training of a dressage horse are applicable to all forms of riding.

Obedience to the aids. A willing and correct response to the rider's aids must be cultivated early in the young horse. First the horse must be taught to move forward in response to the signal from the pressure of the rider's legs on the horse's ribs. The simplest form of this lesson is the halt to walk transition.

The horse must then learn to accept regulation of his forward movement by the action of the rider's hands through the reins to the bit. When the rider closes the hands on the reins and no longer applies leg aids for forward movement, the horse should decrease or cease forward movement. The simplest form of this lesson is the walk to halt transition.

Gradually the horse begins to accept the connection the rider makes from the leg aids to the rein aids and is asked to perform other transitions. This is the process of getting a horse "on the bit." Some of the more basic transitions are walk to trot, trot to walk, trot to canter, and canter to trot.

Suppleness and relaxation. Throughout a horse's training, from the first ride to the most advanced techniques, he must be mentally and physically relaxed in order to perform at his best. It is essential that the horse has accepted the bit, is not afraid to move forward into the bit, and is responsive to signals from it. This takes a fair amount of time to accomplish. The rider encourages the horse to relax by offering steady contact on the reins and allowing the horse to stretch into his natural rhythm. The horse's cadence needs to be regular and energetic.

The rider must follow the horse's movement without interfering with the horse's balance. If the rider is aware of what part of the horse is moving in which way at what time, he or she can influence the horse with aids that ask the horse to emphasize a particular component of his movement. For example, if a rider is in tune with the rhythm of the horse's inside hind leg at various gaits, he or she can apply a leg cue that will energize that hind leg at the moment it is ready to push off from the ground. This increase in power or impulsion will increase the energy of the gait and result in a lengthened stride and swinging back.

Straightness. During this early training of the horse,

The competitive trail riding horse must learn to be patient. These riders on their attentive, well-mannered horses wait for the signal to continue in the race. Tanya and Laurie Arila, on Sir Rouge and Par Ali Hawa. Cherry Hill photo.

102

it is important that he is encouraged to travel straight. His hind legs should follow in the tracks of his front legs, rather than make another set of tracks offset to one side or the other. This straightness is achieved when the rider sits very balanced on both seat bones and has even contact with both legs and both reins.

Most horses have one side that can stretch more easily. Often the opposite side is stronger and its muscles have a tendency to contract. These two facts in combination will make a horse carry various portions of his body to the inside or the outside, referred to as being strong on the convex side and hollow on the concave side. To help straighten a horse, he must learn further obedience, this time to lateral aids.

The horse is introduced to lateral aids by learning to move sideways in response to leg pressure. When the rider applies the right leg, the horse's body should move to the left, the degree of movement depending on the regulation made by the reins and other aids.

To make this lesson most clear, the turn on the forehand is often used (see illustration opposite). While limiting the forward movement of the horse's front legs with the reins, the rider applies a particular leg aid, well behind the girth. This will, in most cases, cause the horse to move his hindquarters sideways, away from the leg applying the cue. For example, the rider will apply the left leg, which will cause the horse to move the hindquarters to the right. Once the horse has mastered the turn on the forehand, he will begin learning a series of lateral maneuvers that ask him to go forward and sideways at the same time, such as leg yielding, the shoulder-in, and the half pass.

The horse will also be asked to apply the lesson of moving away from the rider's leg when he is ridden through corners, arcing turns, and circles. A horse's natural tendency when traveling on an arc is to let his forehand fall to the inside and his hindquarters drift to the outside of the arc. To teach the horse's hindquarters to follow the tracks of the front legs, the rider uses the inside leg ahead of the girth and the outside leg behind the girth. The resulting uniform arc encourages the horse to accept contact with the outside rein. This is the concept of riding the inside leg to the outside hand.

Shifting the balance to the rear. As the horse advances in his training, he is asked to shift his weight rearward. This will make the horse lighter in the rider's

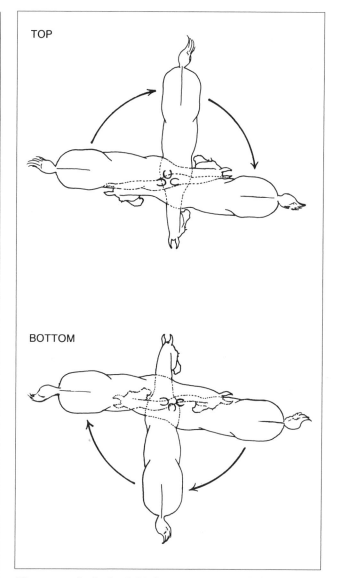

TOP

BOTTOM

The turn on the forehand (hindquarters moving to the left) performed in both the elementary manner (top) where the horse's head is bent away from the direction of movement of the hindquarters and the more advanced manner (bottom) where the horse is required to bend in the same direction as the movement.

hands and will allow the horse to change gait and direction smoothly, without loss of form or impulsion. It is hard physical work for the horse to learn to carry the majority of his and the rider's weight on the rear quarters because horses are built with more weight on the forehand. The process of developing the horse's balance to the rear requires a slow buildup of muscle strength. Although the horse requires steady contact from the rider's hands and legs to perform with such engagement of the hindquarters, the horse is by no means *held* in position. Instead the horse is taught to carry himself in a balanced and proper frame. Dressage riders often check a horse's self-carriage by loosening the rein contact to see if the horse falls apart or holds himself together due to his well-developed circle of muscles.

THE CIRCLE OF MUSCLES

The harmonious flow of energy evident in the fluid moves of a well-trained horse is a precision balance between the contraction and relaxation phases of muscles. Training a horse is actually developing his body. In order for the energy pathway to be continuous without short circuits or glitches, the horse must be obedient, relaxed, and perform in a rounded frame. Perhaps most obvious in the illustration of a highly collected dressage horse, the circular flow is depicted by a flexed poll, elevated head and neck, arched spine, "dropped croup," engaged flow is depicted by a flexed poll, elevated head hindquarters, and flexed abdominals.

In order to maintain equilibrium, the horse assumes a posture or framework in accordance with the horizontal and vertical components and speed of a maneuver, and the placement and movement of the rider. Extended maneuvers are characteristically more horizontal, whereas collected maneuvers are more vertical in nature.

The forces exerted on the various portions of the circle of muscles change with the horse's center of gravity. The center of gravity is altered in respect to the relationship between the horse's skeletal conformation and weight distribution on the frame and the position of his head and neck. At a standstill, the center of gravity is the point of intersection of a vertical line dropped from the highest point of the withers and a line from the point of shoulder to the point of buttock.

Forward movement is dependent on the horse's ability to shift his center of gravity rearward. In order to lighten the heavily weighted forehand for elegant movements, the horse must redistribute his weight, which causes the hindquarters to accept a greater load. The hindquarters are converted from a driving force to more of a supporting force depending on the rider's regulatory aids.

Circle of Muscles: Collection. As a horse collects, he accepts more weight with the hindquarters.

If a 1,275 pound horse carries 175 pounds of rider and tack, he distributes the 1,450 pound total weight differently for various maneuvers. Such a horse with a level top line and average balance and with virtually no influence exerted from the rider would, while standing, bear at least 405 pounds on each foreleg and 320 pounds or less with each hind leg. As the horse performs in a more collected frame, the hindquarters are required to bear an increasingly greater proportion of the load until, in the levade, where all propulsion from the hindquarters has ceased, each hind leg bears 725 pounds. The horse collects by raising the head and neck above the body's mass, contracting the muscles that attach the shoulder to the ribs, contracting the neck muscles, contracting some of the muscles of the chest, and flexing both hocks with the hind feet on the ground.

During forward movement, as the horse's hind foot reaches ahead, the lumbosacral joint (loin) flexes and the sacrum (vertebrae behind the loin) moves down and forward. The pelvis (hip) rotates down and forward by the contraction of the abdominal muscles and is stabilized by the resistance from the longissimus dorsi, the long muscles running along either side of the horse's spine. A dropped croup is a misnomer because it is actually the flexion of the hip joint that rotates the pelvis and produces engagement.

The horse's back stretches between the elastic tension of the croup and buttock muscles, which exert a strong pull down and backward on the back muscles, and the elastic tension of the neck ligaments, which is created by the extension of the head and neck forward and upward. This tension makes it possible for the head and neck to act as a lever on the hindquarters.

The gathered and compacted frame of the collected horse gives the illusion of a shortened top line. The horse's top line is actually the longest when it is in a collected frame due to the stretching of the back.

When a rider introduces the inexperienced horse to collection, however, he or she first must encourage him to lower and lengthen the neck muscles and flex the lower jaw and poll. In gradual progressions, the rider executes half halts while continuing to drive the horse so that it begins to step under its center of gravity with the hind legs. A moderate restraining with the reins causes the horse to begin to round the back and raise the neck.

The horse should be trained and conditioned until it is capable of producing pronounced pulsation of the circle of muscles at the trot. It is easier to achieve success at the trot because it is a balanced gait and naturally cadenced.

When lengthening, remember that the goal is a greater distance covered per stride. Often the rate or tempo is mistakenly increased when in actuality the tempo must be initially slowed to allow for the increased hind limb engagement that will result in a true increase in the length

of stride. The limiting factor in stride length is the ability of the horse to flex the hip joint that carries the femur, stifle, and hock forward.

The more exaggerated the request, the more the horse moves with a springy and elastic forward swing of the hindquarters and back. Additionally, because the spinal column lowers at the rear, the forehand is lightened and the muscles of the shoulder and forearm experience free and lofty movement.

Upper-level movements involve a complex set of contractions and relaxations of superficial and deep muscles. A smooth, coordinated movement is based on the ability of the horse to relax particular muscles in order to allow other muscles to establish supremacy. This results in an efficient contraction for one muscle group while the other muscle group relaxes somewhat but still provides sufficient resistance to prevent dislocations, sprains, and ligament tears.

Some horses have a much more highly developed innate synchronization of muscles than others. Young or underconditioned horses may have poor muscle coordination that results in wobbly, asymmetric, or otherwise unbalanced movements.

The horse's development should neither be rushed nor should a particular frame be imposed upon the horse. The result may be undesirable bulging of certain muscle groups and weakness in others. A horse that is forcibly held in a collected "headset" will often bulge the muscles on the underside of the neck as a means of bracing against the rider's unyielding hand.

If a horse is not encouraged to reach forward for contact with the bit and lengthen the top line of its neck, the under muscles of the neck can thicken. Subsequently, the muscles on the top of the neck receive inadequate development resulting in a flat or ewe neck.

If the rider's driving aids are too forceful or inexperienced to allow the horse to relax the back muscles, the horse will respond by hollowing the back in an attempt to escape the pain and by pushing out the abdominals in a sympathetic response. Because a horse's back is not really designed to carry a load, this hollowing makes the horse even more vulnerable to spinal problems.

A hollow back is structurally weaker than an arched or

Circle of Muscles: Extension. In order to extend, a horse must drive from behind and reach with the front.

flat back. The horse with a pot belly, or weak, bulging abdominals will also have difficulty carrying itself in a collected frame for very many strides.

The rider must effectively train the horse to properly use the neck and abdominal muscles to relieve the back of some of its work. Gymnastics utilizing cavalletti lengthen, strengthen, and stretch the neck muscles; cantering and galloping condition the abdominals.

Two areas of the top line are particularly crucial to the uninterrupted flow of muscular activity: the loin or power transmitter, and the poll or energy transformer. The loin needs to be strong yet supple. The propulsion that the hindquarters generate must be transmitted forward at the same time that the horse bends the spine to accept greater loads with the hind legs. The loin must be relaxed to allow swing and freedom of forward movement.

At the poll, flexor and extensor muscle energy is integrated. The "reaching outward and upward" of the extensors is coupled with the "downward compression" of the flexors and the result is forward movement. To ensure a continuous flow of energy around the horse's body, training should aim to simultaneously strengthen and relax the muscles of the body.

The young horse learning to use himself over a jump.
Major Lindgren, courtesy USDF. Tory Sawyer photo.

CHAPTER SEVEN
TRAINING THE RIDER

THE MENTAL COMMITMENT to riding is the most important criteria to success, no matter what performance event you are pursuing. Although many riders are more concerned with just where a particular aid is to be applied and when, the mechanics of riding only constitute about 20 percent of effort required to become a top-notch rider. In order to get the most out of your lessons, be sure you are relaxed and focused.

Arrive for your riding lesson on time, well rested, and in a good frame of mind. Become familiar ahead of time with the various maneuvers that will be called for during your schooling. Observe another student's lesson to learn your instructor's terminology. Illustration on page 108 shows many of the most common dressage lesson movements. Western instructors may use different terms, but the maneuvers will be similar.

Riding lessons are usually offered on a private, semi-private, or group basis. Group lessons are the least expensive and offer the rider a chance to work with other horses in the ring, but they usually result in less personal attention for each rider and a greater potential for accidents. Private lessons cost more but you will have your instructor's undivided attention.

Every coach has his or her own methods and exercises. However, the basic goals in the training of a rider are the same: to instill safe habits and confidence and to develop the rider's understanding and skills.

Confidence. A horseman must move with sure steps and self-assurance while working around horses and must convey the same poise and control while mounted. If you are timid, your instructor will likely move you through your lessons more slowly so that you can become very familiar with the equipment and the horse's behavior. Familiarity breeds confidence.

Understanding. The theories pertinent to your rid-

Learning the feel of the rein. Carol Story, instructor. Cherry Hill photo.

ing goals are available in books or magazines. Ask your instructor to recommend a text that you can study, or refer to the resource guide in the appendix. In spite of what you read in your studies, always be receptive and open-minded to your instructor's comments during a lesson.

Skills. The largest portion of the student's time is spent on developing skills. English instructors often start their students on a longe line. With the student on the horse, the instructor controls the gaits of the horse with the longe line, allowing the rider to concentrate on developing balance and a confident seat.

Your instructor may design exercises for you to use at home. During your riding lessons, you will likely be asked to repeat certain maneuvers until your instructor feels you have reached an acceptable level of success, or at least know what you are doing wrong and need to work on.

The proper execution of a maneuver in a lesson depends on a combination of factors. You must be able to

Arena Maneuvers:

a. *top: half turn*
   bottom: half turn in reverse
b. *change of rein through the circle*
c. *full circle*
d. *quarter turn*
e. *figure eight*
f. *change of rein on the diagonal*
g. *change of rein through the center, width*
h. *serpentine*
i. *change of rein through the center, length*
j. *cavalletti set for trot*
k. *cavalletti set for walk*
l. *moving off the rail in response to the leg*

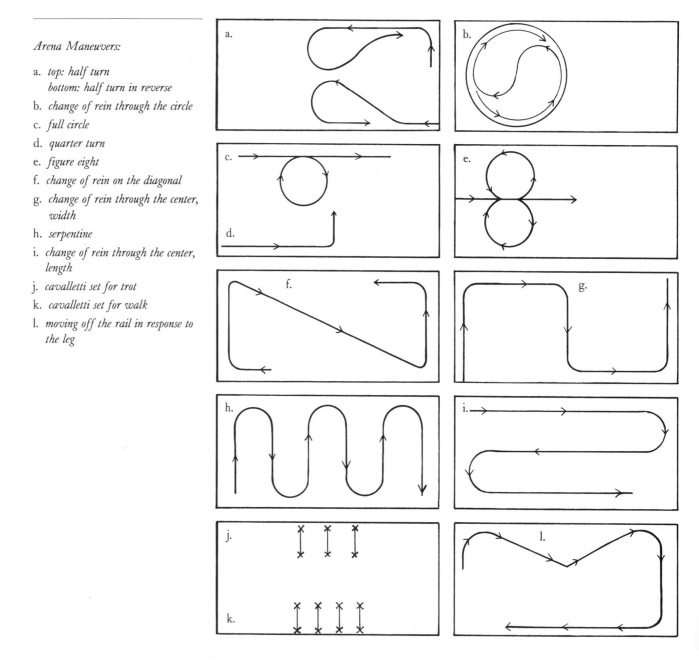

hear the instruction clearly and understand it. Your horse must be obedient and relatively capable of performing the maneuver. And you must have the necessary balance, coordination, and strength to perform the maneuver.

Although I use the development of an amateur reining horse rider as an example of a student's progression, much of the advice will be useful to you, no matter what event holds your strongest interest at this time.

It may take as many as two to three years to make you a top-notch amateur with a solid horse suitable for national competitions. You will first be schooled on an experienced horse to learn cues, develop techniques, and gain confidence, feel, and balance. Lessons may be several times a week at first and from the beginning you will be encouraged to practice at home as well. In addition to working on

specific reining maneuvers that have been covered in the lessons, you will need to keep your horse legged up by riding in the hills or pastures too.

Making mistakes is an essential part of learning. A competent instructor will identify problems and talk you through errors. This feedback will help you develop a feel for what is happening. When a horse loses a pivot foot the instructor will alert you, so that you will first recognize the feeling. Then you will learn how to fix the problem. If you are loping circles and part of the circle is flat, your instructor might go directly to the flat spot and show you where your sense of shape needs improvement. When a rider is right, the horse is right.

Because of the learning process you'll be going through, your horse may need an occasional tune-up by your trainer to smooth over the rough spots created by your trial-and-error method. Each horse eventually gets solid at his own

The footfall patterns of the walk and trot.

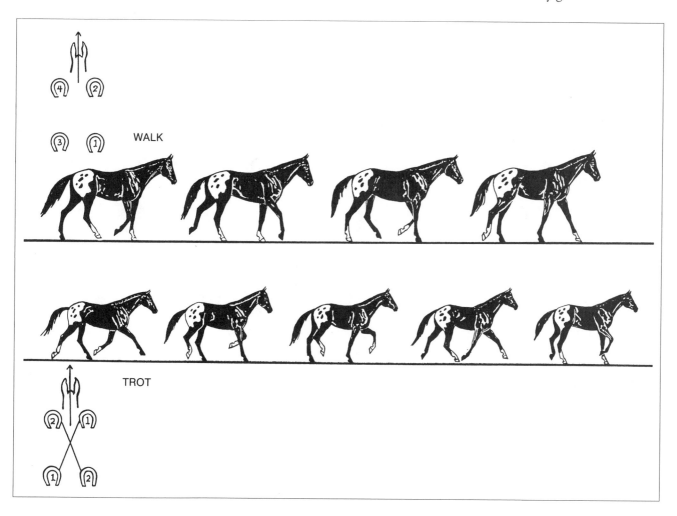

level, reaching a happy medium between what your trainer wants and what you can handle.

Most amateurs experience common problems. Speed control is necessary in the circle work and is achieved by a light balance between the leg and rein. Beginner riders are often stiff and grip the horse's sides, causing the horse to rocket out from underneath them. The goal is to sensitize the horse's sides, ride on a balanced seat, and keep the legs away until needed for a cue.

You should carry your hands in a comfortable position in an imaginary box slightly above the horn rather than reaching down and forward as is often the habit. While schooling, use two hands, which helps keep your shoulders square and the horse balanced and elevated. Neck reining requires an impeccable use of seat and legs

and a lot of finesse with the hands. It will come as you and your horse get more solid and ready for competition.

It is a common error for a novice to over-rein when asking for more speed in a turnaround. Cranking on the bridle locks the horse up and can cause him to turn his head to the outside and shoulder in. You will need to be light with your hands to guide your horse and to use your leg to push your horse around in the spin. Your horse needs room to move and you need to stay out of his way.

Turnarounds can cause disorientation in some riders, so it is best to look at the horse's head or shoulder to prevent dizziness. Watching the horse with direct vision and taking in the environment with peripheral vision allows you to keep track of the number of spins without becoming dizzy.

If a horse scotches (cheats) in his rundowns, it is usually in response to something you are doing wrong. You must

The footfall patterns of the lope/canter on the right and left leads.

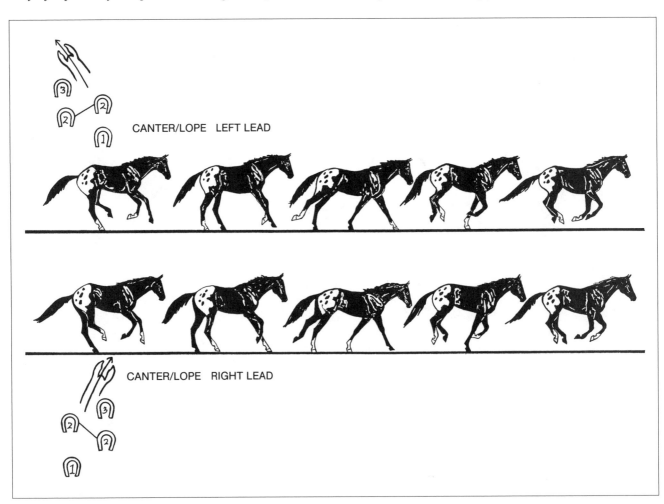

CANTER/LOPE   LEFT LEAD

CANTER/LOPE   RIGHT LEAD

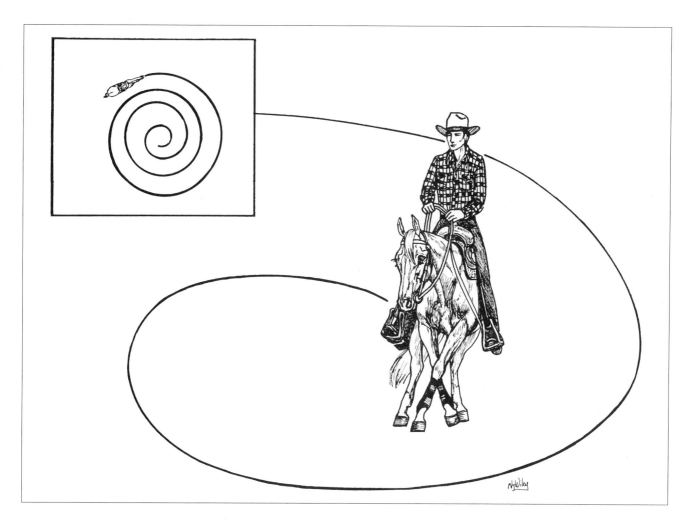

In order to keep the forward movement in a turnaround, the reining horse rider spirals into it.

sit in balance. Standing in the stirrups is an unstable way to approach a stop, and, as a result, you may flounder around giving the horse inadvertent cues. You need to have a steady reining hand and not bump the bit. Starting a rundown at a slow, controlled lope and building speed with each stride teaches the horse that he must speed up into the stop, not slow down before it.

The cues for the stop are much more subtle than you may realize. Rather than driving weight into the saddle and rounding the back, ask for a balanced stop by saying "whoa," using a straight upper body, square shoulders, and elevating your reining hand. If you break in your back and hunker your weight deep into the seat, it can put you behind the motion of your horse and can have the tendency to pop your horse out of what might have started as a deep, hard stop. Learning this finesse takes time and many stops.

Sometimes you can destroy a perfectly good moment in your horse's training by leaning forward and petting him at the wrong time. Because horses link praise to the very last thing they have done, often your good intentions can backfire. If a horse rocks back on his hindquarters and lopes off nicely, and then does a balanced and rhythmic spin, you should ask for a soft stop and then let the horse fill up with air. Rest is a straightforward reward. If, instead, you lurch forward enthusiastically to give your horse a pat on the neck, you force the horse to fall on his forehand. Not only have you lost *your* position, but you have rewarded your horse right as he was thrown off balance. You have praised an undesirable behavior.

Often too much petting can change the relationship

111

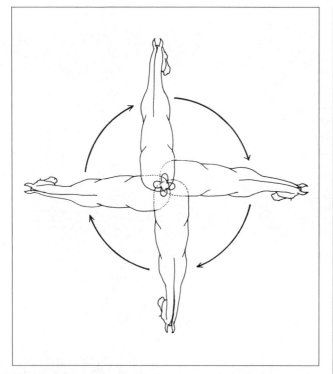

The pivot foot in a turn on the hindquarters (haunches) to the right is the right hind. Your instructor will help you recognize it.

between a rider and a horse. Fondling may encourage your horse to become pushy and dominant. As long as a horse is treated fairly and as a horse, he will like and respect you.

Most of the drills you will practice will begin at slow speeds with an emphasis on accuracy and smoothness. This progressive system provides a basis for understanding and review before you call on your horse for a little more snap.

Walking a horse in a small circle and gradually spiraling the circle into a spin will help you feel the importance of the leg in keeping the horse moving forward (see illustration on page 111). It also will help you learn how to adjust your hands gradually so that when the time comes

to start a spin from a standstill, you can smoothly shape the horse with your hands and guide him into the turnaround. A similar exercise is used by dressage riders to work on the canter pirouette.

To say that you will do a million circles may be no exaggeration. You may be instructed to use a pylon for a center marker and perform five small slow circles, then five large fast circles for twenty minutes or more at a time.

Some of the common exercises used by reining horse trainers are designed to tie several maneuvers together. Practicing these drills will help you with problem areas. The rundown, stop, and turnaround is a good exercise to put forward motion in the spin. Inserting a back between the stop and the spin makes it a more advanced exercise because the horse has to be driven forward in balance before he begins the spin.

Loping circles followed by a stop and a rollback away from the circle keeps the horse thinking about working off his hindquarters in his lope work. Loping circles with stops and turnarounds to the inside helps the horse spin with his head down and into the direction of the spin.

Loping around the entire arena, increasing the reach on the long sides, and rocking the horse back on the ends improves speed control.

Lead changes are rarely practiced because anticipation is common with this particular maneuver. A chargy horse that is "looking for the middle" where the change usually occurs can be discouraged by continuing in the same lead (counterloping) rather than routinely switching leads when changing directions. This exercise adds to overall obedience and helps the horse remain flexible mentally and physically.

As you become more advanced, videotapes of your lessons can be valuable for discussing what you need to improve. It is not a particular concern if, at first, you go off pattern, but your run should resemble the pattern. Freestyle comes later on!

CHAPTER EIGHT
HORSE HEALTH AND CARE

YOUR VETERINARIAN

TRY TO ARRANGE for an equine specialist to be your horse's doctor. Write the American Association of Equine Practitioners for a list of equine specialists in your area and/or ask for recommendations from several professional horsemen.

Once you have selected your veterinarian, be fully cooperative. A good relationship is based on preparation, consideration, and open-mindedness. Make all of your appointments well in advance if possible. Have your horse clean, ready, and quiet when the veterinarian arrives. Your horse should be trained to stand for treatment. If necessary, he should allow the application of a twitch or chain for restraint. Have a strong lead rope and halter of the proper size. Be sure your horse will allow his head, ears, lips, and legs to be handled. Ask the veterinarian how you can assist, where you should stand, and if you should hold your horse. If the veterinarian would rather have the horse tied during treatment, have a safe, strong place to tie him.

For work that requires more time or a greater degree of sanitation, prepare an appropriate area. Be sure it is clean, light, and safe. Familiarize the horse with this place ahead of time by doing something pleasurable in it, such as grooming.

Become familiar with first aid procedures, especially what to do and what not to do in case of a serious injury. If talking is necessary during the veterinarian's treatment, do so in calm, low tones.

PARASITE MANAGEMENT

Although it is virtually impossible to have a parasite-free horse, good management can go a long way in keeping intestinal parasites under control. Removing feces daily from eating areas, rotating pastures, and deworming regularly are recommended.

Classes of dewormers should be rotated because parasites develop a resistance to most chemicals if they are used repeatedly. (Ivermectin may be an exception.) In any deworming program, if a horse's poor appearance does not improve after treatment, it may be helpful to have a fecal examination performed. Some deworming products are more specific for certain parasites than others, so ask for professional advice.

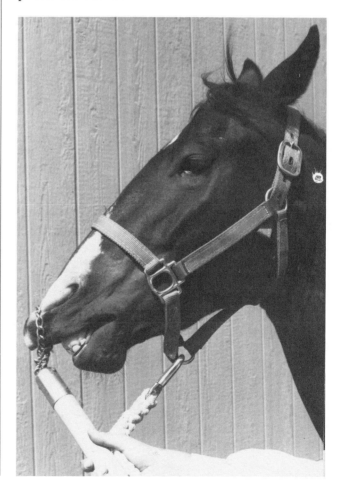

Your horse must learn to accept restraint with a twitch. Richard Klimesh photo.

Young horses generally have a greater susceptibility to roundworm (ascarid) infestation than adults. Bloodworms (strongyles) do the most permanent damage to horses of all ages because the larvae migrate through the body's tissues. Pinworms (oxyuris) can cause troublesome anal itch. During the late summer, bot flies (gasterophilus) lay their yellowish eggs on the horse's leg hairs. Daily removal of the eggs with a "bot block" or "bot comb" is helpful for optimum control.

It is generally recommended that you deworm for roundworms, bloodworms, and pinworms every two months and for bots at least twice a year during the late fall and winter months. Routine administration of paste dewormers is a cost-effective means of parasite control. Be sure to ask your veterinarian for specific recommendations for your farm.

IMMUNIZATIONS

Most equine vaccinations are administered during your veterinarian's routine spring and fall visits. Few horses object to properly administered intramuscular injections.

Veterinary Care: Your veterinarian will monitor your horse's health and soundness.

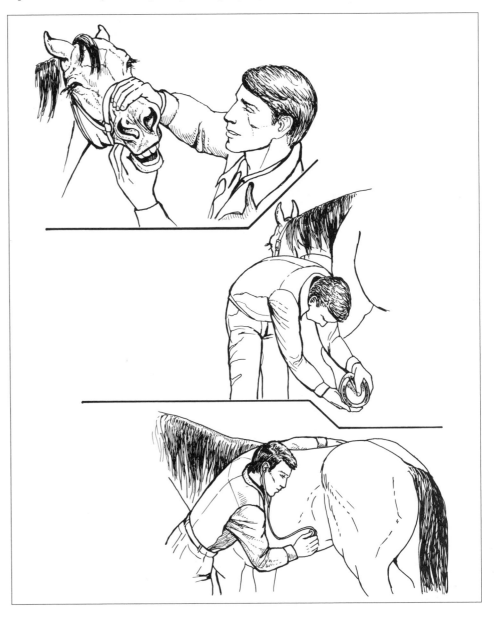

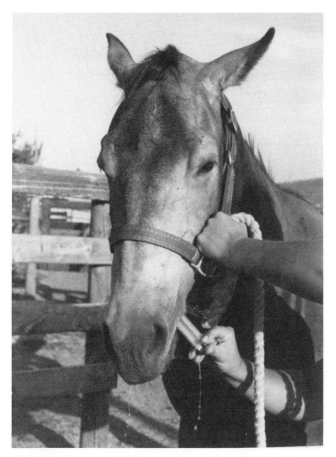

Routine deworming is the first step to overall good health. Cherry Hill photo.

Usually their fear comes from an inexperienced human or insufficient handling before their first vaccination. Rather than take a chance giving the injections yourself, seek the help of your professional.

Horses are usually vaccinated each year in the spring for protection against tetanus, influenza, Eastern and Western encephalomyelitis, and rhinopneumonitis. In addition, it may be recommended in your area to vaccinate for rabies, distemper (strangles), or Venezuelan sleeping sickness.

Currently there is no vaccine for equine infectious anemia, although research is in progress. The Coggins test detects the presence of antibodies in the horse's blood that indicate the horse has been previously exposed to the EIA virus. In order to keep contamination down to a minimum, each state has its own requirements for animals entering and traveling within its boundaries (see appen-

dix). Note that a particular show may have stricter requirements regarding the test for EIA than the state. It is a good idea to have a Coggins test and a health exam performed at least once a year on every horse you are planning to compete with. Although a health exam may not be required by law, some shows may require one. If you have a heavy show schedule that spans many states, it would be wise to have the tests repeated every six months. Carry the certificates with you whenever you travel with the horse.

DENTAL CARE

Horses have two main groups of teeth: twelve incisors at the front of the mouth and twenty-four to twenty-eight molars (or check teeth) at the back of the mouth. The first twelve to sixteen molars are often referred to as premolars; the last twelve are called molars. Through evolution the first premolar (or wolf tooth) has served a progressively less important function, so it has diminished in size and may even be absent.

In male horses, canines appear on the interdental space at about four years of age and are fully developed at five. The canines, also called bridle teeth or tushes, erupt nearer the incisors. Canines can also be present in mares, but are usually small buds.

Tooth problems first show up in the eating habits and unthriftiness of a horse: dropping wads of food, holding the head at an odd angle while chewing, hay and grain in the water pail, etc. Close inspection may reveal an undesirable mouth odor.

Subtle signs that things aren't quite right in the bridled horse's mouth may be an irritable expression of ears or eyes as pressure is applied in a certain way on a rein. Tail swishing, although an indicator of many maladies, can be a substitue behavior for head shaking. If a horse has been taught not to shake his head, he will look for another outlet for his frustration. Maneuvers in a particular direction may all of a sudden become stiff. For instance, the horse may be willing to the right but uncooperative to the left. If the problem affects teeth on both sides of the mouth, the horse may avoid contact with the bit altogether. He may do this by coming above the bit, that is, sticking his head up and out to keep the bit off his bars and tongue. Or he may overflex at the poll and drop behind the bit, letting the headstall suspend the bit in his mouth cavity instead of accepting contact with it.

If during routine bridling your horse tries to move his head away from you and swing his rump toward you or raises his head and pins back his ears, it is past time to get to the "root" of the problem. It may be a case of improper training, but it could also point to the need for dental care.

Floating and wolf tooth extraction are common procedures performed by your veterinarian that will help maintain proper working order of your horse's mouth. Routine floating is the process of filing off the sharp edges of the premolars and molars. The upper jaw of the horse is 30 percent wider than the lower jaw. As the horse grinds his feed in a somewhat side-to-side motion, uneven wear occurs on his molars and premolars. Sharp edges form on the outside (cheek surfaces) of the upper teeth and on the inside (tongue surfaces) of the lower teeth. Even a horse with normal dental conformation and on a regular ration is not immune to the formation of these sharp edges.

Sharp molars can be smoothed and rounded by various types of dental floats. Most veterinarians use files to manually rasp the edges, much the way a farrier shapes a rough hoof wall. The surfaces of the files are usually hard steel or tungsten carbide chips.

Wolf tooth extraction is a routine, on-the-farm procedure today. It lessens the chance for the painful pinching that often occurs in horses ridden with a snaffle bit. Wolf teeth occur more commonly in the upper jaw.

NUTRITION

The five nutrient groups are water, energy, protein, minerals, and vitamins.

Water. Horses drink one-half to one gallon of water per 100 pounds of body weight daily for maintenance. Environmental temperature, level of exercise, and type of feed ration affect water requirements. Always provide good quality, free-choice water. Horses do not necessarily drink when it is convenient for their owners but rather as part of their daily routine. Insufficient water can depress appetite and lead to impaction colic. Be sure the quality of your water is good. If you are in doubt, have it tested for excess sodium, potassium, nitrates, and other harmful substances.

Energy. There are three sources of energy: carbohy-

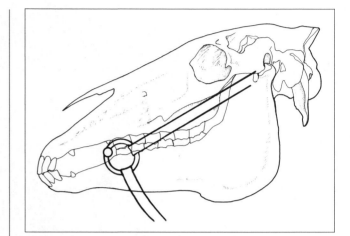

Dentition of the mature horse. From the front of the mouth: incisors, canines, wolf teeth, premolars, molars.

drates, fats, and proteins. Carbohydrates in horse feeds are sugars, starches, and cellulose (predominantly fiber). Most of the energy value of a feed comes from its sugar and starch content. Energy requirements are dependent on the horse's weight, activity level, and, in the case of a nursing mare, her stage of lactation. Feeds for energy should be fed by weight not volume. A 1-pound coffee can holds approximately 1 pound of oats, ½ pound of bran, or 1½ pounds of corn or pelleted feeds. It is advisable to actually weigh the filled can or container to verify the exact amount.

Fats are a concentrated source of energy, providing 2.25 times as much energy as an equal weight of carbohydrates or proteins. The horse can tolerate up to 16 percent fat in his total ration. A horse diet typically contains 2 to 6 percent fat. If a glossier coat or more energy is desired, add 1 to 2 ounces of cooking oil to a horse's ration twice daily.

Protein. Although protein is not economical to feed specifically for its energy content, the horse's body can use excess protein for energy. But feeding high levels of protein can be harmful. Protein is made up of various combinations of the twenty-two amino acids, some of which can be synthesized by the horse's body. Others, called essential amino acids, must be supplied every day in the horse's ration. Feeds high in essential amino acids have high-quality protein. Three amino acids that are typically limited in horse rations are lysine, methionine, and tryptophan. Lysine especially is important for growth, and because feeds vary in the quality of protein they contain, it may be necessary to supplement the ration of the young horse with it.

If more protein is fed than is needed, the horse removes the nitrogen in the form of ammonia from the excess protein and uses the balance for energy. If energy is not needed, it is stored as fat. The ammonia that is removed is the charactertistic strong smell in the urine of horses on high-protein diets.

Excess protein in the diet causes the liver and kidneys to work overtime and increases the horse's water requirements so the body can flush waste products. It can also contribute to bone problems in a growing horse.

Minerals. The amount and balance of minerals are important for many bodily functions. Horses should always have freechoice trace-mineral salt, which provides sodium, chloride, and other electrolytes. In addition, horse owners should be very conscious of the amount and ratio of calcium and phosphorus in the horse's diet.

It is best to keep the calcium to phosphorus ratio in the ration of the growing horse between 2:1 and 1:1 and of the mature horse around 1:1. Hay should be analyzed to determine its actual nutrient composition. Any supplements that are fed should be carefully examined to determine their contribution to the overall calcium-phosphorus balance.

Calcium deficiencies can cause the body to mobilize calcium from the bones, which then weaken the structure. Excess phosphorus can act like a calcium deficiency, which commonly results in leg problems such as enlarged joints (epiphysitis) in the young horse.

Copper and zinc are also essential elements, especially for the young, growing horse.

Vitamins. Most vitamins are present in adequate quantities in the horse's ration. Vitamin A is the only vitamin that may be inadequate if a horse is fed a steady diet of old, bleached forages. The liver, however, can store a six-month supply of vitamin A. Oversupplementation of vitamin A is usually more of a problem than dietary deficiencies.

Feeds

Roughages. Roughages are fed to the horse in the form of hay, pasture, or compressed hay pellets, wafers, or cubes. Hays are generally legume, grass, or cereal grain hay. The major legumes fed to horses are alfalfa and clover. Grasses include but are not limited to timothy, brome, and orchard grass. Oat hay, in which the grain has not been harvested, can make suitable horse forage.

Alfalfa is higher in nutritional value than an equal-quality grass hay, having at least twice as much protein, three times the amount of calcium, and many more vitamins than the grass. If good-quality alfalfa is available, it is highly recommended for the growing horse but may be unnecessary for the adult horse, especially if grain is also fed.

Hay quality is determined by how mature the plants were when the field was cut, growing conditions, field management, and weather during the curing and baling process. Good hay is free of mold, dust, and weeds and has a bright green color and fresh smell. The leaf-to-stem ratio is high and the hay is soft to the touch, with little shattering of leaves but no excess moisture that could cause overheating and spoilage. Because hay is the mainstay of the horse's ration, it behooves the horse owner to spend time locating the very best hay available for the growing horse.

Pasture can provide nutrients plus exercise. One acre of improved pasture with adequate moisture or irrigation can support two horses during the six-month grazing season. However, it may require fifty or more acres of dry rangeland to support a single horse. Local extension agents can assist in choosing the best plant varieties and management procedures.

Hay pellets and cubes are usually available in bulk or in 50-pound sacks. Although they may be more convenient for you to use, they may not be the best choice for every horse. Some horses fed compressed hay products bolt their feed, which can cause choking. Compressed hay products do not satisfy a horse's urge to chew, like long hay does, and so may lead to the bad habit of wood chewing.

Concentrates. Feeds that are low in fiber but high in energy are the grains and protein supplements. Oats have become a traditional horse feed because of the safe ratio of fiber to energy that their hulls provide. A highly digestible grain such as corn, with its thin seed coat, may be too concentrated for the horse's diet. On an energy basis, oats are about the most expensive grain whereas corn is an economic source of concentrated energy. A lot of old wives' tales have circulated about corn: it is a "hot" feed, or it will make horses founder, become fat, or too spirited. The truth is that because of its density, an equal volume of corn has twice the energy value of oats. So if you are feeding by the coffee-can method (volume instead of weight), horses *might* suffer these feared consequences because they are getting twice what they should.

Feeding extra corn in cold weather can actually be counterproductive. Horses gain body heat from the heat of digestion. Because corn is digested relatively quickly, it offers little body heat. Hay, on the other hand, requires a longer digestion time and subsequently warms the body. When a cold snap hits, feeding free-choice roughage is often the best management practice. Feeding corn prior to the cold season to fatten and insulate a horse has some value but is not recommended for young horses. Feeding a balanced, high-quality ration year-round is preferred.

At the head of the protein supplement list is soybean meal. It contains the highest-quality protein and the highest amount of lysine of any plant source, and is the supplement of choice.

Commercially prepared horse feeds are available as pellets or grain mixes. Pelleted feeds may be forages, concentrates, or a combination. "Sweet feed" grain mixes are usually a combination of oats and/or barley, corn, molasses, and a pellet consisting of soybean meal, minerals, and vitamins. Feed mills create different products to correspond to the needs of the various classes of horses and usually have several grain mixes and concentrates from which to choose.

Feeding Practices.

- A laboratory analysis of hay and grain is the simplest, best, and most direct method to determine exactly what a horse is being fed. Your veterinarian or nutritionist can advise you on sampling procedures and can assist in interpreting results and making supplement corrections.
- It is best to feed at least twice a day and at the same time every day.
- Feed areas should be free from fecal contamination.
- Feed roughages at ground level whenever possible.
- Feed by weight not volume.
- Make all increases and decreases of concentrates gradually: Change by half-pound increments and hold for four feedings before making another adjustment.
- Choose safe feeders that horses will not chew on.

Providing balanced nutrition is essential for the wellbeing of your horse. Cherry Hill photo.

- Make all changes from one type of forage to another over a period of several days.
- Be sure a horse has had a "full feed" of hay before turning him out on pasture for the first time each year. Limit the amount of time on pasture initially to a half hour per day and gradually increase it.
- For optimal results, feed each horse his concentrate ration separately. Group forage feeding is acceptable as long as there is enough feed and space for the level of competition in the group.
- Discourage vices such as wood chewing by providing adequate roughage and exercise.
- Monitor the calcium to phosphorus ratio closely.
- Know the difference among horse blocks. There are basically four types of blocks, listed here in order of

increasing palatability: salt, trace minerals and salt, calcium and phosphorus with trace minerals and salt, and protein (usually also contains trace minerals and salt). The protein blocks are tasty and most horses will spend hours at them. Do not buy protein blocks containing urea. As long as a horse's ration remains balanced with the addition of a protein block, it can be a great pacifier.

HOOF CARE

Horses came originally from a semiarid environment, so their external hoof structures are well adapted to dryness. In fact, many hoof problems can be linked to excess external moisture and deficient internal moisture. Horses confined to stalls experience the worst of both evils. Standing in manure, urine, and wet bedding softens the supporting structures of the foot, and the strong acids can decompose tissues and set the stage for further complications. Muddy lots are equally damaging. When the hoof gets wet, it expands. When mud dries around the hoof, it leaches precious internal moisture. This expansion and contraction on a daily basis can destroy the integrity of the hoof horn, causing weak and brittle hooves.

Confinement also diminishes the amount of internal moisture a hoof receives from blood flow. An idle horse has stagnant circulation, resulting in fewer nutrients being delivered to the hoof, fewer waste products being removed, and less internal moisture being distributed.

Keep the hooves clean and dry to prevent thrush, and keep an eye on any tendencies of the horse to develop weak heels and other hoof irregularities such as flares, club feet, or thin soles. Working closely with a veterinarian and farrier can minimize the risk of such problems. Discuss stable management with your farrier and follow his recommendations. He or she cannot wave a magic wand over a horse's feet every eight weeks to counteract mismanagement. Work together toward long-term positive hoof improvement.

A horse should have its feet checked every six to eight weeks. Don't take your horse into a show ring if he is due to be reshod. It will count against you in showmanship and will probably negatively affect your horse's performance. He may stumble, forge, or even lose a shoe in the ring. Try to coordinate schedules so that your horse is shod one to five weeks before a competition.

Before you telephone your horseshoer, make an accurate list of which horses need attention. If your needs happen to change before the farrier arrives, have the courtesy to call so he or she can adjust the rest of that day's schedule accordingly.

Good farriers are scarce and in great demand. Give your farrier the same consideration as your veterinarian. Be sure facilities and equipment are safe and comfortable. Don't expect your farrier to shoe out in the hot sun while your horse is tied to a wire fence with baling twine. Provide a level place for the horse to stand, where it can be tied safely and securely at the level of the withers or higher. Have plenty of fly spray on hand and don't wait until the farrier's visit to acquaint the horse with a spray bottle.

It is not part of the farrier's responsibilities to train your horse. That should be done well in advance of the appointment. Accustoming your horse to regular handling will allow your farrier to do the best job.

Minimizing stress. Veteran endurance rider Paul Baetz cools his horse's feet in some Rocky Mountain water during a rest stop. Cherry Hill photo.

CHAPTER NINE
STRESS

SHOW HORSES are frequently subjected to grueling schedules with temporary accommodations providing inconsistent creature comforts. In addition, they may be exposed to and frightened by any of the following: applause; large crowds; music; loudspeakers; flapping flags, ribbons, banners, and papers; indoor arenas; carts and buggies; small children running nearby; lawn chairs at the rail; tractors, harrows, and water trucks; and, odd as it might seem, ponies and foals. It is no wonder that the show environment can stress a horse beyond his level to cope. Although horses differ greatly in their individual tolerance for stress, certain elements are common to most.

Stress is a demand for adaptation. In the wild, horses have the opportunity to flee rather than confront their fears. Domestication requires that horses learn to live in our world. Each horse has its own stress-tolerance level. When domestication pressures and demands exceed a horse's capacity to adapt, some type of failure results. It can be in the form of behavior abnormalities (vices or bad habits), illness, or injury.

On the other hand, some stress is essential for the mental and physical development of an individual. Usually gradual exposure is used to accustom a horse to a stress. Some situations, however, require that a horse be confronted all at once with a stress.

Interval training is one way to gradually teach a horse to adapt to stress. Stressful episodes are alternated with rest or a nonstressful activity. Stimulation is increased gradually. Change the frequency, intensity, suddenness, and duration of the stress during different training sessions.

For example, if the stress of a gallop is used for conditioning purposes, it can be varied in the following ways: the number of times the horse is galloped during a training session, the speed of each gallop, the length of the pregallop warm-up, the activity immediately preceding the gallop (breaking from a standstill as opposed to galloping from a canter), and the length of time the horse is asked to gallop.

In the same way, you can gradually expose a horse to psychological pressures. If you want to be able to take off your jacket while you are mounted, you begin by allowing the horse to inspect and accept the sight and smell of a soft jacket. Over several sessions, you can gradually increase how suddenly you present the jacket to the horse, and how fast, how intensely, and how long you flap it. Another variation in the intensity of the lessons would be to use a noisy plastic raincoat.

Sometimes it is necessary to confront a horse with his fears all at once, such as tying him up or picking up his feet. You can't gradually tie a horse or pick up his feet halfway. These are some of the all-or-none situations in horse training. If sessions are carefully planned using proper principles, facilities, and equipment, a confrontation can become a positive addition to the horse's experience. During a confrontation, a horse learns in certain terms what works and what doesn't. Horses do not know the difference between "good" and "bad": They merely form habits in accordance with their experiences. When confronted, a horse is likely to learn the lesson if the trainer makes it clear what he or she wants.

Sometimes, if the basics have not been firmly established, a horse can become uncooperative and sullen when confronted. Such a horse has no previous experience of submitting to the will of his trainer. A sullen horse characteristically tunes out the lesson by holding his breath, often biting his tongue, holding eyes at half mast, and leaning into heavy pressure. A sharp noise or flat slap is most effective to snap a horse out of this behavior. The reaction is liable to be sudden as the sullen horse instinctively sucks in air to fill the oxygen debt.

Stress can be a positive building force as well as a debilitating one. Often there is a negative connotation associated with the word "stress." Whereas the word "tension" describes a nervous or edgy animal, "stress" defines the normal and healthy process of an animal faced with a difficult situation or force. How prepared a horse is before encountering a challenge determines whether he will be strengthened or weakened by it.

TYPES OF STRESS
Psychological Stress

Most psychological stress is based on the horse's innate reaction to flee from danger and to seek the security and companionship of his herdmates. Trailering to a show can certainly upset a horse. The show horse may be required to leave home without his buddy and, worse yet, may be stabled next to a hostile horse who has learned to aggressively protect his temporary space. When allowed little positive interaction with his own species, a horse new to traveling on the show circuit can become lonely and insecure.

Lack of confidence coupled with the overstimulation characteristic of a show environment can make a horse doubt his safety. Horse show barn areas are commonly bright, noisy, and bustling, offering few opportunities for a peaceful and satisfactory rest.

Being stabled twenty-four hours a day or being tied to a trailer for long periods of time frustrates the horse's inherent desire to roam. Unless a horse has previously become accustomed to such restraint and long periods of immobility, confinement can make him anxious, irritable, or angry. The result may be the development of a vice such as pawing, weaving, stall kicking, or cribbing.

Because most showgrounds do not offer ample turnout space, it is the exhibitor's responsibility to provide his or her horse with exercise and time out of the stall. Although exercise fulfils an important physical release, it is also essential for a horse's mental well-being. All too often, exercise at the showgrounds consists of either longeing or preperformance warmup riding. Although these types of exercise are helpful, a bit of time invested in other activities can add to the horse's comfort and relaxation. Hand walking is a labor-intensive method of providing exercise, but it allows the horse to slowly unwind his muscles and his mind. Nothing very demanding is asked of him, yet he is allowed to stretch, release tension, and view the scene.

Several medium-length walks per day are more beneficial for the horse than one very long one.

When using riding as a form of exercise, try not to work on problem areas. Working in a long frame, rather than a collected one, and asking for flexible, relaxed movements allows the horse to stretch his body and put his mind at ease. Although it is true that horses are always being trained in one way or another, during a session designed specifically for exercise it is best not to work on anything troublesome or new.

Ensuring your horse's privacy, especially during long trips away from home, will allow him to obtain higher-quality rest. Stall curtains around and over the top of the stall will keep out excess light as well as noise from passersby. If you can afford to pay for a buffer zone of an extra stall between yours and the next exhibitor's, it can be used as a handy tack area and groom's quarters. it will also serve as added insurance that your horse will not be forced to be neighbors with an incompatible horse.

Metabolic Stress

Metabolic stresses affect fit, well-cared-for athletes as well as overweight or malnourished horses. A common condition associated with many cases of metabolic stress is an electrolyte imbalance. The initial cause may be over-exertion, severe injury or illness, or body upsets that result in a horse going off feed or water. A large loss of important body fluids (water or blood), often coupled with the horse's failure to replenish them, can produce an electrolyte deficit or imbalance result. When tissue ion concentrations of sodium, potassium, calcium, or chloride are low or imbalanced, muscles may experience weakness or spasms. The desire to drink or eat is diminished, thereby increasing dehydration.

Dosing a dehydrated animal with electrolyte solution often gives him the necessary interest and energy for recovery. Because body chemistry operates on a delicate balance, it is important that you obtain the assistance of a veterinarian.

It is not advisable to change your horse's hay or grain rations or become involved in a stalemate with him about drinking while you are on the show circuit. A horse that has gone off his feed or water is in danger of developing a digestive disturbance from mild dehydration to severe colic. The balance of electrolytes in a horse's body is necessary for optimum performance.

To assure that a horse drinks ample water away from home, it may be necessary to scent or flavor the water. If a substance is added both at home and away, the horse is less likely to detect subtle odor and taste differences. Some substances you may wish to try include cider vinegar, oil of wintergreen, molasses, Jell-O, or Kool-Aid.

A horse that tends to develop loose manure when traveling may benefit from eating grass hay instead of alfalfa during the show season. The laxative effect that rich alfalfa leaves have on some horses can lead to an unwanted loss of body water.

Nervousness caused by an unfamiliar environment can often be dispelled by offering a horse many small feedings of his hay throughout the day and night. The slow, rhythmic process of eating roughages tends to soothe the horse, as does licking or chewing supplement blocks.

Sometimes inadequate stabling can contribute to metabolic stress. Cold, drafty, or wet conditions keep the horse in a constant state of muscle contraction as he shivers to keep warm. Excess toxic substances can build up in the tissues and create a vicious cycle of muscle tension. Blanket a horse appropriately, use stall curtains to minimize drafts, and keep the bedding dry.

Immunological Stress

Horses are subjected to immunological stress both from their natural environment and from vaccinations. Undesirable stabling conditions can lower the horse's temperature and resistance to disease and challenge his ability to handle immunological stress.

Vaccinations should be strategically planned in advance of seasonal exposure to diseases. The immune system is gradually and repeatedly introduced to disease-causing organisms to build a stong defense. When a horse encounters an antigen (disease-causing organism) from the environment or a vaccine, his body responds by forming an antibody or antitoxin, which then counters the invader in the future. Over time, antibody levels diminish and need to be boosted. Most equine vaccines are reintroduced once a year for optimal protection. The respiratory diseases influenza and rhinopneumonitis usually require

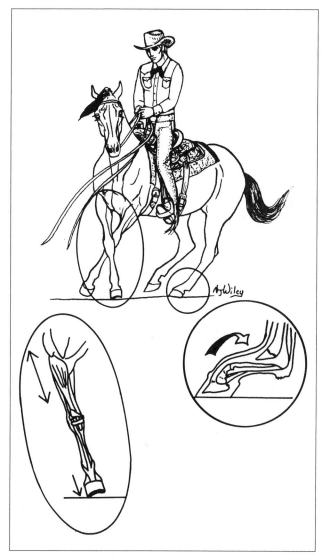

The stress of the turnaround: In a series of very fast hindquarter turns, the inside hind or pivot foot of the spinning horse hyperextends as it accepts nearly full body weight at the same time it contends with the twisting forces of torque. The front legs take turns experiencing stretching forces and asymmetric concussive loading.

more frequent boosters and are recommended every six months or so for horses that will be routinely exposed to new facilities and other horses.

Mechanical Stress

There is often a fine line between a conditioning effect and mechanical overstress. Although horses need a certain amount of bone concussion, muscle fatigue, and tendon stretching to achieve a useful athletic condition, often it is overdue and early signs of overstress go undetected.

For example, working a horse on hard ground may be exactly what he needs to develop tough hooves, durable ligaments, and dense bone columns for eventing or endurance riding, yet it can also become his downfall if in the process he develops sole bruises or arthritis. If a horse is required to do a lot of lateral work, such as the dressage, cutting, or reining horse, his muscles and joints must be able to adapt (see illustration on page 121).

Although a horse can show signs of mechanical stress at home as well as at a show, there are additional factors that

The barrel horse must adapt to lateral stresses at speed. Sandy Martin and Ben. Courtesy of The Appaloosa Horse Club. Harold Campton photo.

make the show environment more dangerous. The arena footing provided for warm-up and performance may be very different from what the horse is accustomed to at home. Hardness, depth, heaviness, evenness, and texture of footing all exert an influence on energy requirements, muscle strain, and joint sprain during performance. It is advisable to condition the performance horse on a variety of terrains to prevent mishaps from hyperextension or concussion.

The fetlocks of hunters and jumpers hyperextend as they land at a fence. It is important to condition these horses so that the demands of the sport do not result in bowed tendons or fractures. Dressage horses must be able to withstand hard-packed, slippery, or deep footing. Arenas at home and away do not have ideal footing at all times. Reining horses can suffer the most from a poor working surface. If an arena is too slippery, the reining

horse may have difficulty loping circles or performing turnaround, and he may lose his footing in the stop causing his hind legs to shoot too far underneath his belly or wildly out to the side. This can result in hock, stifle, or back injury (see illustration (below). If the ground is sticky or heavy, it could create too much grab in the stop, causing an abrupt cessation of forward movement and leading to injuries such as curbs. Condition any horse properly on a variety of footings, inspect the arena footing before you perform, and use protective boots where allowed.

Some classes allow horses to wear leg protection. Boots of various kinds are used to cover the cannons, front, and hind (see illustration on page 127). These may be made of leather, hard plastic, or rubberized synthetics fastened by velcro or buckles. The thickest part of a boot is located in the area of the leg needing the most protection. Therefore, splint boots have an extra wear plate over the inside splint

bone; galloping boots are heaviest over the flexor tendons; and skid boots (for sliding stops) have a thick cup over the hind fetlocks. Leg wraps are used in some events, such as dressage, instead of boots. Bell boots protect the coronary band from a blow from another hoof.

Trailering, one of the greatest mechanical stresses involved with showing, takes place before the horse even arrives on the grounds. Refer to the section on selection of a trailer, and become familiar with trailering procedures to ensure that your horse receives a comfortable ride.

MONITORING STRESS

In order to recognize an abnormal level of stress, you must be thoroughly familiar with the normal ranges in which your horse functions. Except for cases of purely mechanical stress, such as a fractured bone or bowed tendon, the causes and symptoms of various types of stress are interrelated.

One of the simplest means of monitoring stress is taking the horse's temperature, pulse, and respiration. To take the temperature, insert a lubricated rectal thermometer into the horse's anus and leave it for two minutes. The thermometer can be lubricated with petroleum jelly or saliva. Tie a 2-foot piece of string to the thermometer, attach an alligator clip to the other end of the string, and fasten the clip to the horse's tail while the thermometer is registering. In the event the horse defecates during the two minutes, your thermometer will not fall to the ground and break. Normal resting adult temperature is about 100°F.

The horse's pulse can be taken in a number of places, most commonly the inside of the fetlock, the inside of the jaw, and just behind the elbow. Use the fingertips of your index, middle, and ring fingers to find the pulse. If you feel for the pulse just after the horse has exercised, you will have an easier time finding the beat because it will be stronger than when the horse is at rest. Normal resting adult pulse is usually between thirty-five and forty beats per minute.

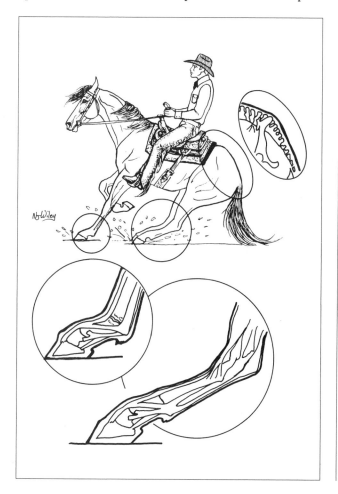

The stress of the stop: As the reining horse drops his croup for a sliding stop, the lumbar vertebrae are repositioned to compensate for the rounding of the back. The hind legs are set well under the horse's body and the hock is required to balance the horse's weight without a vertical supporting column. The front legs alternately flex and hyperextend with a snapping action.

Respiration can be counted by viewing the nostrils or the flank. One breath is measured as one inspiration and one expiration and should be twelve to twenty-five breaths per minute. The ratio of the pulse to the respiration is often a more significant measure of stress than the actual individual figures. A 3:1 to 2:1 ratio is usually normal. If rates become inverted such as 1:2, a horse is having difficulty normalizing his bodily functions and may require the services of a veterinarian.

The pinch test is a quick and easy measure of dehydration. If a fold of skin is picked up in the shoulder area and then released, it should return to its flat position within a second. If the skin remains peaked, it is cause for concern. A standing "tent" of a five- to ten-second duration indicates moderate to severe dehydration.

Inspection of the mucous membranes for a bright pink color and appropriate moisture gives information on the fuctioning of the circulatory system. With the horse's upper lip rolled back, exert firm thumb pressure on the gum. When the thumb is removed, a circular white spot will appear. Within one second, the spot should return to its original color. This is the capillary refill time. If it takes five to ten seconds, your horse is showing signs of circulatory impairment, and you should consult a veterinarian.

Careful palpation and visual examination of a horse's legs, particularly after strenuous work, often reveals localized inflammation. Swelling, heat, and pain are indications of mechanical stress.

A drastic change in your horse's muscle tone could indicate a serious problem. Rigid contractions may be a sign of overall metabolic stress. An example of such a condition is tying up, which is muscle cramping occurring during or after a workout, usually to a horse that has been inconsistently exercised.

Stress is generally manifested as either anxiety or depression. The anxious horse may be in a constant state of agitation resulting in hyperactive intestines that may lead to diarrhea and dehydration. This is a result of the body's reaction to the flight response. A nervous horse that does not feel it is safe to relax may suffer from lack of rest or sleep. A fatigued horse is dull, yet easily startled, and may experience visual distortions and develop hypersensitivity to noise and motion.

In extreme cases, excitability leads to panic. A young

Monitoring stress. An endurance ride veterinarian, Nancy Loving, monitors the level of stress at one of the mandatory veterinary check points at an AERC ride. Cherry Hill photo.

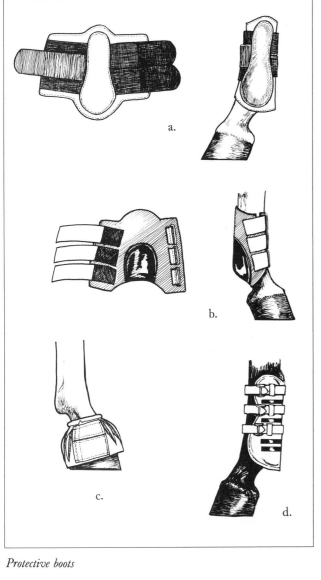

Protective boots

a. *Splint boots*

b. *Skid boots or run-down boots*

c. *Bell boots*

d. *Open front galloping boots*

ritable. Although they may technically do what is asked, they do it in a resentful manner with muscle tension, tail swishing, and negative ear signals.

A depressed horse is more difficult to analyze and deal with than an anxious horse. When a horse has no hope of resolving his frustrations, he may withdraw into a noninteractive shell. As he tunes out the surroundings, exhibiting progressively less interest in feed and water, an apathetic individual with a hanging head and listless expression emerges. The depression may interfere with bodily functions if the horse is not given positive treatment.

PREVENTING STRESS

Exposing a horse to the various elements he will encounter on the show circuit is the best way to ward off stress's harmful effects. Introducing a horse to a variety of experiences builds a confident, independent attitude. Most often a gradual method is successful, but sometimes confrontation is necessary to allay a horse's suspicions. Because a horse does not naturally elect to stay around and ask questions when he encounters a frightening circumstance, you may have to force him to face his fears. Often a single unresolved anxiety can stand in the way of a horse becoming a successful performer.

If a horse's natural instinct is to leave the stadium when he hears applause, for example, yet he is a brilliant jumper, it is worth the effort to devise a suitable program of conditioning to help him deal with the problem. A strong and capable rider may be all that is needed on show day, but perhaps a gradual habituation to the sound of clapping would make the horse safe for even a less experienced rider. Restraining the horse in-hand, in stocks, or in a stall while familiarizing him with live or tape-recorded applause may gradually lesson his desire to flee. Once the horse has begun to accept the clapping, his behavior should be rewarded and encouraged. Feeding him while he is calm during the clapping coupled with positive reassurance from the handler may be helpful. A soothing phrase or pat, once connected with the food reward, will bring a sense of well-being to the horse and can be used in times of trauma to remind the horse that the lesson had a nonthreatening outcome.

horse can become hysterical if improperly prepared for the stresses of showing. Forgetting good behavior patterns and relying on its instinctive response to fear, the panicked horse seeks escape. Breaking a lead rope while tied, running away with a rider, stepping on a handler, or crowding another horse for security are some of the signs that a horse lacks confidence.

Older horses that know they must behave but are still upset with the horse show environment can become ir-

Lessons at home should work toward developing independence in a horse so that he is more self-sufficient when traveling. Varying a horse's neighbors and turnout companions, in addition to providing him with good human relationships, will help a horse feel more confident.

Some horsemen provide their mounts with a companion, such as a goat, for security both at and away from home. This isn't always recommended, however. Although it may give the horse some peace of mind while stalled, he still must perform in the arena alone. And other exhibitors' horses are put at an unfair disadvantage if subjected to an odd animal stabled nearby.

To prevent anticipation, few exhibitors run through exact patterns at home. Yet it is advisable to have a dress rehearsal to expose the horse to as many of the variables he will encounter on show day as possible.

A genuine practice run includes braiding the mane and tail and using the show tack and clothes. Some horses find it irritating to have to stand still to be braided and are in a foul mood afterward; others accept the braiding process

but can't keep their mind on their work with all those little bits of yarn, tape, or rubber bands snugly tying up their hair. It is good to find these things out well before competition and accustom the horse to the necessary requirements for show day.

This advice goes for the rider as well as the mount. Do you feel as though you can ride as well in your show boots and coat as you do in your everyday apparel? Wear your show clothes often enough so that they do not impair your movements and make your riding stiff and ineffective. The converse can also be true though. Saving your perfectly fitted boots and equitation gloves for a special occasion can make you ride with an added bit of confidence and elegance.

Your practice sessions should also include trailering somewhere such as a nearby stable for a lesson, a schooling show, or a ride with a friend. Leave your horse tied to the trailer for a large part of the day. It will be to the horse's advantage to find show day just an extension of regular everyday activities.

CHAPTER TEN

GROOMING

THE TURNOUT, or overall appearance, of your horse plays a large part in his placings in many classes, and if managed properly will positively affect your confidence and self-esteem. The shine of a horse's coat is brought about by a combination of proper feeding, health care, and constant brushing. Grooming involves a lot of hard work. There are no gimmicks that can take the place of elbow grease.

Grooming tools should be kept scrupulously clean and it is best if an individual set is used for each horse.

Purposes of Grooming

- Sanitation: Removes dirt, sweat, glandular secretions, dead skin cells, and hair.
- Warm-up: Provides mental and physical preparation for upcoming work. The massage increases circulation and relaxes the horse.
- Appearance: Cleans the body and brings natural oils to the surface for a glossy hair coat; facilitates shedding.
- Rehabilitation: Can provide the idle recovering horse with a stimulating and soothing interaction.
- Inspection: Allows you to look closely at skin, head, mane, tail, legs, and hooves.
- Training: Accustoms the horse to being handled and desensitizes ticklish areas.
- Stimulation: After hard work, body stropping can invigorate a horse and dispel the waste products of muscle metabolism.

TOOLS OF THE TRADE

The following tools are listed in the order of use:

Hoof pick. Mud, manure, and foreign objects should be regularly cleaned from the clefts of the frog and the sole to prevent disease and injury.

Rubber curry. Used to loosen mud, sweat, and loose hair and bring it to the surface. Soft rubber "nubbins" stimulate the hair follicles to produce oils for a healthy shine. Use in a vigorous circular motion.

Rubber grooming mitt. Serves the same purposes as the rubber curry but designed for sensitive areas such as the legs and head.

Dandy or mud brush. Stiff-bristled brush used to remove the large pieces of dirt and hair brought to the surface by the rubber curry. Used with a flicking motion of the wrist for most of the large-muscle-mass cleaning.

Metal curry comb. Used to keep the bristles of the dandy brush clean. Seldom used on the horse's body. Hold in the hand opposite the brush and run the bristles of the brush over the teeth of the curry every five strokes or so.

Wisp. Woven hay or straw pad used on a dry or wet horse.

Body brush. Short, soft-bristled brush used to further clean the coat after the dandy and rubber grooming mitt.

Terry cloth. Damp or dry cloth used to clean the horse's eyes, nostrils, anus, udder, and sheath. Also handy to keep your hands clean!

Mane and tail brush. You can usually pick through a horse's tail with slightly lubricated hands (use a teaspoon of baby oil or a mane and tail product especially for horses). When brushing is necessary, a human's hairbrush or a dog brush (occasionally lubricated), causes less breakage and pulling than a comb. The lubrication makes brushing easier and less damaging, but it also attracts dirt, so both the brush and the tail will have to be shampooed more frequently. Begin brushing a tail or a long mane from the bottom and work your way up.

Mane pulling comb. Used to shorten or thin the mane. Unwanted strands are wrapped around the comb's teeth and pulled out. Should not be used for routinely combing the mane or untangling the mane or tail because it results in too much hair loss.

Stable rubber. Linen cloth used to remove any remaining dust from the coat and smooth the hair. Always wipe in the direction of hair growth.

BATHING

Bathing is contrary to a horse's natural sense of self-preservation. Baths can be cold and noisy, involve unusual equipment, and are most notably wet. Asking a horse to stand, no questions asked, under a huge rubber snake that is spewing icy water over his back and between his hind legs, is probably a bit unreasonable from his point of view.

It would be ideal if the horse's first bath could come on a hot day, when he might possibly appreciate it. Use body-temperature water, so that the horse won't experience a radical temperature change. First, wet his shoulder area in a nonthreatening manner, perhaps using a bucket and sponge rather than a hose. Move on to the back and hindquarters, then the neck and head. The first bath might consist of just a quick rinse. During later baths, be sparing with the shampoo, or you will extend the bath into a long rinsing session beyond the horse's stage of tolerance.

When you are washing the head of even an experienced horse, avoid using a hose if possible. Spraying the face may cause understandable resentment and could lead to ear and eye irritations. Use a sponge instead. Remove excess water from the horse's body with a contoured aluminum sweat scraper. The dripping water from the belly, especially, can be irritating to some horses.

Either walk the horse as he dries or tie him in a warm but shady place. Because it is difficult to thoroughly dry a horse in the winter, baths are not recommended. If you need to remove sweat marks, use a damp sponge. A solution of one tablespoon of Calgon water softener to a gallon of water is a good mixture for this purpose.

If a horse is well groomed every day, it is not necessary to bathe him often. Once a week before shows or twice a month otherwise would be sufficient. Rinsing daily does not harm, but excessive use of shampoos can contribute to a dry coat.

ADVANCED GROOMING: THE WISP

The wisp that is used for vigorous grooming can be simply a handful of straw or a woven or plaited pad complete with a handle. A wisp can also be made by folding a rough natural fiber material, such as burlap, into a rectangle that will fit the hand. The traditional wisp, however, is made from a twisted rope of straw or hay that is woven into a pad.

The tool has many uses. The coat of a hot horse can be roughed up with a wisp so the skin and hair dry more easily. The vigorous back-and-forth motion creates heat from friction, so a wisp can provide valuable stimulation for a sedentary horse. In addition, a freshly made wisp will absorb sweat, and a clean damp wisp can be useful to set the coat in the final stages of grooming.

Rubbing with a wisp also brings oil up from the follicles and distributes it on the skin and along the hair shafts, contributing to the health of the hair and skin and putting a shine on the coat. This type of grooming is especially important for the confined horse that does not have the opportunity to rub himself by rolling on the ground.

The massaging action of a wisp stimulates the skin's circulation and improves its metabolism. An invigorating rubdown removes scurf, sebum, dandruff, and oils from clogged pores. With the pores opened, the skin cells are able to take in nourishing oxygen. The result is an improvement in overall skin tone and elasticity.

Body stropping invigorates and tones the muscles. The groom slaps the horse with a wisp on the heavy muscles of the neck, shoulder, and haunches. The horse reacts with an isometric contraction. This brings blood to the surface, clears away the muscle waste products that accumulate during exercise, and invigorates the animal. Performed daily on a horse after exercise, this thorough rubdown is guaranteed to give the groom a good workout while providing mental and physical benefits for the horse. Both the groom and the horse are left with a sense of well-being afterward.

To begin stropping, hold the wisp in the flat of the palm 6 to 12 inches from one of the horse's deep muscle masses. Bring the wisp to the muscle with a flat bang and move it smartly off the body in the direction of the hair growth. You should study the growth pattern of the hair when the coat is dry in order to determine the proper direction for the strokes. Repeat the stroke when the horse has relaxed. Once the horse becomes accustomed to the procedure, he will tense and relax in rhythm with the regular strokes of the wisp.

The alternating contraction and relaxation acts as a purification pump, which enables the blood to carry nourishment in and waste products out of the muscles. Strop-

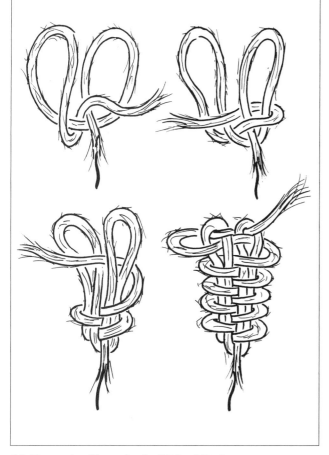

Making a wisp. Illustration by Richard Paul.

ping is only appropriate for the areas of deep muscle mass, such as the neck, shoulder, forearm, croup, and hindquarter. When introduced to the procedure, a horse may adapt immediately or tolerate only several strokes. Once the horse is familiar with the technique he should enjoy the procedure. You can work up to as many as one hundred strokes per muscle group, but this will take as long as forty-five minutes and is strenuous work if properly done.

The wisp is too abrasive for the head, ribs, and legs, but a similar effect can be provided in these areas by hand rubbing with a pair of cotton garden gloves or a rubber grooming mitt. A soothing, circular motion with the hands will allow you to clean and stimulate the delicate and elusive nooks and crannies where bones and joints are close to the surface of the skin.

As a finale to stropping you can cup one hand over each eye and lightly rub. Then move the hands to the ears and strip each ear with several massaging pulls sideways from base to tip. This puts many horses into a state of euphoria.

MANE AND TAIL

A healthy flowing tail and an attractive mane add elegance to most horse performances. More important from the horse's perspective, a long tail and mane make efficient fly chasers.

Many management practices can affect the quality of the keratinized protein that makes up hair. An adequate quantity of good-quality essential amino acids in the diet assures that the horse has the ingredients to produce top-notch hoof horn and hair. If hair is dull or rough or hooves brittle and shelly, the horse's ration should be tested to determine whether it provides adequate methionine and tryptophan. Increased shine of body hair is often evident after six to seven weeks of oil supplementation. Feeding two ounces of vegetable oil twice daily with the grain ration can provide the unsaturated fatty acids that will make a difference.

Problems

Horses that rub their manes and tails usually do so for a specific reason initially, but they may continue the habit long after the cause has been removed. Therefore, it is of utmost importance to locate the problem early. Geldings and stallions most often rub their tails because of a dirty sheath. Fatty secretions, dead skin cells, and dirt accumulate in the sheath area. This black sticky substance, called smegma, should be removed at least four times a year.

The cleaning can be accomplished within the sheath, or the horseman can encourage the horse to "let down" with a tranquilizer or by scratching the horse over the loin, especially when he is relaxed, such as after a workout. If you find a very heavy accumulation of smegma, you may need to apply mineral oil, petroleum jelly, or glycerine for several days to loosen the debris. Oil will also attract more dirt, however, so you must follow this pretreatment with several washings with mild soap and warm water and thorough rinsing.

Often a ball of smegma, called a "bean," will accumulate in a flap of skin near the urethral opening. This can build up to a size that interferes with urination and must be removed.

Whenever you clean your gelding's sheath, use safe procedures. Stand close to your horse facing his hindquarters at the middle of his rib cage with a lot of body-to-body contact. If cleaning from the near side, put your left arm over your horse's back and begin to rub his belly with your right hand. Gradually work your way to the sheath. Use a firm, not a tickling, touch.

Mares produce a similar type of accumulation between the folds of the udder, and they may become tail rubbers if it is neglected. As with a gelding, safety precautions should be observed.

The presence of dandruff on the crest or dock may cause itching. Dandruff is often characteristic of an overweight, underexercised horse. It may also indicate skin irritation caused from overwashing, insufficient rinsing, or nonspecific dermatitis. Dry skin is often caused by biochemical imbalances that interfere with normal sebum production.

External parasites such as lice, mites, and ticks can drive a horse into an itching frenzy. Each must be diagnosed and treated separately.

Bare patches in the hair coat caused by fungus will often follow the midline of the horse, appearing on the face and from the poll, through the mane, at the point of the croup, and through the tail head. Medicated iodine shampoos are often used to treat fungus.

Care of the mane and tail. Routine mane and tail care should start with a daily inspection. Using thread or yarn instead of rubber bands for show braids results in less hair breakage. Tight braids should be undone as soon as possible; gently untangling the tail hairs with the hands results in the least damage. A natural-bristle human's hairbrush is the safest tool. Plastic brushes, plastic combs, and metal combs cause more breakage.

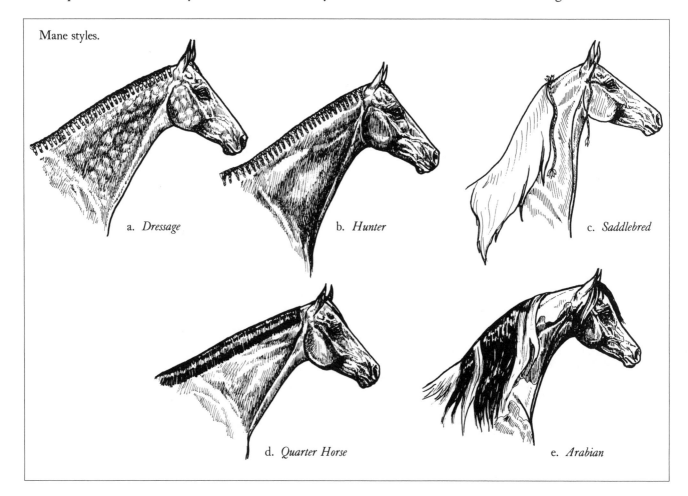

Mane styles.

a. *Dressage*   b. *Hunter*   c. *Saddlebred*

d. *Quarter Horse*   e. *Arabian*

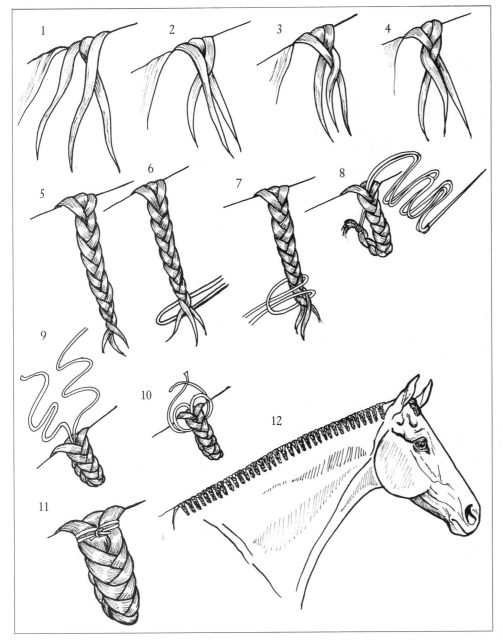

Braiding the Mane.

1–5. *The three-strand braid.*

6–7. *Secure the end.*

8–9. *Fold the braid in half.*

10–11. *Secure with a square knot.*

12. *Finished product*

Shampooing the mane or tail more often than once a week may unnecessarily irritate the skin. Mild soaps are best and should be used primarily on the skin of the crest and dock. Soap residues can make a horse become a tail rubber, so be generous with the rinse water. Following a shampooing with a Calgon rinse is very effective as a final cleansing.

If it is necessary to add moisture to a horse's dock or crest, a good mixture is ten to twenty parts baby oil to one

part Absorbine-type liniment. The liniment is stimulating, cooling, and mildly antiseptic, and the baby oil is absorbed easily by the skin. The mixture should be applied at the roots of the hair. The tail can be wrapped with a cotton bandage for several hours following treatment. If a horse has very sensitive skin, it is best to start with a mixture containing very little liniment or just plain baby oil.

If a long mane or the skirt of the tail lacks moisture, the

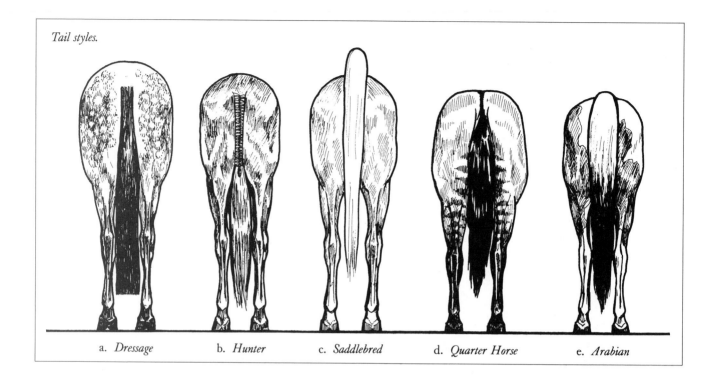

Tail styles.

a. *Dressage*   b. *Hunter*   c. *Saddlebred*   d. *Quarter Horse*   e. *Arabian*

best remedy is to apply a good-quality hair conditioner to freshly shampooed hair while it is still wet. You can use a type specifically designed for horses or the large economy size from your local discount store. Let the horse's mane and tail dry away from the sun's rays, and do not comb or brush them until they are dry.

Long tails can be protected in the nonfly season by a combination of loose braiding and wrapping. A quick-and-easy method requires a 10-foot piece of gauze. For safety, stand off to one side rather than directly behind your horse. Starting at the dock, divide the hair into three strands. Put the midpoint of the gauze behind the middle strand and hold an end of the gauze with each of the outer strands. Braid loosely. When you get to the end of the tail, you should have ample gauze left over to loop the braided tail through itself several times. Secure the loop closed with crisscross or solid wraps. If this is done with moderate but even tension, the tail can be left braided for several weeks at a time with no harm.

Sometimes it is necessary to thin, shorten, or shape the mane or tail. This can be done several ways, but the best results are obtained by pulling. Wrap several of the longest underhairs around a pulling comb and remove them. Doing this gradually over several sessions results in less

irritation to the horse than if it is all done in one afternoon. Numbing the root area or the crest of the mane with a little liniment may make the experience less unpleasant for the horse.

A 5- or 6-inch area of the dock from the tail head to the point of buttock of dressage horses, jumpers, and some animated horses is clipped or pulled for a neat appearance. The clean line of a clipped tail enhances the shape of the hindquarters.

CLIPPING

You should accustom your show horse to the sight, sound, smell, and feel of electric clippers because it will frequently be necessary to use them.

Be sure that the electric cord is out of the way and that the clippers have sharp blades and are functioning properly. Begin by letting the horse smell the clippers. Rub the clippers on the horse's neck with the motor turned off. Then move to the area of the bridle path and ears. Move the clippers down the horse's legs. Now turn the clippers on at a distance from the horse. Turn them on and off several times. Then with them off, lay them on the horse's neck, with the blades away from the horse's skin and turn them on. Let the horse relax to the noise and vibration over the thickly muscled area before you move the clippers to the thin-skinned and bony area where you need to do the clipping. You may have to build up a horse's tolerance to clipping over several sessions.

If you resort to use of a twitch while clipping, you may always have to use one. Twitches, in general, are a last resort or emergency measure and should never be used as a long-term substitute for proper training.

Be careful not to lose patience with a horse. If a horse quivers while staring at the clippers, he is likely acting out of honest fear. Give him the time and training to overcome the fear. If a horse has been previously clipped, but pulls belligerently out of reach and refuses to even look at the clippers, he is likely acting out of willful disobedience. This horse needs experienced discipline.

Acceptable clipping for the show ring varies greatly for each breed and performance. Clipping a 1- to 6-inch bridle path (depending on current style) between the forelock and the mane prevents tangling while bridling and halter-

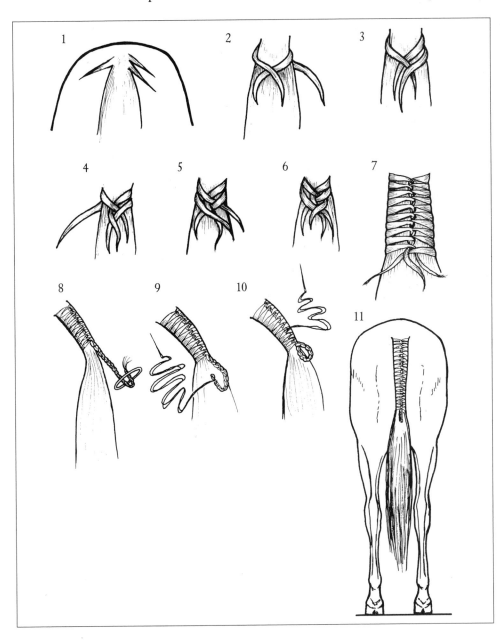

Braiding the Tail.

1–6. *Three-strand braid, adding from sides.*

7. *Quit adding from sides and finish braiding to end.*

8. *Secure.*

9–10. *Loop.*

11. *Finished product.*

Clipping the fetlock. Richard Klimesh photo.

ing. Removing long fetlock hairs is required for almost all events except competitive trail riding. Most show-ring performers have had their whiskers, ears, and eye hairs clipped. Although it gives a polished appearance to the face, it does cause some management problems. Nature provided whiskers for a purpose—to help the horse orient his head in a space that he cannot see, such as a feed bucket, manger, or trailer. Ear hair protects the horse from gnats and flies. Consider these things before you automatically shave your horse.

THE NECK SWEAT

Some horses develop a heavy neck and, if they are to be used as performance animals, you may want to discourage excessive fat deposits. Using a rubberized neck wrap during work sessions will intensify sweating in the target area while continuing to build muscles in other areas. If the horse is eventually to be a breeding or halter animal, any alteration in neck size or shape is only cosmetic. The horse still has the genetic potential for the neck he was born with.

Feeding a conservative but adequate diet to young horses, allowing them to ingest forages from ground level, and providing them with the right kinds of exercise will help minimize the development of a heavy neck.

For last-minute grooming details, see the section on getting ready in Chapter 14.

SECTION THREE
YOUR FIRST SHOW

SECOND PLACE

*S*heila and Connie had been competing against each other all summer in the trail classes at the open shows. Sheila's gray gelding had won year-end awards in this event for several years in a row. Connie and her mare were newcomers, but they were becoming more polished at every show. Sheila was certain there was no chance of being beaten.

At the Silverdust Show, the open trail class was set up to run most of the day in a separate arena. Exhibitors could take their horses through the course whenever their schedule allowed. There were few spectators at the trail course site—in fact, when Connie and her mare took their turn on the trail course, just she, her horse, and the judge were present. Everything went like clockwork. By about the third obstacle Connie knew she really had the judge's attention, so she began doing those extra little things that really show the thoroughness of a horse's training. During the ground tie, for example, she did not need to tell her horse "whoa," nor did she need to sneak away to be sure that her horse would stand still. Rather, she strode boldly away from her horse, walked a broad circle around the mare, and returned briskly to her side. As Connie left the ring, she knew this was their best team effort yet. She praised her mare.

Hours later, in the heat of the afternoon, an announcement stated that the trail class would officially close in fifteen minutes. Connie happened to be within earshot of Sheila's trailer at the time and heard Sheila's husband call out to his wife, "You'd better get ready to go get your trophy." Sheila casually mounted and rode up to the announcer's stand ready to collect yet another prize. Connie, meanwhile, waited nearby with a group of other riders, all nervously chatting and hoping to be called in for a ribbon. Without having seen all of the other contestants perform, it would be impossible for anyone except the judge to predict the placings.

When the announcer called Connie's name to receive the trophy, she reached forward and scratched her mare on the withers and then entered the arena. She smiled graciously, holding her trophy while the other winners were called. Although Sheila had earned the red ribbon, she chose to ignore the announcer and instead rode back to her trailer.

We have arrived! Chris Tufano and Montaro. Courtesy Taft Hill Horse Farm. Cherry Hill photo.

CHAPTER ELEVEN
PAPERWORK

MAKING ENTRY

HORSE SHOWS are rated either by the number of horse entries or by the amount of money available for awards. The variety of classes offered can also affect a show's rating. A rating based on horse numbers is determined after the show, whereas ratings based on cash winnings and classes offered are known well in advance.

"A" shows offer more points and more money and attract professionals and the very best amateurs. They are often scheduled over three or four days or as a series of one-day shows in the same or nearby locations. These "circuits" make it more convenient and less expensive for the exhibitor to show under a number of different judges. "B" shows are almost always one-day shows, but with considerable competition. "C" shows are usually local recognized shows. Nonrated or open shows can be sponsored by a breed or performance association or by a local club or stable and provide a good opportunity to gain experience.

Which show will be your first? If you are a novice you should begin by entering several schooling, or practice, shows in order to become familiar with showing without paying large entry fees. Schooling shows are often held early in the season as a way for the novice and professional alike to practice. A novice may use a schooling show to gain personal experience whereas the pro may use such a show to give a young horse his first exposure to the show ring. Often a schooling show is unrecognized by any organization and unregulated by rules, but is nonetheless a very important step on your way to the bigger shows.

Some schooling shows are designed to be fun, with innovative classes, games, and a casual dress code. Others are part show and part clinic, where you will receive a critique from the judge after your performance. Still other schooling shows are intended to be more formal stepping-stones to regular competitions. Often schooling shows offer classes that are seen nowhere else, such as "First Time Ever," "Pre-Green," "Baby," or "Beginner." Be sure to check whether the class names refer to the rider's or the horse's experience.

Look in an all-breed regional newspaper to find out what shows are scheduled. Complimentary copies of these papers are often available at your local tack or feed store (see appendix). If you are interested in one particular performance event or breed, look for coming events in the appropriate official publication. Contact the American Horse Council for a complete listing of breed and performance associations and their publications. You may also be able to get such information from a local professional who exhibits in the classes that interest you. When you are browsing through the show listings, keep a lookout for words that might indicate a practice show, such as "Warm-up," "Tune-Up," "Fuzzy," "Pre-Show," "Practice," or "Schooling." Once you find a show that is nearby, contact the show secretary by phone or mail, requesting the class list (or show bill), entry forms, and other pertinent information. Sometimes schooling shows, in an effort to keep costs down, are quite informal regarding paperwork. Often you enter the day of the show. The following comments regarding entry apply to larger shows and some of the well-established schooling shows.

Usually a show bill will note the show's affiliation and rating, the judge's name, location of show (often with a map), starting time, health requirements, preentry and postentry information, stabling information, fees, and prize money.

Read all information carefully. Sometimes simply overlooking a piece of information on the application can cause an entry to be ineligible for competition. If membership in a particular organization is required, there may be a space on the prize list that allows you to join simultaneously with your entry. Some shows allow nonmembers to exhibit, providing they pay a fee.

Be sure that your horse qualifies for the class you are considering. Is your horse's level of training adequate for exhibition? Check breeding certificates and registration papers to make sure that your horse fulfills class specifications.

Are you eligible? Make certain that you understand the terminology of the class descriptions, the cutoff points for age divisions, and any requirements regarding horse ownership. For example, if you are an adult wishing to enter your four-year-old horse in a junior class, be sure that the term junior refers to the age of the horse and not the rider. If you will turn twelve during the show season this year and it is not clear which age division you should show in, get a written copy of the organization's system. Some organizations require that in order to show a horse in a particular class, you (or, in some cases, a member of your immediate family) must own it. And, of course, just as you evaluate your horse's readiness for exhibition, you must take an objective look at your own performance.

If you and your horse are both ready and eligible, pick up a pen and begin! Remember that when you fill out and sign an entry form, you are stating that

1. You and your horse are eligible to enter.

2. You will abide by the association and show rules.

3. You are paying for the judge's opinion and will accept all decisions as final.

4. You will not hold the show or association liable in the event of an accident or injury.

After providing all of the information requested on the entry form, attach the following to it, if required: proof of a recent negative Coggins test (see appendix for state requirements), the horse's health exam papers, a photocopy of the horse's registration papers, and a check for the total fees.

Fees commonly include, but are not limited to an entry fee per class, an office charge, a grounds charge, and a drug-testing fee. In addition, there may be a deposit required when exhibitor numbers are distributed. The deposit is refunded when the numbers are returned. Shows that require overnight stabling will request stall reserva-

tions and a deposit or payment in full with your entry.

Showing can get expensive, so it is important to decide your goal early in the season. If you are solely after experience, choose the show closest to home that offers you the level of competition you desire. If you are after points, you will want to go to the larger shows.

Most associations have a national system for awarding permanent points to a horse's or exhibitor's show record. For example, every time a horse places in a Western pleasure class, he will earn a certain number of points, depending on which placing he earned and how many horses were entered in the class. Records of these points are kept at the association headquarters and when a horse accumulates a certain number of points in a particular category, he will be awarded a performance certificate. See chart below for an example of a system used for awarding national points.

POINTS EARNED ACCORDING TO PLACING AND ENTRIES

# of horses in class	1	2	3	4	5	6	7	8	9
			Placings						
5–9	1								
10–14	2	1							
15–19	3	2	1						
20–24	4	3	2	1					
25–29	5	4	3	2	1				
30–34	6	5	4	3	2	1			
35–39	7	6	5	4	3	2	1		
40–44	8	7	6	5	4	3	2	1	
45 & more	9	8	7	6	5	4	3	2	1

In addition, each show or circuit of shows may have a similar but separate system of tallying points for regional or local awards. For example, if a horse wins or places in enough classes at one show, he may be eligible for an overall award, often called a high-point trophy. Some shows offer such an award for exhibitors as well: one for each of the youth age divisions, amateur riders, and open class riders. A further expansion on this same idea is the high-point circuit award. Points earned for each placing at each show of the circuit are totaled. The winner often receives a saddle, a horse blanket, or a cash prize. Yet

CHECKLIST

PAPERWORK

Original or photocopy of registration papers
Coggins test certification
Health exam certification
Proof of ownership
Amateur or nonpro card
Membership card
Proof of age (for youths)
Show bill
Rule book
Paper and pencils

HORSE CARE ITEMS

Grain and feed tub
Grain
Hay net
Hay
Water pail
Water, if necessary
Wintergreen, cider vinegar, Jell-O, or Kool-Aid, if necessary
Manure fork and bucket or basket
Barn broom
Rake
Bedding (shavings or straw)
Barn lime
Horse blanket and hood
Sheet or fly net
Fly repellent

TRAVELING

Traveling blanket
Shipping leg wraps
Tail wrap
Halter and lead rope

TACK

Saddle
Bridle
Martingale
Pad

Girth
Show halter
Lead
Longe line
Longe whip
Cavesson
Whips or crops
Bell boots
Splint boots
Other boots
Tack trunk
Extra halter and lead rope

TACK CARE

Sponges
Cloths
Saddle soap
Polish
Small bucket

GROOMING KIT

Hoof pick
Rubber curry
Dandy brush
Body brush
Wisp
Rubber mitts
Rub rags
Sponge
Sweat scraper
Bucket
Shampoo
Hose
Cornstarch
Baby oil
Hoof dressing
Hoof black
Battery-operated clippers
Comb
Hairbrush
Yarn and needle
Rubber bands
Tape

Scissors
Extra tail wrap

FIRST AID

Iodine-based antiseptic solution
Hydrogen peroxide
Nonstick gauze pads
Self-conforming gauze rolls
Stretch bandaging tape
Elastic adhesive tape
Scissors
Cotton or disposable diaper
Chemical ice pack
Liniment
Sunscreen

FOR THE RIDER

Coat
Pants
Chaps
Shirt
Tie and pin
Vest
Boots
Spurs
Gloves
Hat (show type)
Hat (for sun protection)
Hair net
Pins
Comb
Brush
Safety pins
Mirror
Rain gear
Rubber shoes or boots
Nutritious snacks
Water
Folding chairs

MISCELLANEOUS

Plastic bags
Extra cloths

another type of award based on points is the year-end award. Our local and regional dressage associations, for example, keep track of the placings of the members throughout the show season. At Christmas, gift certificates or other prizes are presented to the top riders at each level.

Except for the difference in entry fees, it costs just about as much to go to a small show as to go to a big one, and big shows award many more points if you happen to be a winner. If you are working toward a title or performance certificate for your horse in a particular event, choose a show that has a history of large entries in that particular class. It is discouraging to haul 300 miles to find only three

or four other contestants in your class. Information on the number of entries in a class in previous years can usually be found in the show results published in breed journals or association newsletters.

CHECKLISTS

Develop a series of checklists you can use each time you prepare for a show. You may wish to keep certain lists in your office, others in your tack room, and a master list in your truck or trailer.

Be sure that you have everything that you think you will need at the show . . . and more! Richard Klimesh photo.

CHAPTER TWELVE
TRAILERING

TOWING VEHICLE

WHAT IS YOUR VEHICLE'S towing capacity? The weight of a towing vehicle should be at least 75 percent the weight of the loaded trailer. Is the wheelbase of your towing vehicle at least 115 inches? Does it have a powerful enough engine to haul the extra 5,000 pounds of a loaded two-horse trailer? Does it have heavy duty suspension to take on the additional load of the trailer? Does your towing vehicle have good brakes and steering? Look in the owner's manual for information on your vehicle or ask your dealer to help you.

TRAILER SELECTION

New trailers will cost from $2,500 for a bare bones two-horse model to $10,000 and higher for a deluxe four-horse model with dressing room and tack room. Many good new trailers can be purchased for $6,000, and used trailers can be found for substantially less. No matter if your budget dictates new or used, there are basic decisions you must make.

Type of Trailer. There are three basic types of horse-hauling vehicles: enclosed trailer, stock trailer, and horse van. Enclosed trailers usually come in two-horse and four-horse models and are the most common trailer seen on the road. The height inside trailers ranges from 72 to 90 inches, with many near 66; length of standing room ranges from 66 to 88 inches (depending on style) with the average somewhere around 70; the width of one stall ranges from 26 to 32 inches with most toward the low end. A sixteen-hand horse can fit into a standard trailer, providing he is levelheaded about loading and unloading. Better suited for large horses are the 7-foot high diagonal load trailers that allow ample space for the tall- and long-bodied breeds. If you are planning to haul a very large horse, you may need to look into a custom trailer or van.

Stock trailers are usually the equivalent of a four-horse trailer in length and basic style, but the sides are slatted rather than enclosed. Horses can be hauled loose in a stock trailer, which comes in handy for mares, foals, and young horses. Horses have less of an enclosed feeling because they can see out of the stock trailer but because of the slatted sides, they get very dusty, cold, and wet.

Vans are horse stalls on trucks. They are more comfortable for the horse than conventional trailers and are the most expensive of the three types.

Construction. The materials and workmanship dictate the cost of trailer. Materials commonly used include steel, aluminum, and fiberglass. A trailer with a frame and skin of steel is sturdy. Substituting an aluminum skin while retaining the steel frame will decrease weight and rusting. Fiberglass is often used for roofs and fenders because it is cool, lightweight, and easy to repair.

Good quality trailer suspension should be sturdy but not stiff. Whether you decide on leaf springs or rubber torsion suspension depends on the quality of each, but the latter gives a more flexible ride. Be sure the suspension is independent, that is, when one wheel hits a bump or a hole, it will absorb the shock apart from the rest of the trailer. Electric brakes are preferred, and there should be adequate operating lights and clearance lights for night-time driving.

Quality workmanship will be evident in the straightness of the frame, the fitting of seams, the finishing of edges, and the paint job.

Design. First, you must decide how you wish your horses to ride in the trailer—facing forward, backward, sideways, or loose. Most trailers are designed for rear loading and place the horses side by side, facing forward. Other options are available if your horse is a difficult traveler. Horses load into a hauling vehicle by stepping up onto the trailer or by walking up a ramp. The step-in style is less expensive and more common. The ramp style is usually safer and more expensive. The length of the ramp dictates the slope the horse must climb. A power-assisted ramp will be easier for you to close.

Are you looking for a bumper hitch trailer or a gooseneck style? A gooseneck trailer attaches to a "fifth wheel," a type of hitch that must be installed in the bed of your pickup truck. What type of tack room do you need: a small compartment for just a saddle and bridle or a larger one that can also be used as a dressing room?

Details. Consider the following options, keeping the price in mind. How many vents, windows, and interior lights do you require? A minimum of one bus-style window on each side of the trailer is suggested. Does the center divider of the trailer need to be removable for hauling a large or difficult traveler or a mare and foal? Does the center divider go all the way to the floor? Most horses travel more comfortably if the divider only goes halfway to the floor. Do you want padding on the sides of the stalls, on the center divider and at the breast? What type of flooring is available? Oak or pine are both fine as long as the quality of the wood is good with no warping or knots. Pressure-treated wood may withstand manure and urine longer than nontreated wood. What type of mats come with the trailer? Removable rubber mats are preferable. What type of release bars are there at the breast or head, the tail, and at the center divider? Check to be sure all

releases work easily. Some are very difficult to operate if the trailer is on less than 100 percent level ground.

Don't assume that just because a trailer looks good it is safe. For example, a well-known manufacturer overlooked one small detail in rear door design that let the doors come off their hinges. This allowed horses to fall out of the trailer or be dragged behind it. Get competent help when you select a trailer.

Alternatives to trailer ownership include sharing trailer rides and expenses with a friend or hiring someone to haul your horse for you. Expect to pay at least 30 to 45 cents per mile for the service.

TRAILER TRAINING

Regardless of whether you are using an owned, borrowed, or hired trailer, you and your horse must be comfortable with the process of loading, unloading, and traveling. Practicing the loading process at home with a new or unfamiliar vehicle can help safeguard against problems on show day. For practice, either hitch the trailer to a vehicle or immobilize its wheels and hitch to prevent it from moving. The area under the entryway should be blocked, with a railroad tie for example, to protect the horse's hind legs from slipping under the sill.

Loading. A horse must become accustomed to several

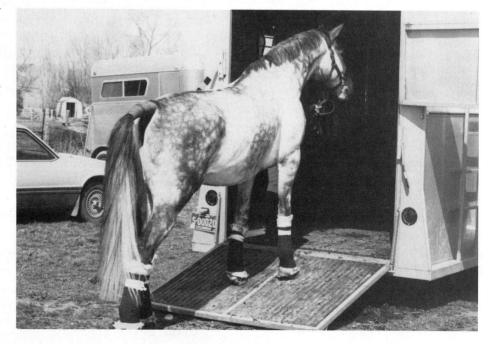

Well before the first show, the horse must be accustomed to leg and tail wraps, the hollow sound of the trailer ramp and floor, and the darkness inside. Cherry Hill photo.

When using a two-horse trailer, it is best to teach the horse to walk on by a voice command. Richard Klimesh photo.

new sensations during trailer loading: the hollow sound of the wooden floor, the rattle of stall dividers as his weight shifts the trailer, the darkness, the confinement, and perhaps the presence of a ceiling most of all.

You can prepare your horse for the loading experience by leading him across ditches, bridges, and into low buildings. Be sure that he will walk forward when asked.

Loading a horse into a trailer is a continuation of the lesson "Walk on." Initially it may take as many as three people to safely load an inexperienced horse: one to lead the horse in, one to close the rear door, and one to fasten the manger snap. Later on, with practice, it will require only one person to send the horse into the trailer.

Even if a horse has been previously loaded into a stock trailer or large van (sometimes called a loose box), he may be apprehensive the first time he faces a two-horse trailer. Initially, you may choose to walk alongside the horse into the adjacent stall. It is best to assume a normal leading position on the horse's near side, aiming the horse into the right stall of the trailer. Walking directly in front of the horse into the same side of the trailer "to show that it's safe" can be dangerous. The horse may lunge forward and trample you or attempt to follow you out of the escape door.

After loading your horse once or twice by leading him and walking alongside him, you will likely be able to send the horse into the trailer by standing at the back door and giving the command, "Walk on." Horses should never be coaxed into a trailer by bribery with feed, but an obedient horse can be rewarded with feed after it has been loaded and is secured. Having someone stationed at the manger to speak reassuringly to the horse will allow the trainer at the rear of the trailer to fasten the butt chain and rear doors. Only then should the horse's head be secured. This is usually done using a 12- to 18-inch rope with panic snap on one or both ends that is secured to a tie ring in the manger of the trailer. A panic snap is designed so that it can be released even if the rope is taut. A normal snap would be impossible to unsnap in such a situation. Be sure to remove the lead rope for safety during travel.

Trailer loading can hold its share of surprises for the novice horseman. The horse can back out immediately after loading, or attempt to turn around in the narrow stall and become wedged, or rear and get his front legs caught in the manger. If you are at all hesitant, seek the help of a professional rather than jeopardizing your safety or your horse's.

Unloading. Often getting the horse to back out of the trailer is more difficult than getting him to enter. In most trailers, it is difficult to get next to the horse to properly

Prepare your horse for loading by leading him over obstacles. Richard Klimesh photo.

cue him. You will probably need someone to help you.

Teaching the horse in advance to back up in-hand and "weaning" him from all cues except the voice command will help in unloading. First, attach the lead rope and unsnap the trailer tie. Then signal your assistant to open the rear doors and unhook the butt chain or bar. Saying "back" will often provide enough of a cue that he will begin shifting his weight rearward. The first step off is a tough one. Preparing your horse ahead of time by leading and backing it over small ledges or obstacles will help give him confidence. Many horses become frightened when they can't feel the ground with a reaching hind leg and jump back into the trailer. Slippery footing can compound such a scare, so never attempt to load or unload a horse on a patch of ice or mud. If you are unloading without a ramp, be sure the horse's legs will not slip under the trailer sill as he backs out. Pulling the horse's tail to signal him to unload is not recommended. *Never* stand directly behind a trailered horse regardless of whether or not the butt chain is fastened.

When it comes time to start the engine and take your new horse on his first drive, I recommend a well-mannered companion. With the manger full of fresh hay and a familiar, seasoned traveler alongside, your new horse will be more likely to relax and enjoy the association with the trailer.

PRECAUTIONS

Trailering can be very hard on a horse's joints. Rough roads, long miles, inexperienced or inconsiderate drivers, and poor trailer suspension all contribute to wear and tear on the equine athlete. To help assure that a horse arrives at its destination refreshed rather than fatigued, make the trailer as safe and comfortable as possible. Organize a maintenance plan for the horse trailer as you would for your car. Periodically lubricate the following when necessary and check for wear: wheel bearings, suspension, shocks, spring shackles, hitch, safety chain, floorboards, mats, hinges, vents, lights, and brakes.

If you take the time to ride in the trailer yourself, you may become more aware of the details that can create stress for your horse: rattling stall dividers, too much draft or not enough fresh air, an inexperienced driver, inadequate suspension, sliding mats, a hornet's nest, etc. Even in a roomy and well-maintained trailer your horse may be nervous. Cotton in the ears and blinders over the eyes may diminish the fear of heavy traffic. Bedding on the floor often encourages a horse to urinate and relax in transit. Frequently, horses are blanketed too heavily for today's airtight trailers and arrive at their destination weakened from sweating and subsequent chilling.

Wrapping your horse's lower legs can prevent serious

injury to the coronary band and bulbs of the heels. Thick padding in this area will likely be torn more often and will require more frequent laundering, but the coronary band and bulbs of the heel is where the protection is required. Use commercial shipping boots, or ask your instructor how to properly apply a shipping wrap.

The horse's tail can be wrapped to protect it from rubbing as he leans on the butt bar or door during uphill travel. Cotton wraps are safe but are often found on the trailer floor upon arrival. Good results are obtained with an ace bandage or Vetrap stretch bandaging tape applied with moderate even tension. Nonslip rubberized tail wraps will stay put but be careful not to apply them too tight or leave them on too long or they can cut off circulation, which may result in sloughed hairs that may grow back abnormally.

Although a trailer ride can provide some psychological concerns for a horse, many of them are based on physical stresses. The fatigue that horses experience from a long trip is caused by an unstable environment. Evaluate the temperature, air flow, humidity, space, noise, footing, air pressure (if you are hauling at high altitudes or flying), and the direction the horse is facing in relation to the direction of travel. Often a small adjustment will dissipate a horse's uneasiness.

ON THE ROAD

Out of consideration to your horse, let him stand peacefully in his stall while you load all of the last-minute items into your truck or trailer. Have your checklists handy and refer to them several times, making certain that every item is accounted for. Give your truck and trailer another once-over to be sure that all systems are go. Double check for that important packet of papers. Be sure you have a spare tire, lug wrench, and a jack to fit the trailer, feed, the trailer registration, and a thermos of coffee or jug of ice water. Then, when you are certain that everything is in order, prepare your horse for traveling and send him into the trailer.

Once he is secured, make a thorough last-minute check to see that all tack and trailer doors are latched, hitch is still fastened properly, and lights are working. Be sure that all wheel blocks are removed and put in the rig before you pull away.

Once you are out of the driveway and on straight, level ground, recheck all of your mirrors for proper alignment. Shortly after you leave home, you should stop for a trailer check. In fact, when I am traveling with horses, I stop every 50 miles or so to stretch, walk around the rig, check the tires, and say hello to the horses. Often you can detect a problem early, such as a soft tire or warm brakes, before it becomes a disaster.

You can also monitor your horse's comfort by slipping a hand under a blanket, if one is used, to assess body temperature. Use the same common sense that you would with your own comfort. Obviously, if a horse is hot to the touch or sweaty under a blanket, he is dressed too warmly. Substituting a sheet or cooler for a heavy blanket will allow him to dry and cool gradually. In time, you will automatically chose the right blanket or sheet for your horse.

During one of your stops along the way, you may wish to clean the manure from the back of the trailer. But be careful. Whenever you open a trailer door alongside a highway, you are taking a chance. The door could blow open and be caught by a passing vehicle, or your horse could think you are unloading him and bolt out the door.

If you are going to be traveling more than eight or ten hours at a stretch with a conventional horse trailer, you will need to unload your horses for exercise and rest. For shorter trips, however, most horses do fine if they have had a good drink of water before leaving home and are allowed to munch hay en route. If the weather is warm, you may wish to offer your horse a drink every four hours or so, although don't be surprised if he doesn't drink until after you arrive at your destination.

Drive safely. Accelerate and brake gradually. Anticipate stop signs and corners. Use your turn signals. Take curves at moderate speed. Keep your senses alert to unusual sounds, smells, and vehicle motions. When you are riding, you need to trust your horse explicitly. When you are trailering him, he is entrusting his safety to you. Keep it between the fences. The showgrounds are just ahead.

Make your horse comfortable. Courtesy NATRC. Judy Wise photo.

CHAPTER THIRTEEN
AT THE SHOWGROUNDS

ARRIVAL

THE LONG-AWAITED MOMENT has arrived. You have made the trip safely, and the showgrounds are in sight. Most shows have a separately designated exhibitor's entrance to accommodate trucks and trailers. First obtain your stall assignment if needed and instructions for parking. One-day shows usually have a specified place for trailers to park that becomes your horse's temporary home and your base of operation. Larger shows that offer stabling usually allow trailers to unload horses and tack near the barns and then require you to park elsewhere for the duration of the show. Allow enough space between trailers so you don't create a danger among horses.

If you are using a stall, first check it over carefully for protruding nails, splinters, unsafe latches, and hinges. Sprinkle barn lime on the bare floor if necessary, and then bed the stall with the shavings or straw you have brought or with the bedding provided by the show management. Add your own water pail to the stall and get a welcoming flake of hay ready for your horse.

Unload your horse. Take off his shipping wraps and tail wrap, and inspect him for any injuries. Then let him become accustomed to the stall.

If your horse will be tied to your trailer during the show, be sure the halter and rope are strong. Don't tie the horse with a long length of rope, or he might get tangled in it. Hanging a hay net on the side of the trailer is convenient, but caution must be used. A full hay net hangs much higher than an empty one, and a pawing horse could get his hoof caught in a low-hanging hay net.

Keep the area around your trailer clean of manure, litter, buckets, hay, and supplies. Dogs do not belong at horse shows. Neither do unattended young children. If you are stabling your horses, keep the aisles near your stalls uncongested.

Once your horse is settled, locate the show office. Check in and receive your number and any additional materials. If you are attending a one-day show, you will likely fill out your entry form at the show secretary's table. Be sure to bring all of the paperwork on the checklist with you to the show office (see page 141).

Take a quick tour around the grounds and locate water for your horse, the wash rack, the warm-up ring, and the lavatories. Note where the farrier and veterinarian are set up and whether there is a human first aid station. Check the location of the nearest telephone.

You may wish to familiarize your horse with the showgrounds before your first class by either leading or riding him. Accustoming the horse to the sights and sounds around the arena can prevent him from being startled when he is making the first pass around the ring.

SHOW PERSONNEL

Show manager. The responsibilities of the show manager are immense and varied. He or she is responsible for paying all the bills incurred by the show and must have a thorough knowledge of horse shows and rules. Although the manager of a large show may have various committee heads to whom duties can be delegated, he or she is still responsible for seeing that everything is arranged properly.

Many details regarding the facilities must be arranged by the show manager, who customarily also oversees the work of the judge selection, awards, and equipment committees. He or she submits the necessary paperwork to assure that the show is approved, ensures that arrangements have been made for exhibitors' numbers and officials' badges, hires or selects show personnel, sees that patterns are posted on schedule and conform to the rule book, and makes sure scores are posted promptly. The show manager may need to make impromptu decisions regarding the effect of weather on a competition.

Sometimes the show manager, in lieu of a steward, is designated to enforce rules at a show, handle protests, and disqualify exhibitors committing an offense. The person in this position also sees that results are sent in to the national association.

Show secretary. The show secretary, with his or her assistants, establishes order in handling the paperwork associated with a show, and maintains that order in spite of the seeming chaos that is characteristic of every horse show. The secretary works closely with the show manager in designing the prize list and entry blanks, maintains a current mailing list of exhibitors, and develops a system of taking entries, recording placings, calculating points, and posting scores.

Steward or technical delegate. Some larger shows hire or appoint a rule book expert who also functions as a liaison between the exhibitor and the judge. An official steward may assist with the enforcement of the rules and the completion of required reports. He or she may be assigned to make an inspection of courses for possible rule infractions. In some instances the steward may function as an official timekeeper. In general, the steward's role is to point out, in a diplomatic manner, any violation of the rules.

Judge. Judges have the authority to decide the relative aesthetic and financial worth of individual horses by ranking their performances. In a like manner, judges influence riding techniques and styles by their evaluations of rider equitation.

Judges are usually experienced horsemen and showmen themselves. However, due to the restrictions listed in most rule books, it is difficult for a person to be an active member of the horse business community and also a judge. There could be questions of conflict of interest in the placings. For that reason, some judges are not involved in horse sales, training, showing, teaching, or boarding.

In the past, Western trainers came up through the ranks from working ranches, and English trainers came from a strong fox hunting and/or Pony Club background to become judges. Today's professional judges usually have the additional qualification of a professional apprenticeship or an academic equine background. In any event, a good judge has spent enough time in the saddle to recognize a good-minded and free-moving horse.

It is difficult to be an expert in all of the events represented in today's horse shows. That is why the American Horse Shows Association and other organizations have ways of certifying judges for specific events. Open-show or mixed-event breed show judges must make a sincere attempt to appreciate and understand competitions other than those of his or her personal interest. If a judge places a hunter class as if it were a group of stock horses, the bias will be noted by the exhibitors.

Goal-oriented breeding programs, specialty trainers, and more sophisticated exhibitors require that a judge not only be aware of the overall specifications of various classes but of the subtleties as well.

A good judge is open-minded about the various styles of horse use and an exhibitor's personal characteristics. Each exhibitor should receive equal consideration. A judge that automatically gives an advantage to a horse because of who is riding or leading it is doing a great disservice to the owners of other horses in that class and to the horse industry in general. Placing horses according to the reputation of the handler could result in an elite club and an undesirable equine gene pool.

Judges need to make prompt, accurate decisions. A judge who has a clear mental picture of a top performance or of the type of horse that will improve the breed usually can spot it quickly. This requires a wealth of knowledge, experience, and keen eyesight.

More often than not, there is more scheduled to judge in one day than seems humanly possible. Good overall health and stamina are imperative. It is physically abusive to stand or sit relatively immobile for twelve hours eating dust. Most judges would probably be more comfortable spending the day in the saddle.

A judge needs to have a wide view of the horse world. He or she must be able to see the "big picture": where the horse business is coming from and where it is headed. The judge must know if the development of a particular breed is traveling in a desirable direction and how to influence the course if it needs alteration.

Every judge has a picture of an ideal horse in his mind: one that is functionally sound, trainable, healthy, and aesthetically pleasing. The conformation horse must be chosen with performance in mind. Each type of competition makes different requirements of the horse, but some things are common to all events. The horse must be sound, a fluid and correct mover, coordinated, and coop-

Keep the area around your trailer safe and neat. Cherry Hill photo.

erative. The selection made at horse shows must move toward these goals.

Desired change often comes slowly. Judges must avoid the temptation of rewarding a temporary fad. Choosing an otherwise mediocre horse simply because it possesses a trait that is currently in vogue spells economic disaster for breeders. By the time breeding programs are producing the whim, the fad has changed. In addition, overemphasis of a single trait in a breeding program tends to slow down the improvement of other characteristics or even make them regress. A good judge of horseflesh recognizes the classic blue ribbon horse.

Besides deciding what kind of horses will be available for exhibitors to ride in the future, judges also determine riding styles. When a judge pins an equitation or horsemanship class, he has helped to set the standard for excellence in riding. He chooses the best horseman, not the most impressive tack or appointments or the prettiest smile (although honest smiles do make judging much more fun!). Here again, the judge has a classical picture in his mind. Equitation should be functional, effective, and harmonious. The horse and rider should work as a unit: the rider elicits responses with confidence and fluidity, and the horse performs with obedience and relaxation.

On the way to becoming a judge, an experienced horseman may apprentice to several accomplished judges. There are formal ways to do this in some organizations, such as the learner-judge program in the AHSA and junior judging in some breed associations. Individuals who make application to become judges are carefully evaluated, and various types of references are required. Even after becoming approved, judges must attend seminars periodically to keep up on new rules and judging techniques.

Ringmaster. The person chosen for the position of ringmaster has the responsibility of managing the activities in the show ring. Very often, the ringmaster is a volunteer who has not been tested or licensed and so has no official capacity. The ringmaster is there to ensure the safety of the exhibitors and to do what the judge requires so that the show runs efficiently.

Cooperative team effort between the judge and other show officials can make the difference between a sloppy and an efficient show. A judge often meets with the ringmaster and the announcer before the show to discuss a particular manner of running the various classes.

Routines of specific judges have evolved to provide the opportunity to make specific observations. In the rail classes (flat classes), for example, transitions are extremely important. That is why gaits are called for in a particular order and at specific times. If the announcer and ring-

Catching a few winks between classes. Richard Klimesh photo.

Before the horses enter the ring in a group show-ring class, a gate person should be checking individual exhibitor numbers to ferret out any misplaced or improperly numbered individuals. Once the gate has been closed, the judge, ringmaster, and announcer should all compare their total exhibitor count. This three-way check ensures accuracy in reporting to the official association and is vitally important when issuing points earned by the winners.

During competition where exhibitors perform individually, the judge often sits in a judge's box outside the ring. He or she is often assisted by a ringmaster or scribe.

While the judge is evaluating the contestants, the ringmaster should stand near enough to hear the judge speak in a normal conversational volume, but not so close that he is looking over the judge's shoulder. Some judges prefer to work from the corner of the arena to allow an unobstructed view of the entire arena, which is especially helpful during critical transition calls. In that case, the ringmaster should stand as a buffer between the judge and the flow of traffic. For example, if the horses are tracking left, the ringmaster should stand on the judge's left side. Other judges, who operate from the center of the arena (or one of its long sides), may want the ringmaster behind and slightly to the side opposite the direction of travel, to guarantee a clear view at all times. It depends greatly on the judge's preference. Some like to see the horses tracking toward them; some want to see the movement as they are tracking away; some like a close-up profile; and some prefer a distant view on the rail.

In some situations, such as dressage, the judge has an assistant, called a scribe, who records the judge's scores and comments. Otherwise, judges may elicit the help of the ringmaster in recording scores and numbers or may prefer to do the tabulating and reporting themselves. It is easy for anyone to transpose numbers in a score or record an incorrect exhibitor number, and the judge is ultimately held responsible for errors.

The ringmaster, as much as the judge, sets the tone of the show. Courtesy to the judge and the exhibitors is paramount. The ringmaster can smile and be friendly without becoming lax in his or her responsibilities. Chatting with the exhibitors, letting horses in after the gate has been closed, or not paying close attention to the judge's needs can result in disorganization and unnecessary delays.

master understand the judge's plans and devise an effective system of signals ahead of time, it contributes to a smooth show.

The ringmaster is expected to be thoroughly familiar with the rules of the association sponsoring the show. He or she needs to formulate a plan of action ahead of time for each class that enters the ring, anticipating potential problems and having solutions in mind. In no way, however, is the ringmaster expected or allowed to interpret the rules for the judge or, for that matter, to talk with a judge unnecessarily.

Conversation with a judge should be limited to official business. Once informal chatting begins, it is all too human for the ringmaster to slip and mention specifics about a particular exhibitor. Common infractions in this regard are such remarks as, "Did you see the big horse blow his lead just now?" "I can't help you in the next class. My son is in it," and "The liver chestnut horse won under both judges yesterday." These types of comments are not allowed.

ApHC JUDGES SCORE CARD
REINING

Judge: _____

Event: _____

Date: _____

Class: _____

MANEUVER SCORES

-1½: Extremely Poor -1: Very Poor -½: Poor

0: Average ½: Good 1: Very Good 1.5: Excellent

1. The following will result in no score:
   a. More than 1 finger between reins.
   b. Changing hands; 2 hands on reins.
   c. Failure to drop bridle to Judges.
   d. Willful abuse to an animal while in the show arena.

2. The following will result in a score of 60:
   a. Failure to complete pattern as written.
   b. Performing the maneuvers other than in specified order.
   c. The inclusion of maneuvers not specified.
   d. Equipment failure that delays completion of pattern.
   e. Balking or refusal of command where pattern is delayed.
   f. Running away or failing to guide where it becomes impossible to discern whether the entry is on pattern.
   g. Jogging in excess of one-half circle or one-half the length of the arena while starting a circle, circling or exiting a rollback.

   h. Overspins of more than ¼ turn.

3. The following will result in a reduction of five (5) points:
   a. Freezing up in spins or rollbacks.
   b. Spurring in front of cinch.
   c. Use of free hand to instill fear.
   d. Holding saddle with free hand.
   e. Fall to the ground by horse or rider.

4. Break of gait will be penalized 2 points. The break of gait penalty will not be applied in the event of a canter departure when starting a circle maneuver for the first ¼ of a circle.

5. Starting circles or eights out of lead, delayed change of lead or eights out of lead will be judged as follows: Delayed change of lead by one stride will be penalized ½ point. From start to ¼ circle, deduct 1 point. From start to ½ circle, deduct 2 points. From start to ¾ circle, deduct 3 points. From start to ¾ circle, deduct 3 points. For the complete circle, deduct 4 points.

6. Deduct ½ point for starting circle at a jog or exiting rollbacks at a jog up to 2 strides. Jogging beyond 2 strides but less than ½ circle of ½ the length of the arena, deduct 2 points.

7. Deduct one-half (½) point for over or under spinning up to one-eighth (⅛) of a turn; deduct one (1) point for over or under spinning up to one-quarter (¼) of a turn.

8. Where a change of lead is specified immediately prior to a run to the end of the pen, failure to change lead will be penalized as follows: 1 point if lead is picked up within 2 strides; 2 points if lead is corrected prior to the stop; 3 points if lead is not corrected. In patterns 3, 5, 8 and 9 the horse is required to be on the correct lead when rounding the end of the arena. Failure to be on the correct lead will be penalized 1-4 points depending on the distance travelled out of lead with 4 points denoting a complete failure to be on a specified lead.

9. Deduct 2 points for failure to go beyond markers.

POSITION	ENTRY No.	MANEUVER	1	2	3	4	5	6	7	8	COMPOSITE	PENALTIES	SCORE
1		PENALTY 70 SCORE											
2		PENALTY 70 SCORE											
3		PENALTY 70 SCORE											
4		PENALTY 70 SCORE											
5		PENALTY 70 SCORE											
6		PENALTY 70 SCORE											
7		PENALTY 70 SCORE											
8		PENALTY 70 SCORE											

The judge must choose a horse in the conformation classes that is able to perform.

In certain classes, such as pleasure driving, the presence of the ringmaster is vital to the maintenance of safety. During jumping and trail classes especially, the ringmaster needs to keep his or her eyes on the entire arena. Noting details such as the need to reposition equipment can be a real time-saver and assure fairness for all exhibitors. In showmanship, many judges choose a pattern that uses the ringmaster as a reference point for the showman.

Because the ringmaster's job is so critical to the success of a show, the show committee should select the most qualified individual for the position. An inexperienced adult can do a fine job as long as he listens and does as the judge advises. Experienced ringmasters are flexible and cooperative because they realize that each judge has his or her own system for class routines. It is more efficient for the same individual to serve for the entire show than for the judge to break in several people during the day.

Serving as ringmaster provides an opportunity to view the horse show from the center of the ring. Helping a judge with the details of a show is an important and interesting assignment.

Scribe. The dressage show scribe has the responsibility of transferring a judge's scores and verbal comments into official written show records. Most dressage show schedules do not allow judges the time required to completely review each score sheet after each ride, so the judge depends on the scribe's accuracy.

Exhibitors, too, depend on the scribe to produce an accurate, legible assessment of their performance. Many riders save their score sheets for comparison and as a means for checking progress. Often the comments are much more important to the rider than the actual scores, so a scribe who can get all of the judge's comments down in writing is much appreciated by contestants.

The volunteer scribe must arrive for duty promptly and wear a watch set to the official show time. The scribe uses pencil for AHSA tests and ink for FEI tests.

It is essential that a scribe has good hearing. It simply doesn't work to constantly be asking a judge to repeat comments. The scribe must have a good understanding of the tests and their corresponding score sheets. In the event the judge fails to give a comment, or perhaps even a score for a particular movement, the scribe must be cognizant of that fact and skip to the next movement. When the opportunity presents itself, usually at the end of the test, the scribe should call the omission to the judge's attention. A scribe in such a situation who is unfamiliar with the test may make the error of writing many scores and comments in the wrong boxes.

In order to keep up with the verbally fluent judges, a

JUDGES' SCORE CARD — HUNTERS

Class No. _____

1	6
2	7
3	8
4	9
5	10

Entry	Fences										Pace - Style Manner - Conf. Notes	Scores				Total	Jog
	1	2	3	4	5	6	7	8	9	10		(Under) 60's	70's	80's	90's	Aver-age	Order

scribe must be able to write quickly and legibly. Using some abbreviations and symbols is all right as long as they are easy to decipher. After writing a few tests for a particular judge, one can get a feel for favorite phrases and ways of expression. If the first time a term is used, the scribe follows it with an abbreviation in parentheses, then the abbreviation alone can be used thereafter on the same score sheet. Some examples follow:

impulsion	(imp)
balance	(bal)
cadence	(cad)
collection	(coll)
irregular	(irr)
engagement	(eng)
self-carriage	(SC)
on the forehand	(OF)
not on the bit	(NOB)

In addition, the scribe may find a judge uses such phrases fequently: "needs more impulsion," "needs more extension," or "not straight," "not precise." Using the entire phrase the first time and "NM imp" or "NM ext" thereafter should suffice.

After the test has been ridden, some judges prefer to write their own collective marks and comments. During this brief time, the scribe should see that the judge is not interrupted.

Show veterinarian. An official show veterinarian may be hired for one or several of the following reasons:

• To be responsible to show management as a consultant and advisor regarding unsoundness.

• To be in attendance to provide services to exhibitors on a private basis.

• To enforce the U.S. Department of Agriculture Horse Protection Act by inspecting for "sored" horses.

• To conduct drug and medication testing by the specific rules as outlined by the sponsoring organization.

• To enforce state regulatory requirements for vaccination certification, negative Coggins tests, or other health requirements.

Show farrier. A qualified horseshoer, preferably an American Farrier's Association certified journeyman farrier, may be hired by show management for one or both of the following reasons:

• To make emergency repairs during a class if permissible. This must usually be done within a time limit of about two minutes.
• To provide services to exhibitors on a private basis.

Course designer. For shows offering hunter, jumper, or trail classes, a course designer is hired or appointed to develop the courses. This involves design, layout, construction (if necessary), and proper measurement with safety and good performances in mind.

Ring crew. A group of people usually volunteer or are hired to set up hunter and jumper courses and raise the jumps when necessary, to set up and maintain trail courses, and to manage the stock during cattle classes. They should be present during the running of the class so that if equipment is altered or damaged by a performance, it can be straightened or replaced for the next horse. In addition, the ring crew is often in charge of maintaining desirable footing in the arena by harrowing and watering during available breaks.

It is best if there are designated individuals to operate the in-gate and the out-gate for the entire show. The in-gate person, or paddock master, has the responsibility of checking in each exhibitor number as the contestants enter the ring.

Show photographer. Show management often makes arrangements for a professional photographer to be present to provide exhibitors with a memento of their show experience. Customarily, all of the exhibitors in the ring are photographed. The official show photographer is one of the only people allowed in the arena while classes are in progress; in some cases, governing bodies specify exactly where the photographer may stand.

Usually at the end of each day, the film is either developed on the showgrounds or rushed to a laboratory, so that prints can be made available to the exhibitors the next day. Riders can view the proofs and order additional copies. Negatives are numbered so that prints can be ordered any time after the show.

In addition to arena action shots, most photographers offer formal posed settings complete with drapes, artificial turf, flowers or shrubs, and usually a banner with the name of the competition on it. Often these are ordered by clients for advertising purposes.

The photographer must be an astute judge of horse performances and well versed in what constitutes a good moment in a variety of classes. Most show photographers say that riders are more sensitive to imperfections in their horse's appearance than to their own, and that makes sense. After all, the horse is a reflection of the rider's effectiveness.

Announcer. The person most capable of affecting the mood of the audience is the professional horse show announcer. With one eye on the judge and ringmaster, one on the show schedule and results, and with an ear tuned to the secretary who is usually close at hand, the announcer must be on top of it all. The best are also able to add interesting anecdotes and information for the benefit of the spectators.

Awards person. Often a young but precocious future equestrienne is allowed to hand out the ribbons to winners at small shows. At larger competitions, and especially those with prestigious awards, a special attempt is made to select an appropriate individual to present the prize to the winner.

CHAPTER FOURTEEN
SHOW TIME

Showground etiquette. From the moment you arrive on the grounds, a certain code of ethics, attitude of sportsmanship, and set of manners should govern your actions. Know the rules of the sponsoring organization and abide by them, and follow the Golden Rule when dealing with fellow exhibitors.

Try not to monopolize facilities that are provided for the benefit of all exhibitors. Be organized, so that time spent at the wash rack or in the warm-up ring is minimal and allows all exhibitors access to these common areas.

Getting ready. About an hour or so before you are due in the show ring, you will need to add the finishing touches to your and your horse's appearance. Have your attire organized and laid out, but before you put on those good show clothes, attend to your horse's final preparation.

I am assuming that your horse is already bathed and braided. With a bucket and a brush, clean your horse's hooves, top and bottom, and let them dry while you take care of other details. With a damp sponge, remove any dirt or manure stains that have appeared since your horse's bath. Check for straw or shavings in your horse's mane and tail.

To highlight your horse's facial features, you may wish to apply a light coat of baby oil to his muzzle or eye area. Be careful not to get the oil in his nostrils or eyes. And be aware that if you are using oil on a horse with a white muzzle, you may be setting him up for a painful sunburn. Either wash the oil off when it is not needed or use a sunscreen product. Some exhibitors use a dusting of cornstarch to highlight a horse's leg markings.

If it is customary for your horse's breed or event, you may wish to apply hoof polish. Be sure to check the rules. In some cases you may be able to use black, other times clear, and in other cases, none at all. Wax polish will give a dull natural look, is not very harmful to the hoof, but requires more time to apply. Liquid hoof polishes are shinier and quicker to apply but some solvent-based hoof

lacquers are very drying. Sanding the hooves removes their natural protective layer and results in dryness through evaporation of internal moisture.

Once your horse is groomed and tacked, have someone watch over him while you quickly change into your show clothes. Present yourself to a friend for inspection—full-length mirrors are rarely available on showgrounds. Be sure your hair is neat, your hat is on securely, and your number is clearly visible.

Make a final check of your horse's tack, mount up, and head to the warm-up arena.

Warm-up. Warming up a horse consists of a different routine for each horse. A "fresh" horse must be worked enough so that he doesn't want to play in the arena, but over-riding a "mellow" horse may take all the sparkle out of his performance. In most cases, begin by riding your horse in a long, stretched-out frame for ten minutes or so. Then ask the horse to perform a few maneuvers that will be required of him in the class. In the warm-up, the reining horse might be asked to stop once and perform one spin. The hunter may be taken over a practice jump several times. The horse needs to be physically warm and mentally in tune with what the rider will be asking him during the class.

The warm-up ring is specifically provided for those who will shortly be riding in a class. It is not designed for an entire string of horses to receive their daily training sessions. Longeing, coaching lessons, and exercise riding should be done elsewhere on the grounds.

When in the warm-up area, be alert and use caution and common sense when you pass another horse and rider. If all horses are traveling in the same direction, give a horse on the rail a wide berth as you pass or, better yet, make a circle to delay your passing or cross the arena to an open spot on the rail. Even if your horse needs extra work in one direction, be courteous and change your direction of travel with the rest of the group in the warm-up ring. If horses

Bathing at a show should be a routine procedure that does not alarm your horse. Courtesy of The American Paint Horse Association. Catherine Van Der Goes photo.

are traveling in both directions in the warm-up ring, they generally are to pass left shoulder to left shoulder.

Horses working at the fastest gait should have the rail but often this is not what happens in a warm-up ring. It makes no sense for the horse that is cantering or loping to be forced to the middle of the ring, while those walking or jogging hug the rail. If you want to practice a sliding stop or canter pirouette in the warm-up ring, plan carefully around the other traffic.

If you are jumping, keep track of others using the practice jumps. Do not monopolize the equipment. If you carry a whip, take care as you pass other horses: They may react more strongly to a whip than your own horse does.

Just before heading to the show ring, you should limber up your arms, stretch your back muscles, and relax your neck. Take several deep breaths. Visualize your pattern as you learned to in your lessons. Think of the parts of your performance that will go especially well and give your horse a kind word and a pat as you head to the in-gate.

Into the ring. Be aware of the order of classes and arrive promptly at the in-gate. Don't crowd the entrance, but be ready to go in as soon as the gate person begins checking in numbers. Assist him by calling out your number as you ride in. If you have a question for the gate person, be patient and courteous.

Watch out for other exhibitors in the ring. When passing is necessary in the show ring, leave the rail several horse lengths behind the horse you are going to pass. Move adequately to the inside and then return to the rail, being sure not to cut off the horse you have just passed. Causing the horse behind you to break gait in order to avoid rear-ending your horse can cost you an equitation or horsemanship class. And such inconsiderate behavior will make other exhibitors feel unkindly toward you. Try to ride the full arena without cutting corners.

Pay attention to the announcer's instructions and the positions of the judge and the ringmaster.

Continue showing your horse until the class has been judged. Some judges will have the entire group of competitors continue to work on the rail as the winners are being called to the center. Other judges bring all exhibitors to the center to line up and the winners are called out of the lineup.

Although you can relax somewhat once the results have been handed in, you should not lose control of your horse. As the placings are being called, keep an open mind even though you feel your ride deserved the blue ribbon instead of the out-gate. Remember, if you were concentrating on your riding, you did not have a chance to see other contestants' performances. An exhibitor who scurries out of the ring frowning may miss the opportunity to hear a helpful comment from a judge who may have basically liked his or her performance. Although judges often do not have time to talk with exhibitors, an effort is sometimes made to provide bits of advice to young people and amateur riders.

If you don't wish to exhibit in classes you have already entered, you should notify the show secretary immediately that you have scratched. If this is not attended to, valuable time is lost while the judge and the entire show wait for an exhibitor who is not coming. Often there is a three-minute gate hold for late contestants. It doesn't take many of these to upset a show schedule.

Tack changes, too, can delay a show. If it is necessary to change attire, saddles, or horses between classes, be organized ahead of time so that you can make the change quickly.

In most cases, a judge's opinion is indisputable. If an exhibitor has a question about a placing, he should first go to the exhibitor's representative or the show steward for

This exhibitor shows that her horse is a pleasure to ride.

disqualifications can occur after the class has been judged and placings awarded. If it is discovered that a horse has an illegal substance in its blood or that it has been treated in an illegal or inhumane way on the showgrounds, its winnings may be revoked.

In some instances, the representative or steward may need to confer with the judge for a clarification and, on a rare occasion, the judge will talk directly with the exhibitor. If an exhibitor wants to protest a judge's or a steward's ruling, he must formally file a complaint with the show management, usually within twelve hours. The procedures vary with each organization and usually are quite involved. Most complaints simply arise from a difference of opinion between the exhibitor and judge, and of course that is understandable. There is only one winner in each class, and only one person goes home with the blue ribbon!

UNITED STATES RIBBON COLORS

First Place	Blue
Second Place	Red
Third Place	Yellow
Fourth Place	White
Fifth Place	Pink
Sixth Place	Green
Seventh Place	Purple
Eighth Place	Brown
Ninth Place	Dark Gray
Tenth Place	Light Blue
Grand	Blue, Red, Yellow, and White or Purple
Reserve Grand	Red, Yellow, White, and Pink or Purple and White
Champion	Blue, Red, and Yellow or Purple
Reserve Champion	Red, Yellow, and White or Purple and White
Note: In Canada, first prize is red and second is blue.	

WINNING AND LOSING

In addition to ribbons, class winners can earn points, money, and trophies. Sweepstakes prizes consist of entry fees plus an added purse. The total is distributed among the winners according to previously determined percentages.

clarification. Ninety-five percent of problems are cleared up by an explanation of rules that were misinterpreted by the exhibitor.

Disqualifications can occur for many reasons and are handled in different ways according to the rules of the organization. Some disqualifications occur at the paperwork stage, such as a horse without the proper registration certificate or proof of ownership. In such a case, the horse is not allowed to participate in the class. Other disqualifications occur when the horse enters the ring. The horse may be wearing illegal tack. Some shows will have a steward to point out the infraction to the exhibitor and the contestant will be asked to leave the ring. In other cases, the improper tack may not be discovered until the entire group is working on the rail. In such a case, the horse is allowed to work with the class, but will not be placed. Still other

Lead-Line winner Cari Baker on Porvenir Gay Bobby with Brook Baker Leading. (Note: Most shows require the attire of both showmen to be the same style.) Courtesy of Moondrift Morgan Farm.

Some trophies are awarded permanently to a winner and others remain the property of a show. In most cases, however, they become the permanent property of the winner. Trophies are not limited to decorative, dust-collecting memorabilia but can be useful items such as horse blankets, coolers, halters, saddles, and so on.

A challenge trophy is one that has been donated by a person or a business to the show committee, and the winner earns possession of it for one year. Some challenge trophies eventually become the property of the winner if won a prescribed number of times. A perpetual trophy, however, is never awarded permanently to a contestant. Instead annual winners are awarded token replicas.

Whether or not you have won a prize, congratulate the winners and accept compliments graciously after your class. Do not blame the judge, your horse, the arena conditions, the show management, or the person you bought the horse from if you do not leave the arena with the blue. Look to yourself for ways in which you can improve your next performance.

Commend your horse for a job well done by taking care of him properly whether you won or lost. Never attempt to relieve the frustration of losing by schooling your horse excessively after a class. This may serve to alienate him further from performing well at a future show. If, however, your horse exhibited willful disobedience in the ring when he was asked to do something he knew well, you may need to school him after a class. At a time like this, it is safest to follow the advice of your coach.

After your horse is comfortable in his stall, return to ringside so that you can once again observe what makes a winning ride. Discuss the class you participated in with an experienced, objective observer. Don't expect your family or friends to provide an unbiased critique. Plan future lesson goals with your trainer or instructor. This will increase your chances of winning the next time. Make some specific notes on the details of your performance while it is fresh in your mind.

And think about this. You were probably originally attracted to horses for the same reasons that I was. They are beautiful animals with great athletic potential, diverse talents, and a willingness to cooperate if treated fairly. Don't lose sight of this fact, and your show-ring experience will be much richer.

SECTION FOUR
APPENDIX

ADDRESS LIST

Breed Associations, Performance Organizations, and Professional Organizations.

American Association of Equine Practioners
410 West Vine Street, Lexington, KY 40507

American Driving Society
P.O. Box 160, 16 East High Street, Metamora, MI 48455

American Endurance Ride Conference
1915 I Street NW, Number 700, Washington, DC 20006

American Farriers Association
P.O. Box 695, Albuquerque, NM 87103

American Horse Council
1700 K Street NW, Number 300, Washington, DC 20006

American Horse Shows Association
220 E. 42nd Street, 4th Floor, New York, NY 10017

American Morgan Horse Association
P.O. Box 1, Westmoreland, NY 13490

American Paint Horse Association
P.O. Box 18519, Fort Worth, TX 76118

American Quarter Horse Association
2701 I-40 East, Amarillo, TX 79168

American Saddlebred Horse Association
4093 Ironworks Pike, Lexington, KY 40511

American Vaulting Association
20066 Glen Brae Drive, Saratoga, CA 95070

Appaloosa Horse Club
P.O. Box 8403, Moscow, ID 83843

4-H
7100 Connecticut Ave., Chevy Chase, MD 20815
Or contact your local extension agent.

International Arabian Horse Association
P.O. Box 33696, Denver, CO 80233

National Cutting Horse Association
P.O. Box 12155, Fort Worth, TX 76121

National Reining Horse Association
28881 SR 83, Coshocton, OH 43812

North American Trail Ride Conference
P.O. Box 20315, El Cajon, CA 92021

The United States Pony Clubs
329 South High Street, Westchester, PA 19382

United States Combined Training Association
292 Bridge Street, South Hamilton, MA 01982

United States Dressage Federation
P.O. Box 80668, Lincoln, NE 68501

Check your horse in transit. Richard
Klimesh photo.

FAIRS

California International Horse Expo
Tulare County's International Agri-Center
Tulare, CA
May
209-627-0122

Equifair and Breeds of the World
Spruce Meadows
Calgary, Alberta, Canada
September
403-256-4977

Harness Expo
Pompano Park
Pompano, FL
November
502-582-1672

Hoosier All-Breed Horse Fair
Indiana State Fairgrounds, West Pavilion
Indianapolis, IN
April
317-299-2027

Horse Expo
Western Idaho Fairgrounds
Boise, ID
May
208-537-6664

Horses
Tacoma Dome Complex and Convention Center
Tacoma, WA
August
206-631-1355

International Thoroughbred Exhibition and Conference
Lexington Center
Lexington, KY
June
502-582-1672

Iowa Horse Fair
Iowa State Fairgrounds
Des Moines, IA
April
515-262-3111

Maryland Horse Fair
Prince George's Equestrian Center
Upper Marlboro, MD
May
301-952-4740

Michigan Annual International Stallion Exhibition and Trade Show
Lansing Civic Center
Lansing, MI
March
517-628-2577

Mid-American Horse Festival
Saint Charles Fairground
Saint Charles, IL
July
312-557-2575

Midwest Horse Fair
Dane County Coliseum
Madison, WI
April
219-672-8229

Minnesota Horse Exposition
Minneapolis Auditorium
Minneapolis, MN
April
612-933-3850

Oregon Horse A-Fair
Lane County Fairgrounds, Horse Coliseum
Eugene, OR
April
503-746-6564

GUIDE TO INTERSTATE HEALTH REQUIREMENTS

This guide to health requirements for horses being shipped interstate was supplied to the American Horse Council by Dr. Joan Arnoldi of the Wisconsin Department of Agriculture. Each state establishes its own rules for animals entering its borders. These requirements are amended frequently, so it is advisable to check with the State Veterinarian at your destination (listed in the Directory) prior to shipment.

Regulations In Effect As Of April, 1988

State	EIA Test Required	State Health Certificate*	Temp. Reading
Alabama	Yes (6 months)	Yes	No
Alaska	Yes (6 months)	Yes (A,B)	No
Arizona	No	Yes	No
Arkansas	Yes (6 months)	Yes	Yes
California	Yes (6 months)	Yes (C)	No
Canada	Yes (6 months)	Yes (G)	Yes
Colorado	Yes (12 months)	Yes	No
Connecticut	No	Yes (B)	No
Delaware	Yes (12 months) (D)	Yes	Yes
Florida	Yes (12 months)	Yes	Yes
Georgia	Yes (12 months)	Yes	Yes
Hawaii	Yes (90 days)	Yes (A)	No
Idaho	No	Yes	No
Illinois	No	No	No
Indiana	Yes (12 months)	Yes	No
Iowa	Yes (12 months)	Yes	No
Kansas	No	Yes	No
Kentucky	Yes (12 months) (D)	Yes	No
Louisiana	Yes (12 months)	Yes	No
Maine	Yes (6 months)	Yes (A)	No
Maryland	Yes (12 months)	Yes (A)	No
Massachusetts	Yes (6 months)	Yes	No
Michigan	Yes (6 months)	Yes	No
Minnesota	Yes (12 months)	Yes	No
Mississippi	Yes (12 months)	Yes	No
Missouri	Yes (12 months)	Yes	No

State	EIA Test Required	State Health Certificate*	Temp. Reading
Montana	No (E)	Yes (B)	No
Nebraska	Yes (12 months)	Yes	No
Nevada	No	Yes	No
New Hampshire	Yes (6 months)	Yes	No
New Jersey	Yes (30 days)	Yes (A)	No
New Mexico	No	Yes	No
New York	Yes (12 months)	Yes (F)	No
North Carolina	Yes (6 months)	Yes	No
North Dakota	No	Yes	No
Ohio	Yes (6 months)	Yes	Yes
Oklahoma	Yes (6 months)	Yes	No
Oregon	Yes (6 months)	Yes (B)	No
Pennsylvania	Yes (12 months)	Yes	No
Puerto Rico	Yes (6 months)	Yes (A)	No
Rhode Island	No	Yes	No
South Carolina	Yes (6 months)	Yes	No
South Dakota	Yes (12 months)	Yes	No
Tennessee	Yes (12 months)	Yes	No
Texas	Yes (12 months)	Yes (B)	No
Utah	Yes (12 months)	Yes	No
Vermont	Yes (12 months)	Yes (B)	No
Virginia	Yes (12 months)	Yes	No
Washington	Yes (6 months)	Yes	No
West Virginia	Yes (6 months)	Yes (A)	Yes
Wisconsin	Yes (12 months)	Yes	No
Wyoming	Yes (12 months)	Yes	No

* Health certificate filed with the state veterinarian in state of origin is required.

(A) Health certificate must be approved in state of origin prior to shipment.

(B) Permit from the state of destination is required prior to entry.

(C) Copy of health certificate and $2 filing fee must be sent to California by date of shipment.

(D) Delaware requires tests within 6 months for sale or auction; Kentucky requires a test within 6 months for sales.

(E) A Coggins test is required for horses from certain Southern or Gulf Coast states.

(F) Thoroughbred stallions used for breeding must have a negative viral arteritis test within 30 days prior to shipment.

(G) U.S. origin health certificate endorsed by a USDA approved veterinarian.

NOTE: Certificates are valid for only 14 days for return to the U.S. The Coggins test is valid for U.S. return for 180 days.

COURSES AND DEGREES

The Harness Horse Youth Foundation, Inc. publishes *The Equine School & College Directory*, a 64-page directory of schools and colleges that have certificates, majors, or degrees in equine sciences. The directory, published yearly, also includes a partial list of scholarships available within the equine industry.

The publication costs $3.00 for postage and handling. To order, write or call:

Margaret H. Vild
Executive Director
The Harness Horse Youth Foundation
3386 Snouffa Road
Worthington, OH 43085

(614) 764-0231

BIBLIOGRAPHY

BOOKS

Corley, G.F., D.V.M. *Riding and Schooling the Western Performance Horse.* New York: Prentice-Hall, 1982.

Crabtree, Helen K. *Saddle Seat Equitation.* Garden City: Doubleday, 1982.

Crossley, Anthony. *Training the Young Horse.* London: Stanley Paul, 1978.

Dunning, Al. *Reining.* Colorado Springs, CO: Western Horseman, 1983.

Evans, J. Warren. *Horses: A Guide to Selection, Care, and Enjoyment.* San Francisco: Freeman, 1981.

German National Equestrian Federation. *The Principles of Riding.* New York: Arco, 1985.

Harris, Susan E. *Grooming to Win.* New York: Scribner's, 1977.

Hill, Cherry. *The Formative Years: Raising and Training the Young Horse from Birth to Two Years.* Millwood, NY: Breakthrough, 1988.

Hyland, Ann. *Endurance Riding.* Philadelphia: Lippincott, 1975.

Klimke, Reiner. *Basic Training of the Young Horse.* London: J.A. Allen, 1985.

Lewis, Lon D. *Feeding and Care of the Horse.* Philadelphia: Lea and Febiger, 1982.

Littauer, Vladmir. *Commonsense Horsemanship.* New York: Arco, 1974.

Loriston-Clarke, Jennie. *The Complete Guide to Dressage.* Philadelphia: Running Press, 1987.

Miller, Robert W. *Western Horse Behavior and Training.* Garden City: Dolphin, 1975.

Morris, George H. *Hunter Seat Equitation.* Garden City: Doubleday, 1979.

Museler, Wilhelm. *Riding Logic.* New York: Arco, 1981.

Podhajsky, Alois. *The Complete Training of Horse and Rider.* Garden City: Doubleday, 1965.

Podhajsky, Alois. *My Horses, My Teachers.* Elverson, PA: Bright Books, 1987.

Schusdziarra, H., M.D., and V. Schusdziarra, M.D. *An Anatomy of Riding.* Millwood: Breakthrough, 1985.

Seunig, Waldemar. *Horsemanship.* Garden City: Doubleday, 1956.

Strickland, Charlene. *Show Grooming.* Millwood: Breakthrough, 1986.

Swift, Sally. *Centered Riding.* New York: St. Martin's, 1985.

White-Mullin, Anna Jane. *Judging Hunters and Hunt Seat Equitation.* New York: Arco, 1984.

Wilde, Louise Mills. *Guide to Dressage.* San Diego: Barnes, 1982.

Willcox, Sheila. *The Event Horse.* Philadelphia: Lippincott, 1973.

MAGAZINES

Horse Care

Equus, P.O. Box 932, Farmingdale, NY 11737

English Riding

Practical Horseman, P.O. Box 927, Farmingdale, NY 11737
Chronicle of the Horse, P.O. Box 46, Middleburg, VA 22117

Western Riding

Horseman, P.O. Box 1990, Marion, OH 43305

Regional (examples)

Horseman's Yankee Pedlar, 785 Southbridge St., Auburn, MA 01501

Equine Market, 111 Shore Drive, Hinsdale, IL 60521

Horses West, P.O. Box 1590, Boulder, CO 80306

California Horse Review, P.O. Box 2437, Fair Oaks, CA 95628

Horses All, P.O. Box 550, Nanton, Alberta, T0L 1R0 Canada

Breed and Performance

See address list at beginning of appendix.

GLOSSARY

ACTION. Degree of flexion of the joints of the legs during movement; also reflected in head, neck, and tail carriage. High snappy action is desired in some classes whereas easy, ground-covering action is the goal in others.

AGE (of the horse). Computed from January 1 of the year in which the horse is foaled.

AIDS. Signals from the rider to the horse. Natural aids are the mind, voice, hands, legs, and weight. Examples of artificial aids (which are extensions, reinforcements, or substitutions of the natural aids) are whips, spurs, and nosebands.

AIKEN. Jump made of vertical rails and a mound of fir boughs.

AMATEUR. Rider over eighteen who does not get paid for riding.

AMATEUR-OWNER. Class open to horses whose owner or member of owner's immediate family is the rider.

APPOINTMENTS. Tack and equipment (attire is sometimes included).

ATTIRE. The rider's clothes.

BACK. Two-beat diagonal gait in reverse.

BAD HABIT. Undesirable behavior during training or handling. Examples are rearing, halter pulling, and striking.

BALANCE. In regard to movement, a state of equilibrium; in regard to conformation, desirable proportions.

BALK. To refuse or cease to move forward.

BANK. Solid earthen ramp or wall that is used as a drop jump.

BARN SOUR. Herd-bound; a bad habit that may result in a horse bolting back to the barn or to his herdmates.

BARS. Part of the saddle's tree that runs along each side and parallel to the horse's spine; interdental space between incisors and molars where the bit lies.

BASCULE. The desirable arc a horse's body makes as it goes over a jump.

BASE. The rider's seat and weight.

BELL BOOTS. Protective boots, usually of rubber, which encircle the coronary band and bulbs of heels.

BIGHT. Traditionally a loop in a rope. With closed reins, such as with an English bridle, bight refers to the ends of the reins. Even though Western reins are often split, their ends are also referred to as the bight.

BIT GUARD. Rubber or leather ring that lies between the horse's cheek and the snaffle bit ring to prevent skin pinching.

BITING. Bad habit common to young horses, stallions, and spoiled horses. It can result from hand-fed treats, petting, or improper training.

BLEMISH. Visible defect that does not affect serviceability.

BLOODLINES. The family lineage.

BOLTING. Gulping feed without chewing; running away with rider.

BOSAL. Rawhide noseband used in Western training and showing that works on the principles of balance, weight, and pressure.

BOT BLOCK. Porous synthetic black "stone" whose uniformly abrasive surface will remove bot eggs from the horse's hair. The block can be "sharpened" by drawing it across a hard edge.

BOWED TENDON. Damage to a tendon usually caused by overstretching due to improper conditioning, overwork, or an accident.

BREED CHARACTER. The quality of conforming to the description of a particular breed.

BREEDING CLASS. Conformation class.

BRILLIANCE. Flash or dazzle, as related to performance.

BRUSH. Jump made of shrubs and brush with a clearly visible bar.

CADENCE. The rhythmic clarity of a gait.

CANTER. English term for a three-beat gait with right and left leads. The canter has the same footfall pattern as the lope.

CANTLE. The back of the seat of the saddle.

CAVALLETTI. Ground rail suspended between two wooden Xs designed to provide three different heights for working horses. A very small jump.

CAVESSON. Leather noseband (customarily used with the English snaffle bridle) which encourages the horse to keep its mouth closed; a longeing cavesson is a leather or nylon headstall with a weighted noseband that has metal rings for various attachments of the longe line.

CHAMPION. Highest award in a particular division.

CHANGE OF DIAGONAL. Rider changes the diagonal to which he is posting. *See* DIAGONAL.

CHANGE OF LEG OR LEAD. Change of the leading legs at the canter or lope.

CINCH. Band that fastens a Western saddle in place.

COGGINS TEST. Laboratory blood test used to detect previous exposure to equine infectious anemia.

COLD-BLOODED. Refers to horse having ancestors that trace to heavy war horses and draft breeds. Characteristics might include more substance of bone, thick skin, heavy hair coat, shaggy fetlocks, and lower red blood cell and hemoglobin values.

COLIC. Gastrointestinal discomfort that can range from a mild "stomachache" to a violent frenzy.

COLLECTION. Gathered together; a state of organized movement; a degree of equilibrium in which the horse's energized response to the aids is characterized by elevated head and neck, rounded back, "dropped croup," engaged hindquarters, and flexed abdominals. The horse remains on the bit, is light and mobile, and is ready to respond to the requests of the trainer.

COLOR. Class in which coat color and pattern, not conformation is a deciding factor (e.g., Palomino, Dun Factor, etc.).

COLT. Young male horse to age four.

COMBINATION. Series of two or more fences within 39 feet 4 inches of each other that must be taken as a pair; an in-and-out.

CONDITIONING. The art and science of preparing a horse mentally and physically for the demands of an event.

CONFORMATION. The physical structure of a horse compared to a standard of perfection or an ideal.

CONFORMATION HUNTER. Class judged 40 percent on conformation and 60 percent on performance.

CONTACT. The horse's stretching forward into the bit and accepting the taut rein as a means of communication with the rider.

COUNTERCANTER. Deliberately asking the horse to canter on the lead opposite the direction of movement. For example, in a circle to the right, requesting a countercanter would result in a canter left lead.

COURSE. Prescribed route that the horse and exhibitor must take, usually in hunter and jumper classes.

CRIBBING. Vice whereby a horse anchors its teeth onto an object, arches its neck, pulls backward, and swallows air. It can cause unthriftiness, tooth damage, and other physical disturbances. It can be socially contagious.

CRYPTORCHIDISM. Retention of one or both testicles in the abdominal cavity.

CUE. Signal or composite of trainer aids designed to elicit certain behavior in a horse.

CURB. Type of English or Western bit that has shanks and works on the principle of leverage; a curb may have a solid or jointed mouthpiece. Also an unsoundness of the hind leg.

CURB STRAP. Leather strap that is affixed to the bit below the reins and lies across the chin groove. When used with a curb bit, it creates pressure on the chin groove from the leverage action of the shanks. When used with a snaffle, it prevents the snaffle from being pulled through the horse's mouth.

DIAGONAL. Pair of legs at the trot, such as the right front and the left hind. The rider sits as the inside hind hits the ground or "rises and falls with the (front) leg on the wall." Also a maneuver from one corner of an arena to another through the center.

DISUNITED. Cantering or loping on different leads front and hind.

DOCK. Flesh and bone portion of the tail.

DOUBLE BRIDLE. Bridle consisting of two separate headstalls and bits. The snaffle bit (bradoon) is very small.

DRESSAGE. French for "training" or "schooling." The systematic art of training a horse to perform prescribed movements in a balanced, supple, obedient, and willing manner.

DROPPED NOSEBAND. Piece of tack worn lower than a cavesson and used in conjunction with a snaffle bridle. Worn over and below the bit, it enhances sensitivity to the snaffle by positioning it on the bars and encouraging salivation.

ELIMINATION. Disqualification from placings because of an infraction of a specifically stated rule, such as a fall, going off pattern, etc.; a process of selecting semifinalists from a very large number of riders.

ENGAGEMENT. Use of the horse's back and hindquarters to create energy and impulsion to forward movement. An engaged horse has a rounded top line, dropped croup, flexed abdominals, and elevated head and neck.

EQUESTRIAN. Of or pertaining to horseman or horsemanship; a rider.

EQUESTRIENNE. Female rider or performer.

EQUITATION. The art of riding.

EVASION. Avoidance of an aid; for example, a horse that overflexes or gets "behind the bit" to keep from accepting contact with the bit.

EVENTING. Combined training including dressage, cross country, and stadium jumping.

EXTENSION. Lowering and lengthening of a particular frame and stride while maintaining the original rhythm.

EXTENSOR. Muscle responsible for opening the angle of a joint.

FALL. For a horse, shoulder and hindquarter on the same side touch the ground; for a rider, separation between the rider and horse necessitating remounting.

FAULT. Scoring unit to keep track of knockdowns, refusals, or other offenses.

FEI. Federation Equestre Internationale or International Equestrian Federation, the organization governing international competitions.

FENDER. Part of the Western saddle that protects a rider's leg from the rigging.

FIADOR. Knotted rope throatlatch, used in conjunction with a bosal, browband headstall, and horsehair reins. The knots of the fiador are the hackamore, the fiador, and the sheet bend.

FIGURE EIGHT NOSEBAND. Noseband popular with eventers; straps cross in an X on the bridge of the horse's nose.

FILLY. Female horse to age four.

FLASH NOSEBAND. Cross between a cavesson and a figure-eight noseband.

FLAT. Class without jumping.

FLEXION. Characteristic of a supple and collected horse, there are two types of flexion: 1. vertical or longitudinal, which is often mistakenly associated with "headset," when in reality it is an engagement of the entire body: abdomen, hindquarters, back, neck, and head. 2. lateral, which is side-to-side arcing or bending characteristic of circular work.

FLEXOR. Muscle responsible for closing the angle of a joint.

FLOATING. Process of filing off sharp edges of a horse's teeth.

FLYING LEAD CHANGE. Change from one lead to another without changing gait.

FOREHAND. That portion of the horse from the heart girth forward.

FORK. Part of the swells of a saddle that makes up the gullet.

FREE WALK. Walk on a loose rein to allow the horse to stretch its neck and lower its head.

FUTURITIES. Those events for young horses that require entering long (often years) before the actual event.

GAITED HORSE. Animated horse such as the Arabian, American Saddlebred, Morgan, or Tennessee Walking Horse with flashy gaits.

GELDING. Castrated male horse.

GIRTH. Strap around the horse's heart girth that fastens an English saddle in place.

GO-ROUND. One heat or elimination round in a class with a large number of entries.

GRADE. Unregistered horse.

GRAND. The champion overall.

GRAND PRIX. Top caliber classes in dressage and show jumping, often offering large cash prizes.

GREEN. Inexperienced horse or rider, relatively speaking. In hunter classes, the horse can be any age and is rated according to awards won in past performances.

GROUND TRAINING. When the training works the horse from the ground, rather than being mounted. Includes in-hand work, barn manners, longeing, and ground driving.

GULLET. Area under the fork, swells, or pommel of the saddle.

HACKAMORE. Americanization of *jaquima*, which is Spanish for the composite of a bosal, fiador, headstall, and mecate.

HACK CLASS. A flat class.

HALF-PASS. Variation of travers, executed on the diagonal instead of along the wall. The horse should be nearly parallel to the long sides of the arena, with the forehand slightly in advance of the haunches.

HALTER CLASS. Conformation class.

HALTER PULLING. Bad habit in which a horse pulls violently backward on the halter rope when tied.

HAND. Measurement calculated from the highest point of the withers to the ground. One hand is 4 inches.

HANDY. Prompt and athletic in response to the rider.

HAUNCHES. Hindquarters.

HEAVES. Damage to the lungs, resulting in labored breathing.

HOGBACK. Three-rail jump with the center element the highest.

HONEST. Quality in a horse that makes him dependable and predictable.

HORSEMANSHIP. Exhibition of a rider's skill, usually referred to as the Western style of riding.

HOT-BLOODED. Refers to horses having ancestors that trace to Thoroughbreds or Arabians. Characteristics might include fineness of bone, thin skin, fine hair coat, absence of long fetlock hairs, and higher red blood cell and hemoglobin values.

HUNTER. Type of horse, not a breed, which is suitable for field hunting or show hunting.

IMPULSION. The energy and thrust forward characterized by a forward reaching rather than a backward pushing motion.

IN-AND-OUT. Combination fence.

IN-HAND CLASS. One in which the horse is led by the exhibitor.

IRONS. Stirrups on an English saddle.

JACKPOT. All entry fees are pooled and awarded in a pre-determined fashion, such as 40 percent for first, 30 percent for second, 20 percent for third, and 10 percent for fourth.

JOG. Slow Western trot.

JUMPER. Horse judged on jumping performance based only on faults and time. Touch faults are sometimes also used. Preliminary jumpers are those horses having won up to $1,000; Intermediate up to $3,000; Open over $3,000.

JUMP-OFF. In the event of a tie, a course may be altered and the two tied horses asked to jump again.

JUNIOR. Rider under eighteen years of age as of January 1. Horse four years of age and under.

JUNIOR HUNTER. Horse of any age ridden by an exhibitor eighteen years or younger.

KUR. Musical freestyle in dressage.

LATERAL. In anatomy, away from the midline as opposed to toward the midline.

LATERAL MOVEMENTS. Work in which the horse moves with the forehand and haunches on different tracks. Shoulder-in, haunches-in (travers), haunches-out (renvers), and half-passes are the lateral movements.

LATIGO. Cinch strap on a Western saddle.

LEAD. Specific footfall pattern at the canter or lope in which the inside legs of the circle reach farther forward than the outside legs. Working to the right, the horse's right foreleg and right hind leg reach farther forward than the left legs. If a horse is loping in a circle to the right on the left lead, he is said to be on the wrong lead or is countercantering.

LEG YIELDING. Exercises designed to teach the horse to move away from leg pressure.

LIMITED. Type of class with entry restrictions for the horse and/or the rider, related to prior winnings at specified shows. May be based on number of blue ribbons (usually six) or monetary earnings.

LONGE. To work a horse in a circle on a 30-foot line around the trainer.

LOPE. Three-beat gait with an initiating hind leg, a diagonal pair including the leading hind leg, and finally the leading foreleg.

MAIDEN. Division open to a rider (or horse) who has not won a blue ribbon at specified shows.

MANNERS. The energetic yet cooperative attitude of a horse, particularly emphasized in ladies and youth classes.

MARE. Female horse over age four.

MARTINGALE. Piece of training equipment designed to fix a horse's head position. Common types include running, standing, and German.

MATURITIES. Those types of events for aged horses (five and older).

MECATE. A 22-foot horsehair rope, ⅜ to ¾ inch in diameter, which is fastened to a bosal to make reins and a lead.

MEDAL CLASS. AHSA equitation competition. National champions are chosen annually at Harrisburg, Pennsylvania, in hunter seat, saddle seat, and stock seat and a dressage class for juniors.

MEDIUM GAIT. Between collected and extended.

MODEL HUNTER. Judged 100 percent on conformation but horse must be shown over fences in the same show in order for points to count toward a championship.

NEAR SIDE. Horse's left side.

NONPRO. A nonprofessional by specific definition from each association such as NRHA, NCHA, and AHSA; may replace "amateur."

NOVICE. In general, an inexperienced horseman; a division for horse (or rider) who has not yet won three first-place ribbons at specified shows.

OFF SIDE. Horse's right side.

OPEN. Competition available for professionals, nonpros, amateurs, and youth. Anyone can enter.

OXER. Parallel bar-type fence with two rails. A square oxer has even rails. A step or ascending oxer has a lower front rail.

PACE. A two-beat lateral gait in which right feet move and land together.

PACING. Continuous stall walking. Often an unhappy horse's reaction to confinement.

PANIC SNAP. Safety snap often used in horse trailers and crossties. The design allows the snap to be released even if there is great pressure on it.

PARK HORSE. Horse with a brilliant performance, style, presence, finish, balance, and cadence and usually animated gaits.

PARROT MOUTH. Unsoundness characterized by an extreme overbite.

PASSAGE. Very collected, elevated, and cadenced trot characterized by a pronounced engagement of the hindquarters, more exaggerated flexion of the knees and hocks, and a graceful elasticity of movement.

PATTERN. Prescribed order of maneuvers in a particular class such as reining or trail.

PAWING. Bad habit usually caused by nervousness and/or improper ground training; can also be a sign of colic.

PEDIGREE. Listing of a horse's ancestors.

PELHAM. Single bit that is used with four reins and combines the effects of a snaffle and curb.

PERFORMANCE. Exhibition of gaits or other required routines.

PIAFFE(R). Highly collected and cadenced trot in place.

PIROUETTE. Circle executed on two tracks with the radius equal to the length of the horse, with the forehand moving around the haunches and maintaining the exact rhythm and sequence of footfalls of the gait being used.

PIVOT. Crisp, prompt turn on the hindquarters.

PLEASURE. Rail class designed to showcase smooth movers.

POINTS. Coloring of the legs, mane, and tail.

POLL. Junction of the vertebrae with the skull; an area of great sensitivity and flexion.

POMMEL. Front portion of the saddle including the swells.

PONY. Horse that stands 58 inches (14.2 hands) or less.

POSTING. *See* DIAGONAL.

PRESENCE. Personality, charisma.

PROFESSIONAL. The definition varies among associations but most term professional the following activities of a person over eighteen: being paid for riding, driving, or showing at halter; for training or boarding; for instructing; for conducting seminars or clinics; in some situations for being employed as a groom or farrier; for use of name or photo in connection with advertisement; for accepting prize money in classes.

PULSE. Normal adult resting heart rate varies among horses but is usually forty beats per minute.

QUALITY. Overall degree of merit: flat bone and clean joints, refined features, and fine skin and hair coat.

RAIL. Western term for a flat class.

RATING. Means of classifying the size of a show, sometimes done beforehand according to prizes offered, and sometimes after according to number of entries.

REARING. Bad habit in a horse of raising up on his hind legs when he is being led or ridden. An extremely dangerous habit that should be dealt with by a professional only.

REFINEMENT. Quality appearance, indicating good breeding.

REGISTERED. Horse whose purebred parents have numbered certificates with a particular breed organization.

REIN-BACK. To back; a two-beat diagonal gait in reverse.

RENVERS. Haunches-out. The opposite movement to travers, with the tail instead of the head to the wall.

RESERVE CHAMPION. Second place or runner-up in a particular division.

RESPIRATION. Normal adult respiration rate varies among horses but is usually twelve to fifteen breaths per minute. One breath consists of an inhalation and an exhalation.

RIGGING. Style and configuration of the front and rear cinches on a Western saddle.

RINGBONE. Arthritic unsoundness of the pastern joint.

RING SOUR. Poor attitude in a horse who does not enjoy working in an arena and looks for ways to leave the arena or quit working.

ROACHED. Mane or tail that has been clipped to the skin.

ROARING. Breathing disorder.

ROMAL. Type of Spanish-style braided reins used with a Western bridle.

SCHOOLING SHOW. Warm-up or practice show early in the season.

SERPENTINE. Series of half circles and straight lines crossing from one side of the centerline to the other, requiring a change of direction each time the horse passes over it.

SET-UP. Putting a horse in the proper stance for the judge to evaluate him in a halter or conformation class.

SHANK. Lead rope or "stud" chain. Also the arm extending from the mouthpiece of a curb bit to where the reins attach. Pressure on these reins exerts leverage.

SHOULDER-IN. Horse is slightly bent around the inside leg of the rider, and his inside legs pass and cross in front of the outside legs.

SHOWMANSHIP. In-hand class that is judged on the exhibitor's ability to show his horse.

SHYING. Horse spooking or becoming startled by a movement or object. It may or may not include a sudden jump sideways or bolting.

SIDEBONE. Inflammation followed by an ossification of the lateral cartilages of the foot.

SIDE PASS. Full pass: moving the horse sideways, with no forward movement. Often used in trail classes.

SIMPLE LEAD CHANGE. Change from one lead to another with a walk, trot, or halt in between.

SNAFFLE. Bit with a solid or jointed mouthpiece that has no shanks and works on principles of direct pressure only.

SORED. Having physical evidence of inhumane training practices.

SOUND. Having no defect, visible or unseen, which affects serviceability; the state of being able to perform without hindrance.

SPAVIN. Unsoundness of the hock that can involve soft tissues (bog spavin) or bone (bone spavin or jack spavin).

SPAYED MARE. Neutered female horse.

SPLINT BOOTS. Protective covering worn around the cannons of the front legs to prevent injury.

SPLINTS. Term commonly applied to inflammation of the attachment of the splint bone to the cannon; older cases of splints are identified as bony enlargements at various points along the splint bone.

SPOOKY. Easily startled horse.

SPORT HORSE. Purebred or crossbred horse suitable for dressage, jumping, eventing, or endurance.

SPREAD. Type of fence that requires jumping the width from front to rear.

STAKES CLASS. Money-earning class.

STOCK HORSE. Western-style horse of the quarter horse type.

STRIDE. Distance traveled in a particular gait, measured from the spot where one hoof hits the ground to where it next lands. Ten to 12 feet is the normal length of stride at a canter, for example.

STRIKING. Bad habit of reaching out with a front foot to hit the handler, equipment, or another horse. A problem calling for professional help.

SUBSTANCE. Strength and density of bone, muscle, and tendons or an indication of large body size.

SUITABILITY. Appropriateness for a particular purpose and/or a type or size of rider.

SULLEN. Sulky, resentful, or withdrawn.

SWELLS. Exterior projection of the fork of a Western saddle.

TACK. Horse equipment or gear.

TAIL RUBBING. Habit that may originate from anal or skin itch or a dirty sheath or udder. Even when the cause is removed, the habit often persists.

TEMPERAMENT. General consistency with which a horse behaves.

TEMPERATURE. Normal adult temperature varies among horses, but will usually range from 99.5^0 F. to 100.5^0 F.

THOROUGHBRED. Breed of horse registered with the Jockey Club. Not meant to be used as a synonym for purebred.

THOROUGHPIN. Swelling in the web of the hock that may be an unsoundness or a blemish.

THRUSH. Disease of the hoof often associated with unsanitary conditions that causes decomposition of the frog and other hoof structures.

TOP LINE. Includes the proportion and curvature of the line from poll to tail.

TRACTABLE. Quality in a horse's disposition that makes him cooperative and trainable.

TRANSITION. Upward or downward change between gaits, speed, direction, or maneuvers.

TRAPPY. Course with sharp turns.

TRAVEL. The path of the flight of each limb during movement.

TRAVERS. Haunches-in. The horse is slightly bent around the inside leg of the rider. Its outside legs pass and cross in front of the inside legs. The horse is looking in the direction in which it is moving. Performed along the wall or on the centerline, at an angle of about thirty degrees to the direction in which the horse is moving.

TRIPLE BAR. Ascending staircase jump consisting of three bars that add spread and increase in height.

TROT. Two-beat diagonal gait.

TURN ON THE FOREHAND. Maneuver in which the horse's hindquarters rotate around his forehand.

TURN ON THE HAUNCHES (hindquarters). Maneuver in which the horse's forehand rotates around his hind end.

TURNOUT. Overall appearance of a horse (and rider).

TWITCH. Means of restraint. A nose twitch is often a wooden handle with a loop of chain applied to the horse's upper lip.

TYING UP. Form of metabolic muscle stiffness caused from irregularity in feed and work schedules.

TYPE. Particular style of horse embodying certain characteristics that contribute to its value and efficiency for its intended use.

UNDERLINE. The length and shape to the line from the elbow to the sheath or udder.

UNSOUNDNESS. Defect that may or may not be visible but does affect serviceability.

VERTICAL. Straight or upright fence.

VICE. Abnormal behavior in the stable environment that results from confinement or improper management and can affect a horse's usefulness, dependability, and health. Examples are cribbing and weaving.

VOLTE. Circle with a 6-meter diameter (20 feet).

WALK. Four-beat flat-footed gait.

WEAVING. Rhythmic swaying of weight from one front foot to the other when confined. Can be socially contagious.

WESTERN BANDING. A grooming technique using tiny rubber bands to make thirty or forty little pony tails out of the mane.

WOOD CHEWING. Common vice that damages facilities and can cause abnormal wear of teeth and possible complications from wood splinters.

WORKING GAIT. In dressage, a gait that is regular and unconstrained, energetic but calm, with even, elastic steps.

WORKING HUNTER. Hunter that must, above all, be sound and a good performer. It is not necessary that the horse be pretty.

YOUTH. Exhibitor eighteen and under. Additional age divisions are often created to separate children further.

INDEX